D1288192

The Weight of Command

STUDIES IN CANADIAN MILITARY HISTORY
Series editor: Andrew Burtch, Canadian War Museum

The Canadian War Museum, Canada's national museum of military history, has a threefold mandate: to remember, to preserve, and to educate. Studies in Canadian Military History, published by UBC Press in association with the Museum, extends this mandate by presenting the best of contemporary scholarship to provide new insights into all aspects of Canadian military history, from earliest times to recent events. The work of a new generation of scholars is especially encouraged, and the books employ a variety of approaches – cultural, social, intellectual, economic, political, and comparative – to investigate gaps in the existing historiography. The books in the series feed immediately into future exhibitions, programs, and outreach efforts by the Canadian War Museum. A list of the titles in the series appears at the end of the book.

CANADIAN WAR MUSEUM
MUSÉE CANADIEN DE LA GUERRE

J.L. Granatstein

THE WEIGHT OF COMMAND
Voices of Canada's Second World War Generals
and Those Who Knew Them

UBCPress · Vancouver · Toronto

25 24 23 22 21 20 19 18 17 16   5 4 3 2 1

Printed in Canada on FSC-certified ancient-forest-free paper
(100% post-consumer recycled) that is processed chlorine- and acid-free.

Library and Archives Canada Cataloguing in Publication

Granatstein, J.L., author, editor
   The weight of command: voices of Canada's Second World War generals and those who knew them / J.L. Granatstein.

(Studies in Canadian military history)
Includes bibliographical references and index.
Issued in print and electronic formats.
ISBN 978-0-7748-3299-1 (hardback). – ISBN 978-0-7748-3301-1 (pdf). –
ISBN 978-0-7748-3302-8 (epub). – ISBN 978-0-7748-3303-5 (mobi)

   1. Generals – Canada – Interviews. 2. Generals – Canada – Biography. 3. Command of troops – History – 20th century. 4. World War, 1939-1945 – Canada. 5. Canada – History, Military – 20th century. I. Title. II. Series: Studies in Canadian military history

U54.C2G75 2016   355.0092'2   C2016-901796-6
                                                                  C2016-901797-4

Canadä

UBC Press gratefully acknowledges the financial support for our publishing program of the Government of Canada (through the Canada Book Fund), the Canada Council for the Arts, and the British Columbia Arts Council.

This book has been published with the help of a grant from the Canadian Federation for the Humanities and Social Sciences, through the Awards to Scholarly Publications Program, using funds provided by the Social Sciences and Humanities Research Council of Canada.

Publication of this book has been financially supported by the Canadian War Museum.

UBC Press
The University of British Columbia
2029 West Mall
Vancouver, BC V6T 1Z2
www.ubcpress.ca

For Shirley, Elaine, Linda, Carole, and Tess –
the women in my life

Contents

Illustrations

Abbreviations

ADC	Aide de Camp (junior officer who assisted general officers)
CCRA	Commander, Corps Royal Artillery (the senior artillery officer in a corps)
CGS	Chief of the General Staff (the head of the army in Canada)
CMHQ	Canadian Military Headquarters (the administrative headquarters of the Canadian Army in Britain)
CO	Commanding Officer (lieutenant-colonel leading a battalion or regiment)
CRA	Commander, Royal Artillery (the senior artillery officer in a division)
GOC	General Officer Commanding (commander of a division or corps)
GOC-in-C	General Officer Commanding-in-Chief (commander of an army or of home defences on the coasts)
GSO1, 2, 3	General Staff Officer, Grade 1, 2, 3 (key staff officers)
HQ	Headquarters
NDHQ	National Defence Headquarters (the headquarters in Ottawa)
PF	Permanent Force (the regular full-time army)
RMC	Royal Military College, Kingston (Canada's military college)

Acknowledgments

I CONDUCTED THE interviews presented in this book on my own, but I had access to interviews with senior officers done at various times by other scholars. They are not printed here, but they informed my research and writing. I am grateful to Terry Copp, the late Reg Roy, Jonathan Vance, Bill McAndrew, and the late Ben Greenhous for letting me use their transcripts. Happily, military historians enjoy sharing their research more than most scholars, and I have tried to be as generous to other historians with my interviews and research materials.

I had splendid aid in researching *The Generals* from a number of graduate assistants at York University, notably Dean Oliver and Penny Bryden; their work almost twenty-five years ago informed that book and this one. Norman Hillmer and Dean Oliver read the manuscript of this book most helpfully. Lieutenant-Colonel Dr. Doug Delaney at Royal Military College also assisted greatly.

I have been greatly impressed by the very professional staff at UBC Press, who have made it easily the pre-eminent scholarly press in Canada. Emily Andrew, Holly Keller, and especially Deborah Kerr did fine work in making this book better.

I will always be grateful to Linda McKnight of Westwood Creative Artists, my long-time literary agent, and to my best reader, my wife, Dr. Linda Grayson.

The Weight of Command

INTRODUCTION

IN 1993, I PUBLISHED *The Generals: The Canadian Army's Senior Commanders in the Second World War*, a study of the men who led the Canadian Army in the 1939-45 war.[1] This was a collective biography of the officers who held the rank of major-general or higher, and it was based on extensive archival research and more than seventy interviews in Canada and the United Kingdom. These interviews are collected here.

At the beginning of the 1990s, Canadian military history was in a parlous position, most especially in the universities. The academic historical profession had moved away from political, foreign policy, and military subjects, and relatively little had been or was being written on military topics. Canada was and always had been a peacekeeper, or so the myth had it. In consequence, the Second World War had faded from the public memory, so it seemed, not to return until the fiftieth anniversaries of D-Day and V-E Day in 1994 and 1995 received massive television coverage and sparked public and some academic interest. Thus, when I began this book in 1990, it seemed as if I were working in a vacuum. There were the fine army official histories, there was excellent work by Terry Copp, Desmond Morton, Lieutenant-Colonel Dr. John A. English, Stephen Harris, and a few other historians, but certainly no one had ever examined the senior leaders who mobilized, directed, and led Canadians in battle against the Wehrmacht and SS. There was one too-laudatory biography of General A.G.L. McNaughton, but there was no biography of Harry Crerar, none of Guy Simonds, Charles Foulkes, E.L.M. Burns, and Kenneth Stuart, key army commanders in the Second World War. No one had studied the General Officers Commanding the divisions in the First Canadian Army, and few historians could name even one General Officer Commanding.

....

1 J.L. Granatstein, *The Generals: The Canadian Army's Senior Commanders in the Second World War* (Toronto: Stoddart, 1993).

What I wanted to do was to examine the generals as a collectivity. I had written *The Ottawa Men: The Civil Service Mandarins, 1935-56,* in 1982, and the collective biography approach I used there could also, I hoped, be made to work with the generals.[2] First, I had to find out who the generals were (which turned out to be surprisingly difficult), which ones, if any, were still alive, and which ones had left papers. Second, I wrote letters, followed leads, searched through archival records and personnel files, and built up my database. Finally, then came the interviews, begun only after I thought I had read much of the surviving documentation.

I talked at length with the generals whom I could find, their key staff officers, the members of their families that I could track down, and officers who had fought under their command. I had no template that I followed in asking questions, but there were certain things that I was after. I wanted to know what kind of men the generals were and where they came from, their education, their own professional training (or lack thereof), and how they trained their troops. I was interested in how they survived the sharp, elbows-up politics of the military and in assessing their battlefield success or failure. Above all, I sought to understand why some officers rose in rank and others stagnated. I knew almost nothing when I began this project, but it quickly became the most engrossing subject I had ever written about.

I wanted to know about the generals' social class and family background. Why had so few francophones risen to become senior officers? How many of the generals had attended Royal Military College (RMC) in Kingston, the country's sole military college, which, during the interwar years, took its cadets from elite private schools and many sons of former (and still-) serving officers? How were RMC-educated officers perceived by Permanent Force (PF) army officers who had not attended the college? And by officers from the army's part-time soldiers, the Non-Permanent Active Militia? What happened to the Great War veterans in the officer corps? What were relations like between these "dugouts," as some called them, and the younger officers who joined the PF in the 1920s and 1930s? Between PF and Militia officers? Were the odds stacked in favour of the PF as the army struggled during the war to find younger men capable of commanding troops in the field? If not, why not? If they were, how can we explain how and why some Militia officers rose?

....

2   J.L. Granatstein, *The Ottawa Men: The Civil Service Mandarins, 1935-56* (Toronto: Oxford University Press, 1982; Oakville, ON: Rock's Mills Press, 2015).

All those questions arose in the interviews. There were more. How were the officers trained in the PF and the Militia? The interwar army was tiny – in early 1939, there were only 4,300 in the PF, of whom some 450 were officers, many too old or ill for active service, and at most 50,000 officers and men in the largely untrained Militia. Almost none of the Militia officers were initially competent to command even a thirty-man platoon in action or to train it for war. The PF, where promotion had been glacial, was little better: in early 1939, the three PF infantry regiments – the Royal Canadian Regiment, the Princess Patricia's Canadian Light Infantry, and the Royal 22e Régiment – had only eight captains and nineteen lieutenants under the age of forty. In other words, most regular officers in the infantry were probably too old to handle the strain of modern mechanized war.[3] There were no great commanders ready to lead, no field marshals' batons stowed in officers' kit bags.

Making matters worse, there was and continued to be tension between the Militia and the PF, discord that is amply revealed in the interviews collected here. The PF officers were the professionals, the experts at making war and preparing for it, or so they believed. In fact, Canada's interwar regular army was almost a joke, its officers too old, as indicated above, too untrained, too ill-equipped. Many of the senior Militia officers, the "Saturday night soldiers" who trained in their local armouries until they went to summer camp for a few days of outdoor training, were also too old, veterans of the Great War trenches who believed in their regiments and the need for Canada to be prepared. Their Militia units had less equipment than the PF, which, of course, had almost none. But there was competition for what little money and equipment existed, and resentment among many Militia officers and men at the ill-treatment they believed they received from the PF officers and sergeants who were assigned to train them and with whom they regularly dealt. In essence, the PF viewed the Militia as amateurs, and the Militia largely believed that PFers were know-it-all layabouts who drank too much. Drink was the curse of the PF, they said.

This antagonism lasted throughout the war (and after, up to the present day), as competition for command billets intensified. The PF had seen Militia minister Sam Hughes relegate the PF officers to very few positions in the first contingent in August-September 1914, and the General Staff in Ottawa was

....

3 Brian Reid, *No Holding Back: Operation Totalize, Normandy, August 1944* (Toronto: Robin Brass Studio, 2005), 22.

determined that this would not happen again in September 1939. The important posts in the 1st Division initially went to the PF, and the key posts thereafter – the army GOCs-in-C, the corps GOCs, most of the division GOCs, and the Chiefs of the General Staff in Ottawa – stayed in PF hands throughout the war. But because it drew on a broader base, the Militia produced its stars who could not be denied. By 1945, Generals Bert Hoffmeister, Bruce Matthews, and Holley Keefler were commanding divisions in action and doing so with skill. The mutual antagonism faded as the meritorious rose – and there were fine officers in both the PF and the Militia. Faded, but did not disappear: one Militia officer who spoke bluntly about the shortcomings of PF officers was Major-General Bert Hoffmeister (see pages 28-32).

What must be remembered was that Canada began the war in 1939 with nothing. There had been no defence budget to speak of for the twenty years from 1919 to 1939, no modern equipment, nothing to hold things together but regimental pride and a conviction that another great war was on the horizon. Once the army began to mobilize after the outbreak of war in September 1939, how was it to be trained and equipped? There were far too few trained staff officers, graduates of the British Army Staff Colleges at Camberley in England and Quetta in India and the Imperial Defence College, for even a division of troops, let alone a corps or a field army. Where were such potential officers to be found, and how were they to be trained? And how capable would they prove to be in the field?[4]

Almost thirty years ago, historian Stephen Harris wrote that "it took more than a keen mind, a scientific education, and attendance at British army staff courses to make good generals out of majors and colonels who may have commanded a platoon or company in the Great War, but who had not been in the field since."[5] That was certainly correct. To succeed in battle, recent field experience, a willingness to learn and adapt, and the ability to lead and inspire were essential. No Canadian officers had all those qualities at the beginning of the Second World War, and there were few keen military minds among them. Harris, again rightly, noted that it was unsurprising "that eight

---

4 John A. Macdonald's very good 1992 RMC master's thesis, "In Search of Veritable: Training the Canadian Army Staff Officer, 1899 to 1945," is the best treatment of staff training.
5 Stephen Harris, *Canadian Brass: The Making of a Professional Army, 1860-1939* (Toronto: University of Toronto Press, 1988), 210-11.

of the twenty-two major-generals and above who commanded divisions, corps, or the army overseas were fired for incompetence before they saw action; that two more were relieved after their first battle; and that another survived only nine months."[6] Other national armies had similar problems, of course, notably the British and American, but the Canadian record was far from stellar. In *The Generals,* which was based on archival research and my interviews, I tried to determine what caused these failures – and, as important, how and why successful commanders emerged.

There were highly placed senior officers in both the Permanent Force and the Militia at the outbreak of war and in the first few years. Andrew McNaughton, George Pearkes, E.W. Sansom, F.F. Worthington, and Harry Crerar were the PF commanders who played key roles in raising, training, and beginning to prepare the troops to fight. C.B. Price, Victor Odlum, A.E. Potts, Price Montague, and others were the initial well-connected Militia officers in the spotlight, but as Harris pointed out, most of them – and most of the senior PF leaders too – did not last through the increasingly critical process of hard training and evaluation after 1941. The interviews collected here make clear why such officers, mostly from the "old brigade" of Great War veterans, had to be replaced. They were, as General McNaughton told a journalist in an unguarded moment, the "cover crop, to help the younger men through the wilting strains of the first responsibilities, in the same way that older trees are used to shelter saplings through the heat of the day."[7] Sadly, Andy McNaughton himself would prove to be part of the cover crop.

As the war went on, younger officers came to the fore from both the PF and the Militia, men such as Guy Simonds, Charles Foulkes, E.L.M. Burns, Chris Vokes, Rod Keller, Harry Foster, Bert Hoffmeister, Dan Spry, George Kitching, and Bruce Matthews. Of these, only Burns had served in the Canadian Expeditionary Force during the Great War, and only he held a rank higher than major in September 1939, but the war gave them all the chance to rise with dazzling speed. For Permanent Force officers, as publisher and wartime soldier John Bassett said during his interview (page 156), the war was as if they'd died and gone to heaven. After years with the slowest of promotion and without troops or equipment, suddenly they were generals, and they had everything they wanted and needed – except battle experience.

....

6 Ibid., 211.
7 C.J.V. Murphy, "The First Canadian Army," *Fortune,* January 1944, 164.

Serving under the First Canadian Army's General Officer Commanding-in-Chief, the skilled military politician and survivor General Harry Crerar, these were the men who led the divisions and corps of the First Canadian Army in Italy and Northwest Europe. These were the generals whose careers and qualities, triumphs and failures, emerged from these interviews.

Then there were the areas where Canadian domestic politics intersected with the military. Conscription, a subject whose history dated back to the Great War's Military Service Act of 1917 and the huge controversies it created, was the central question. Historians generally agree that manpower was handled better by Prime Minister Mackenzie King in the Second World War than it had been by Sir Robert Borden in the Great War. Not all senior officers were of that view, however, and there were sharp divisions as a result. The Permanent Force officers, most of them having served in a tiny army where almost all the officers knew each other, split apart on this issue and on others as the ties that bound them together snapped and their willingness to bow to civilian control wobbled dangerously in the autumn of 1944.[8] The struggle for power, higher rank, and bigger commands went on in wartime, exactly as in peacetime, but the casualties to friendships were heavier during wartime.

It must be remembered that all the men I interviewed – there were no female officers at the front, though the spouses and daughters of the generals sometimes lived in England during the war years – were very old when I saw them at the beginning of the 1990s. They had fought the war and survived into their eighties and nineties, whereas many of their friends had been killed or wounded or relegated to unimportant posts because they proved wanting in action, training, or administration. The officers to whom I spoke had been trained in a rigid system that believed in loyalty up to their superiors and loyalty down to their subordinates. During the war, several of the officers whom I interviewed had refused to be disparaging about the abilities of their leaders, despite probing questioning. They had no such qualms in disparaging politicians, but the passage of decades and the gaining of perspective relaxed such instinctive attitudes in many interviewees' remarks on their comrades. The comments by PF officers on their peers, as a result, are sometimes

....

8   See J.L. Granatstein and J.M. Hitsman, *Broken Promises: A History of Conscription in Canada* (Toronto: Oxford University Press, 1977; Oakville, ON: Rock's Mills Press, 2015).

very sharp; the remarks of Militia officers on the PF are also frequently very critical. Some of what I recorded was indiscreet, self-serving, and gossipy, no doubt, but almost all of it seemed to me to be the truth as interviewees saw it almost five decades after the war.

CANADIANS KNOW VERY LITTLE of their nation's role in the Second World War. This is a terrible shame, for the 1939-45 war in so many ways shaped modern Canada. A nation of 11 million people, trapped in the morass of the Great Depression, somehow doubled its gross national product between 1939 and 1945, while simultaneously putting 1.1 million men and women into uniform. As striking, 1 million of those in the military had volunteered to fight and serve anywhere, demonstrating that Canadians believed in the rightness of their cause. Those at home endured long separations – some soldiers went overseas in December 1939 and did not return until late 1945 or early 1946; some 42,000 servicemen never returned, and their graves lie around the world in Hong Kong and Japan, Britain, France, the Low Countries, Italy, and elsewhere.

While the war was being fought overseas, Canada mobilized the home front very successfully, and the government controlled the domestic economy well.[9] Canadians ate better than they had in the bleak 1930s, and this despite rationing and controls. They had more work at good pay, and many families saw all their members working hard, getting as much overtime as they wanted, and saving money.[10] The nation's workers on the farms and mines produced vast quantities of food, minerals, and metals, and the factories and shipyards turned out 16,400 aircraft ranging from tiny trainers to Lancaster bombers, ships of all kinds from lighters to big Tribal Class destroyers, and some 816,000 military vehicles. From a standing start, Canadian war production reached a value of $9.5 billion in 1940s dollars, making Canada fourth in Allied war production behind only the great powers.[11] The war was a tragedy for many at home, those who lost sons, brothers, and fathers overseas, but it

....

9   See J.L. Granatstein, *Canada's War: The Politics of the Mackenzie King Government, 1939-45* (Toronto: Oxford University Press, 1990; Oakville, ON: Rock's Mills Press, 2015).

10 Graham Broad, *A Small Price to Pay: Consumer Culture on the Canadian Home Front, 1939-45* (Vancouver: UBC Press, 2013).

11 J.L. Granatstein, *The Best Little Army in the World: The Canadians in Northwest Europe, 1944-1945* (Toronto: HarperCollins, 2015), Chap. 1.

was simultaneously very good for Canada and most Canadians, and the long postwar boom had its basis in the wartime economy.

Those who directed the nation's remarkable war effort deserve much more credit than they have yet received. The civil service mandarins provided the brainpower that controlled inflation and directed the economy, and the Canadian wartime economic record was superb.[12] The war years also saw the establishment of unemployment insurance, family allowances, the Veterans Charter, and a huge pot of money for postwar reconstruction.[13] Canada began its move into the welfare state during the war.[14]

The mandarins, led by a strong Cabinet and the "Minister of Everything" C.D. Howe, and greatly aided by dollar-a-year men from industry and commerce, also directed the nation's stringent financial regime, which raised taxes, imposed controls, and battled waste. So efficient were these processes that the government was able to lend or give billions of dollars in aid to Britain and other allies, and to keep economic and military relations with the United States close and integrated but not subordinated to the emerging superpower next door.[15] And the fractious tendencies between French- and English-speaking Canadians over compulsory military service overseas largely stayed in check, thanks to the political leadership of Mackenzie King and his Cabinet.

Mackenzie King was not the most attractive politician in our history, but he was surely one of the most successful, and the Second World War was the capstone of his career. He never inspired his 11 million countrymen, and he scarcely made any effort to win a place at the table with Prime Minister

....

12   Michael Stevenson's *Canada's Greatest Wartime Muddle* (Montreal and Kingston: McGill-Queen's University Press, 2001) argues that military and domestic manpower mobilization was a shambles.

13   James Struthers, *"No Fault of Their Own": Unemployment and the Canadian Welfare State, 1914-1941* (Toronto: University of Toronto Press, 1983); Raymond Blake, *From Rights to Needs: A History of Family Allowances in Canada, 1929-92* (Vancouver: UBC Press, 2009); the best book on veterans is Peter Neary, *On to Civvy Street: Canada's Rehabilitation Program for Veterans of the Second World War* (Montreal and Kingston: McGill-Queen's University Press, 2011).

14   See Granatstein, *The Ottawa Men.*

15   R.D. Cuff and J.L. Granatstein, *Ties That Bind: Canadian-American Relations from the Great War to the Cold War* (Toronto: Samuel Stevens Hakkert, 1977); R.D. Cuff and J.L. Granatstein, *American Dollars – Canadian Prosperity: Canadian-American Economic Relations, 1945-50* (Toronto: Samuel Stevens, 1978).

Winston Churchill and President Franklin Roosevelt, who led the Western Allies' war effort. He did host the Quebec Conferences of 1943 and 1944, but though he was present for some of the photo opportunities, his role was merely to provide the food and drink for Churchill, Roosevelt, and their entourages. The inescapable reality was that Mackenzie King and Canada were relatively minor players, effectively shut out from the big decisions.

Nonetheless, Mackenzie King was a leader who directed a remarkable overall war effort that ranked Canada fourth among the Allies, behind only those of the great powers, the United States, the United Kingdom, and the Union of Soviet Socialist Republics. He struggled to manage sharp disputes over the conscription of manpower by hedging, trimming, moving forward, and then back; but he was generally successful, keeping the situation in French Canada under control while not completely losing his standing in the rest of the country. That he won the election of 1945, narrowly to be sure, was the best indicator of his success. Winston Churchill, the leader who many believed had saved the world, could not match that feat.

But the military probably did not share even the public's "hold its nose" view of Mackenzie King. He cut a pudgy unmilitary figure and was thought to be antipathetic to the armed forces. He was no soldier's idea of a wartime leader. From the army's point of view, the government mistakenly created a home defence army, the conscripts recruited under the National Resources Mobilization Act who had to be cajoled into volunteering for service overseas. Another mistake in the eyes of some senior army officers was the establishment of a large air force and navy that took away the best-educated junior leaders and men,[16] who, many generals believed, might have been better employed in khaki, leading platoons of infantry. Still, with a total enlistment of some 700,000, the Canadian Army was almost three times the strength of the Royal Canadian Air Force and seven times that of the Royal Canadian Navy. The army's peak strength in the early months of 1945 was just under a half million volunteers for service anywhere, a substantial force by any measure.

Once the men were mobilized, equipped, and trained, the real question was how the army was to be employed. Mackenzie King's primary political aim was to avoid conscription for overseas service, and he had promised this

....

16 See, for example, Alan English, *The Cream of the Crop: Canadian Aircrew, 1939-45* (Montreal and Kingston: McGill-Queen's University Press, 1996).

for the first time in March 1939 (interestingly, his pledge had been preceded two days earlier by one from Conservative leader Dr. R.J. Manion) and repeated it in September 1939 and during the election campaign in early 1940. In the first days of the war, the Prime Minister had even hoped that Canada might avoid sending a single infantry division to Britain, but his ministers and the English Canadian public, their memories of the battlefield victories won by the Canadian Corps in the Great War still fresh, forced his hand.[17] He then selected Major-General A.G.L. McNaughton to be the 1st Division's General Officer Commanding. Andy McNaughton had been a hugely successful and innovative artillery officer in the Great War and Chief of the General Staff in the 1930s. He picked Brigadiers George Pearkes, Armand Smith, and C.B. Price to lead his brigades, the first a Victoria Cross–winning PF officer, the latter two from the Militia, one a jam maker from the Niagara peninsula, the other the manager of a Montreal dairy. From England, McNaughton would oversee the expansion of his 1st Canadian Division into, first, one corps, then a second, and finally by 1942 into the First Canadian Army with its two corps, three infantry and two armoured divisions, plus two additional armoured brigades. This force, raised in Canada between 1940 and 1942 under the direction of the Chief of the General Staff, Major-General (Lieutenant-General from November 1941) H.D.G. Crerar, was potentially a very powerful army, provided that it could be well trained, well equipped, well led, and reinforced once it went into battle. These were not simple challenges, and the nation struggled to deal with them for the rest of the war.

As Chief of the General Staff, Harry Crerar was also responsible for the creation of the home defence army. The government had passed the National Resources Mobilization Act on 21 June 1940, immediately after the fall of France and the evacuation of what was left of the British Expeditionary Force from Dunkirk. Mackenzie King had introduced the bill in Parliament on 18 June, stating that "this legislation will relate solely and exclusively to the defence of Canada on our own soil and in our own territorial waters." He added that a national service registration would be held in the near future: "Let me emphasize," he said, "that this registration will have nothing to do with recruiting citizens for overseas service."[18] Initially, the term of enlistment for conscripts was thirty days, but this was extended to four months in

....

17 See the account in Granatstein, *Canada's War,* 9-11, 25.
18 Canada, *House of Commons Debates* (18 June 1940), 854.

February 1941, and then in April of that same year for the war's duration. General Crerar wrote privately that these progressive steps "represent[ed] several bites at the cherry – the cherry being conscription for service any-where."[19] Many of the home defence conscripts decided that army life wasn't too bad and volunteered for general service, as service anywhere the army wished was called. Others joined the Royal Canadian Navy or the Royal Canadian Air Force. But many resisted "going active" and remained in Canada, hoarding grievances against the government and the military. These sixty thousand "Zombies," so named by pro-conscription zealots after the soulless dead of Hollywood movies, would serve abroad, they maintained, only if the government had the courage to order them to do so. This did not occur until the end of 1944, after a political crisis that saw ministers resigning, the Prime Minister talking of a military "revolt," and a political uproar that almost destroyed the government.[20]

But this was all in the future. The original plan in the autumn of 1939 was that the 1st Canadian Division would train in Britain before moving into the Allied line in France, but events quickly made that impossible. The collapse of France in May and June 1940 before Hitler's panzers came with stunning speed, and the attempt to re-create a defence line in western France, a line to be manned in part by the 1st Canadian Division, went nowhere. The Canadians were lucky to get back to England with some of their recently issued equipment still in hand. Their mission now was the defence of Great Britain – even half-trained, the 1st Division was the best-equipped formation left for this task in the British Isles. The 2nd Division soon joined it in the Canadian Corps,[21] but with Major-Generals George Pearkes and Victor Odlum in command of the two divisions, training went ahead slowly and, to some younger officers, seemed mired in the trenches of Great War thinking. Not until the British Lieutenant-General Bernard Montgomery, commanding the area of southeast England in which the Canadians served,

....

19 Directorate of History, National Defence Headquarters, H.D.G. Crerar Papers, file 958.009 (D12), Crerar to McNaughton, 19 May 1941.

20 The history of the National Resources Mobilization Act is detailed in Daniel Byers, *Zombie Army: Canada, the Canadian Army, and Conscription in the Second World War* (Vancouver: UBC Press, 2016). See also Granatstein and Hitsman, *Broken Promises,* Chap. 6.

21 The best account remains C.P. Stacey, *Six Years of War,* vol. 1 of *The Official History of the Canadian Army in the Second World War* (Ottawa: Queen's Printer, 1955).

began to push the troops hard and to force out older and laggard officers did training begin to become more realistic.[22]

The debacles at Hong Kong and Dieppe, the first two major Canadian Army operations of the war, demonstrated the need for better training – and better military intelligence. Canada sent two infantry battalions and a brigade headquarters to the British Crown colony off the China coast in the autumn of 1941, and the entire force was lost when Japan captured Hong Kong by Christmas Day. Senior Canadian commanders in Britain also sought active participation in the Dieppe raid of August 1942, an attack planned by Admiral Lord Louis Mountbatten's Combined Operations Headquarters. Fearing that the troops were bored with training and wanting action, General Crerar, acting in command of the corps while McNaughton was ill in Canada, persuaded the British that the 2nd Canadian Division, led by Major-General Hamilton Roberts, should get the job. But the raid was a disaster, the Canadians landing under high cliffs on the English Channel coast of France and in the face of deadly fire that left the dreadfully planned and miserably executed raid in ruins. The bloody casualties and the military lessons of Hong Kong and Dieppe made clear that much remained to be done, including the acquisition of battle experience, before the Canadian divisions could confidently face a first-class enemy. The generals, as the following interviews reveal, had much to learn about fighting a war. So too did their soldiers.

But where could battle experience against the Germans be gained? The British and Americans had landed in North Africa in November 1942, and within six months, they had linked up with General Montgomery's British Eighth Army and were in complete possession of the southern shore of the Mediterranean. Plans were under way to invade Sicily and mainland Italy. But General McNaughton insisted that his First Canadian Army not be tapped for troops for these invasions, preferring to keep his countrymen together

....

22   See the account in Granatstein, *The Generals*, 30-32, 68-69, and passim. In 1942, Harry Crerar said of Pearkes that he was a forceful leader and able trainer but a man of limited scope who would be better as a battalion commander than a brigadier or better as a brigadier than a division commander. He felt that Pearkes was a man of narrow vision who could see only one thing at a time and who had no interest in long-term plans. A first-class fighting soldier, he would handle his men with determination but might produce negative results. Library and Archives Canada, L.B. Pearson Papers, vol. 3, Crerar to Pearson, 25 April 1942. Of Odlum, McNaughton claimed in September 1941 that he was "showing signs of advancing years ... I will have to make a change in command." Quoted in Granatstein, *The Generals*, 37-38.

under his command for the inevitable landing in France. The difficulty was that senior British generals had begun to doubt McNaughton's command capabilities; so too did many of the Canadians, including Crerar, commanding a corps in England, Kenneth Stuart, the Chief of the General Staff in Ottawa, and J. Layton Ralston, the Minister of National Defence. The government forced the decision to send the 1st Division and the 1st Canadian Armoured Brigade to be part of the Sicilian invasion. This was the first sign that McNaughton had lost his sway. Then, after a political and military struggle, McNaughton, the General Officer Commanding-in-Chief who had been built up almost to demi-god status by government propaganda at home, was toppled, the hugely ambitious and politically astute Crerar picked to be his successor.[23] The most important result, however, was that Canadian troops saw action, beginning the process of becoming battle-ready as they fought in the British Eighth Army. Able commanders emerged, officers such as Guy Simonds, Christopher Vokes, and Bert Hoffmeister proving themselves in action. The cost in Sicily and Italy was heavy casualties and the daunting task of maintaining the long supply lines for men and materiel that proved very difficult for a small nation to sustain.

The Canadians were in Sicily and the Italian mainland from mid-1943 into February 1945, moving over the switchback roads of Sicily and up the Italian boot. At Ortona at Christmas 1943, they fought first-rate German paratroopers for the town and, at a terrible cost in lives, beat them. The 1st Division was nearly spent at the end of that battle. Its next major action, joined by the 5th Canadian Armoured Division, both serving under I Canadian Corps HQ, did not come until May 1944 on the Hitler Line south of Rome. Lieutenant-General E.L.M. Burns's first battle in command of the corps, the Hitler Line struggle was another costly success, leaving the dour and unsmiling Burns out of favour with the Eighth Army's commander. The corps moved north through Rome and Florence to the Adriatic coast and the Gothic Line by the end of August 1944. Here Bert Hoffmeister's 5th Canadian Armoured Division played the starring role in cracking the line and forcing

....

23 There is a good account of McNaughton's removal in Paul Dickson's study of Harry Crerar, *A Thoroughly Canadian General* (Toronto: University of Toronto Press, 2007). On McNaughton, see also John Swettenham, *McNaughton*, 3 vols. (Toronto: Ryerson, 1968-69); and John Rickard, *The Politics of Command: Lieutenant-General A.G.L. McNaughton and the Canadian Army, 1939-1943* (Toronto: University of Toronto Press, 2010).

a major German withdrawal. Many historians consider this the most successful Canadian action of the war, and Hoffmeister, a Militia company commander in Vancouver's Seaforth Highlanders in 1939, arguably the best military leader Canada produced in the Second World War.[24]

In Canada, General McNaughton became Minister of National Defence during the conscription crisis of October and November 1944. He soon arranged the move of the I Canadian Corps back to Northwest Europe, where Guy Simonds's II Canadian Corps had been heavily engaged since the Allied landings on the Normandy coast on D-Day, 6 June 1944. At last, the First Canadian Army had been reunited under command of Harry Crerar, five divisions and two armoured brigades strong. The II Canadian Corps had fought its way over the Normandy beaches, helped close the Falaise Gap, cleared the channel ports, and fought a gruelling battle to open the Scheldt estuary to shipping. The casualties had been horrific, and infantry reinforcements had been swallowed in wholesale. Brigade, division, and corps commanders did not always recognize that battalion effectiveness had changed because of casualties. Orders often failed to account for the cumulative losses of the campaign in killed, wounded, and psychological casualties, or the grinding fatigue of near-continuous action. Companies and platoons with fewer men could attack and hold less ground, mustering less firepower than they had in June. Ever greater numbers of killed and wounded were frequently the only result. The dispatch of sixteen thousand home defence conscripts overseas, that question being the primary cause of the autumn 1944 political crisis in Canada, and the transfer of I Canadian Corps from Italy to Northwest Europe had provided a respite, a period without much fighting for the Canadian divisions. But there were again heavy casualties in the last weeks of the European war from February through to V-E Day in May. The Canadians, the British, and the Poles serving under Crerar's command cleared the Rhineland, crossed the Rhine River, and liberated Holland, and the First Canadian Army, its reinforcement pools full again, finished the war with its ranks in relatively good shape, its performance first-rate. Having begun the war with almost nothing, Canada ended it with a powerful force

....

24   On the Italian campaign, see G.W.L. Nicholson's *The Canadians in Italy, 1943-1945,* vol. 2 of *The Official History of the Canadian Army in the Second World War* (Ottawa: Queen's Printer, 1957); and Douglas Delaney's fine biography of Hoffmeister, *The Soldiers' General: Bert Hoffmeister at War* (Vancouver: UBC Press, 2005).

of well-trained civilians in uniform. In the eyes of its commanders and soldiers, it had become the best little army in the world. In fact, with some 185,000 men in the field, it wasn't so little.[25] Significantly, by 1945 the only army, corps, division, or brigade commander in the First Canadian Army who had Great War experience was General Harry Crerar, the GOC-in-C. Canada's fighting generals were all young men.

All these commanders had learned their hard trade on the job as Canada's army played its genuinely important part in the war. While many of the generals made or lost their reputations during the Second World War, their officers and men paid a heavy price in lives during the learning process. In all, the army suffered 22,917 killed or died of wounds, 81,011 wounded or injured, and 6,433 officers and men taken prisoner.[26] There inevitably was a high cost when fighting the Germans, but some of the casualties were certainly the result of the interwar neglect under which the Permanent Force and Militia had laboured.

Ottawa spent $5.64 billion on the army over the six years of war, a huge sum in wartime dollars, and a vastly bigger sum in present-day money.[27] Some 700,000 men and women served in the army during the Second World War, all but a handful in the overseas units, fighting as volunteers. Of the major Allied armies that fought in Europe, only the Canadian Army could say that, and the fact that so many Canadians volunteered to serve in the struggle against Nazism – 1.1 million men and women, or one in ten of the entire population, if one counts the navy and air force – says something important about Canadians. It really was Canada's war.

ORAL HISTORY PRESENTS challenges for a researcher. Memory is fallible, interviewees may wish to protect themselves or settle scores with long-dead enemies, and others simply cannot remember events from a half-century ago with clarity. What most of the interviewees for this book did sharply recall, however, was their reaction to the personalities of those with whom they served. My task, the task of every interviewer, was to be well prepared and

25 See C.P. Stacey, *The Victory Campaign*, vol. 3 of *The Official History of the Canadian Army in the Second World War* (Ottawa: Queen's Printer, 1960); and Granatstein, *The Best Little Army*.
26 Stacey, *Six Years of War*, 524-25.
27 Ibid., 527.

able to help them with chronology and names, but not to lead them where they did not want to go or into expressing views that they genuinely did not hold. I decided not to use a tape recorder, because I believed that it inhibited conversation. Instead, I jotted notes and, as soon as the interview ended, wrote up a memorandum for myself with key comments in quotes. The collected interviews, edited here for coherence and to minimize irrelevant subjects, military jargon, and abbreviations, were a key part of my research for *The Generals*.

In what follows, there are four interviews with generals, all wartime officers of major-general rank, twelve with officers who fought under the generals, twenty-seven with senior and junior staff officers and men, and twenty-six with family members. The ranks given at the beginning of each interview are the highest attained. I have also included one interview with the Rt. Hon. J.W. Pickersgill, who worked with many of the senior officers in Ottawa when he was Mackenzie King's wartime advisor; this can be found in Chapter 3.

The interviews range widely over issues, personalities, and battles, and the categories used for the chapter organization are the generals, the fighters, the staff, and the families. Some of these categories are arbitrary: generals usually served on staff and as battalion or brigade battlefield commanders before reaching the rank of major-general; most staff officers also fought; and some fighters became brigadiers or staff officers. Within the chapters, I have grouped the interviews so that they focus primarily on the key military figures. But, again, staff officers, for example, moved between postings and frequently worked for more than one senior commander. Those who were interviewed are indicated in **boldface** when they are mentioned in others' interviews.

The interviews vary in length and quality, as might be expected, but many are superb in content and revealingly frank. There is naturally substantial repetition in the comments on some commanders such as Generals McNaughton, Crerar, Simonds, Burns, Foulkes, Keller, Matthews, and Hoffmeister, the key leaders of the First Canadian Army and the I and II Canadian Corps, but there are major differences too. Because old men do forget, some interviews do contain factual errors. I have corrected in footnotes the most egregious mistakes.

Readers can and will use these interviews to form their own assessments of men and events. Some will read through the entire book to create an overview of Canada's high command. Others will dip in for specific pieces of information. But for me, what emerged from the collected interviews, what was and remains so striking, was that so many of the key Canadian military commanders lacked the leadership skills, the personality, and the capacity to inspire their men. Andy McNaughton had all of these in 1939 and 1940, but he gradually lost his appeal to his officers and soldiers by focusing too much on his own interests in the technical side of war and not enough on the training of his command for war. As Brigadier-General R.T. Bennett observed (page 196), McNaughton "could dissect any problem," but he had to do it himself. When he was forced out as GOC-in-C in late 1943, the men of the First Canadian Army scarcely noticed. Careful and able as he was, McNaughton's successor, Harry Crerar, had the charisma of a turnip, and Charles Foulkes, who was Harry Crerar writ small, completely turned off many of those whom he ineffectually led. Guy Simonds ranked with the very best Allied commanders in battlefield skill and tactical imagination, but he seemed locked into the role of the stern taskmaster who frightened many of his subordinates rather than making them eager to follow his lead. As his RMC classmate and friend Chris Vokes colourfully said after the war, Simonds was "the finest Canadian general we ever had," but he was not worth "a pinch of coonshit" as "a leader of men."[28] Vokes of the 1st and then the 4th Armoured Division and Rod Keller of the 3rd Division, on the other hand, were self-styled "tough guys" who were popular with their troops. But Keller lacked the tactical skills, self-discipline, moral and physical courage, and intelligence to command effectively in action, and the more able Vokes's favourite word, it was said, was "frontal," a reference to the assaults of his troops, which always seemed to be aimed into the teeth of the enemy's defences.

All these commanders had emerged from the tiny prewar Permanent Force. None had a trace of the fire and charisma combined with competence that made Field Marshal Sir Bernard Montgomery, thoroughly detested by many senior officers as "a nasty little shit," extremely popular with the confident British – and Canadian – troops that he led to victory.[29] On board ship heading for the invasion of Sicily, a Canadian NCO wrote home that

....

28 Granatstein, *The Generals,* 159. See Roman Jarymowycz, "General Guy Simonds: The Commander as Tragic Hero," in *Warrior Chiefs: Perspectives on Senior Canadian Military Leaders,* ed. B. Horn and S. Harris (Toronto: Dundurn, 2001), 107-41.
29 See the useful discussion on British Army leadership styles in Brian Bond, *Britain's Two World Wars against Germany: Myth, Memory and the Distortion of Hindsight* (Cambridge: Cambridge University Press, 2014), 57ff.

"Monty say[s] we can do it and that is good enough for all of us." After the landings, one officer noted to his family that "Monty visited us the other day, and told us what great fighters the Canadians were. He surely has the common touch – gets in amongst them," the officer continued, "motions them to gather round, and then talks to them as if they were all planning together some operations and he needed their advice ... He has a touch of 'genius' all right."[30] Canadians sometimes like to sneer at the British as overly class-conscious and hopelessly stuffy, but the best British commanders had a practised ease of manner that few wartime Canadian senior officers could ever hope to match.

Of the Canadian leaders in the field, only Bert Hoffmeister and Bruce Matthews, the GOCs of the 5th Armoured and 2nd Divisions, successfully practised a consensual style of leadership, and perhaps it was not coincidental that both men rose from the prewar Militia. In their Vancouver and Toronto Militia units, they had learned to stay close to their men, and they carried that instinct into their leadership roles. Their battlefield skills, honed in four years of training and two years in action, were at least on a par with those of their Permanent Force peers, but their soldiers admired them and wanted to win battles for them. Montgomery and US General George Patton could move men to attempt the impossible; sadly, almost none of the Canadian leaders had this facility, and only Hoffmeister seemed able to use his charismatic personality and his care for his troops to inspire his entire division. The 5th Canadian Armoured Division, with its maroon shoulder flash, was nicknamed Hoffy's Mighty Maroon Machine, and it was Hoffmeister who had made it mighty. When I interviewed him (page 25), he was eighty-five years old and confined to a wheelchair after a stroke, but General Hoffmeister still radiated a powerful presence. I could understand why his soldiers had been proud to serve under his command.

Hoffmeister also spoke quite frankly about the difficulty of giving orders that sent men to kill or be killed. He was a commander who understood that even if his plans were perfect, even if his orders were carried out and the enemy was smashed, some of his men would be killed, wounded, or taken

. . . .

30　Library and Archives Canada, Censorship reports, Microfilm reel T-17294, quoted in Robert Engen, "The Canadian Soldier: Combat Motivation in the Canadian Army, 1943-45," mss., 142.

prisoner. This thought always weighed on him. As a company commander in England in 1941, he had suffered a nervous breakdown because he knew he had not been militarily schooled well enough to lead his men successfully against the Germans. In Sicily and Italy, after he had been to Staff College and was now well trained, he had proven his great competence in battle and led his regiment, his brigade, and his division with great courage and skill. And yet, the weight of command always bore down on him, the awful knowledge that his orders sent soldiers to their deaths. That, said Colonel Clement Dick (page 193), was why Hoffmeister went forward to the front so often. He felt the need to share his soldiers' risks. Tearing up during his own interview, Hoffmeister said that after making several visits to see his wounded men, he could no longer bear to go to the hospitals for fear that seeing such sights would weaken his resolve as a commander. Bruce Matthews, the other very successful Militia GOC, felt the same: he tried to avoid hospital visits, he said, something he managed to do because the wounded were evacuated so promptly. Matthews recalled that he was appalled by the casualties, tried to talk to the troops about this, and made every effort to assure them that he was attempting to minimize them. Hoffmeister and Matthews – and indeed all the Canadian generals – understood that the war had to be won and that casualties were the inevitable price of battle, and they carried on. That was leadership in action. But as Brigadier Stanley Todd, one of the great artillerymen of the First Canadian Army in the Second World War, said in his interview, it was a "frightening thing" to command thirty thousand men in action (page 186). It was pleasant to wear a general's red tabs in peacetime but not in action. The weight of command was a heavy burden to bear.

Mrs. Betty Spry, the wife of Major-General Dan Spry, who fought in Italy as a battalion and brigade commander and in Northwest Europe as a division GOC, recollected that he frequently woke up with nightmares long after the war. Spry drank heavily during the war, as did Generals Charles Foulkes, Rod Keller, and Harry Foster, their way of dealing with the high stress of command. Guy Simonds was sometimes wound tight as a drum, so much so that Harry Crerar once asked a military psychiatrist to determine whether he was fit for command in Italy.

These senior officers were not alone in experiencing stress. In the Great War, battlefield breakdown was known as shell shock; in the Second World War, the phrase was battle fatigue; now we call it post-traumatic stress disorder. Front-line infantrymen suffered when they saw their comrades killed and as the manifold terrors of the front wore down their nerves and courage. Commanders at all levels bore heavy responsibilities, and they saw the results of their decisions every day in dead and maimed men, both enemy and their own. The toll that this took was enormous. Their PTSD may not have been diagnosed, but the weight of command was very real.

1 | THE GENERALS

I INTERVIEWED FOUR Second World War major-generals for *The Generals:* Bert Hoffmeister, George Kitching, Harry Letson, and Bruce Matthews. These four, the only survivors of their rank whom I found in the early 1990s, had contrasting backgrounds that said something about the makeup of Canadian senior officers. Strikingly, none were graduates of the Royal Military College of Canada (though Kitching attended RMC Sandhurst in Britain), none were in the Permanent Force, and none had the coveted "psc" indicating that they had passed Staff College. (Kitching and Hoffmeister, however, did complete wartime staff courses.) These men rose on the leadership they had demonstrated before and during the war.

Hoffmeister and Matthews came from the Non-Permanent Active Militia, the first from the Seaforth Highlanders, a Vancouver infantry regiment, the second from the 7th (Toronto) Regiment of the Royal Canadian Artillery. Matthews's father was the Lieutenant-Governor of Ontario in 1939 and had been a wealthy investment broker. Hoffmeister came from working-class origins and was a middle manager in the H.R. MacMillan timber companies. The Militia was important for both men and, they believed, for the country. Matthews took advantage of the gunnery training courses on offer to militiamen and had the money and time to complete them. Hoffmeister, in contrast, devoted himself to regimental life, training, playing sports, and building ties with his men. At the outbreak of war, both were majors, Matthews commanding a battery, Hoffmeister a company.

Kitching was quite different from both men. A graduate of Sandhurst, he had served as a regular officer in the Gloucestershire Regiment in the British Army and came to Canada in 1938, evidently to escape debts and a bad marriage. On the outbreak of war, he joined the Royal Canadian Regiment as a lieutenant, where, his experience immediately evident, he stood out. As the Canadian Army expanded overseas, he rose quickly into command and staff appointments. Historian Brian Reid noted acerbically in critiquing the qualities of both Kitching and his less talented contemporaries that "as a one-eyed man in an army of the blind and near-blind, Kitching had risen rapidly."[1]

Harry Letson had served overseas with the Canadian Expeditionary Force in the Great War and was seriously wounded, losing a leg. Despite this disability, he continued to serve in the Militia while teaching at the University of British Columbia and commanding the university's Canadian Officers Training Corps. He was unfit for active service in 1939, but he nonetheless helped build the wartime army, as did so many other Great War veterans. By 1942, Letson was the Adjutant General, the chief administrative officer at National Defence Headquarters in Ottawa.

Hoffmeister and Matthews served in a variety of roles overseas before rising to the command of divisions. They were the country's two best division commanders by the end of the war, Hoffmeister playing a distinguished role as a battalion and brigade commander in the 1st Division before becoming GOC of the 5th Canadian Armoured Division in Italy and the Netherlands. After commanding a Medium Artillery Regiment, Matthews became Commander, Royal Artillery, in Guy Simonds's 1st Division in Sicily and Italy, then Commander, Corps Royal Artillery, in Simonds's II Canadian Corps in Normandy, and subsequently GOC of the 2nd Canadian Infantry Division in Northwest Europe in 1944-45. Kitching also held a variety of staff positions, many under his mentor and friend Guy Simonds, and he took command of the 4th Canadian Armoured Division prior to D-Day. But his meteoric rise ended in the Canadians' struggle to close the Falaise Gap in August 1944, when his division – under the critical eye of Simonds – fell short of its objectives. Simonds unhesitatingly fired Kitching; he was dropped one rank and soon returned to Italy to become Brigadier General Staff under Charles Foulkes in the I Canadian Corps.

Three of the interviews are quite striking. Kitching was fit and vigorous, still a very handsome man in his eighties, and he remained almost obsessed with the way that Simonds had sacked him, which he still believed unfair. Matthews and Hoffmeister were ill when I interviewed them, but both were very sharp, clear in their recollections, forceful and forthcoming in their comments and opinions, and proud of their roles. Hoffmeister, in fact, was a compelling figure even in a wheelchair. Only the comments of General

....

1   Reid, *No Holding Back,* 58.

Letson, very old and terribly ill when I spoke with him, did not rise above generalities.

All had strong opinions about their superiors, some not very flattering. All were impressive, capable men who had been tested, survived, and ultimately did well in battle. All seemed to remember slights, and all, especially Hoffmeister, could become emotional as they recalled the war, the burdens command had placed on them, and its human costs. For his part, Matthews recollected that when he returned to Toronto after six years overseas, one of his five-year-old twin sons whom he had never before seen asked, "Mommy, who is that man?" The Second World War took its undoubted toll on the survivors, regardless of their ranks.

MAJOR-GENERAL BERT HOFFMEISTER (1907-99)

INTERVIEW | VANCOUVER, BC, 2 MARCH 1992

A militiaman from Vancouver, Hoffmeister served in the Seaforth Highlanders in Canada and England, commanded the regiment in Sicily, led a brigade through the fighting at Ortona, and then took over the 5th Canadian Armoured Division. He led the division for the rest of the war and was chosen to command the division intended to fight against Japan. After the war, he returned home to become a senior executive at MacMillan Bloedel.[2]

Hoffmeister was eighty-five when I interviewed him at his home. He had had a stroke and was in a wheelchair, but he still retained his compelling personality.

The interview began with his time in the Seaforth Highlanders of Canada.

The unit, Hoffmeister said, wasn't very well trained when he joined. He was a cadet from 1919 to 1927, when he took a commission. The training left a great deal to be desired, and anything the unit accomplished was the result of hard work. Still, the Seaforths stood out on inspections and on the rifle ranges. They had a sense of purpose and of history, but the soldiers weren't prepared for war, except insofar as they developed leadership.

....

2 Douglas Delaney's stellar biography of Hoffmeister is *The Soldiers' General*.

Hoffmeister said he came from a poor family and had worked in a saw-mill for twenty cents an hour after graduating from high school. The idea of attending Royal Military College (RMC) at Kingston, Ontario, never entered his head, and he couldn't afford university. It was difficult to get into the Seaforths, and he was questioned by the Adjutant, who feared he couldn't afford uniforms. His father helped with costs. The officer's formal mess kit, he thought, cost sixty-five dollars.

The regiment had obsolete Lewis machine guns, but the soldiers nonetheless became proficient. There were courses at Work Point Barracks in Victoria and lots of drill. The Seaforths had no forward-thinking people. They did stage some combined operations with the Royal Canadian Navy, and they could get about three hundred soldiers out on Monday training nights; on ceremonials, they were first class. They had a number of RMC graduates who were well trained in drill and gymnastics – that helped with tournaments. The ex-cadets in the Seaforths impressed him – they knew how to exert their authority.

Training in England

When war came, he was married with a child, but it never occurred to him not to go active. He believed that the regiment could not stand up to German troops, and he worried that he had no experience with leading men in battle. The Seaforth officers had been told that their men would be taken for training while they themselves learned tactics, but this didn't happen. Brigadier George Pearkes, whom he admired as a splendid soldier, was steeped in trench warfare, and they did time in mock trenches at Pirbright, England. Everyone felt this was already passé as the blitzkrieg rolled over Europe. The Seaforths' Commanding Officer, thinking he had the best company commanders, refused to let them go on course to train them for battle. This bothered Hoffmeister, who pleaded to be allowed to learn his trade; the only course he went on was the Canadian Junior War Staff Course at Staff College in Kingston.[3] Before that point, he didn't even know how to write an Operations Order.[4]

In 1941, all this wore on him to such an extent that he had a nervous breakdown over the agony of coping with poor training and his sense that

....

3 Macdonald's "In Search of Veritable" discusses the problematic Canadian staff situation through the Second World War.
4 A military Operations Order lays out the situation, the enemy and friendly forces, the mission, and the execution of the plan.

he was untrained. One day, he ran a bath, put his left foot into the water, and felt nothing unusual. But when his other foot went in, he discovered that the water was scalding hot and realized that his left side was virtually paralyzed. He went into hospital, where he met an army psychiatrist who introduced him to a brand new philosophy that guided him thereafter: If you're given a job, it's because your superiors think you're capable of handling it, and they expect your best. Do your best and don't let worries accumulate. After the war, he called on the psychiatrist, Dr. H.H. Hyland, with whom he'd become friendly, to thank him. Hoffmeister had never thought that, in light of this breakdown, he might not be given higher command. "Not many knew of it," he said, although he added that it must have been on his personnel file.[5]

After his recovery, Hoffmeister returned to his regiment and then went to Brigade Headquarters as a Staff Learner.[6] As such, he went to the south coast of England and became familiar with it, so much so that when General Bernard Montgomery, commanding South Eastern Command, came to visit, Brigadier A.E. Potts and the Brigade Major, who'd not even checked out the area, had to be shown round by Hoffmeister.[7] (He added that when Potts took over the brigade, he became preoccupied with his social duties.) Potts then sent him to the Canadian Junior War Staff Course in Kingston. Hoffmeister thought this posting was the end of the world as he wanted to be only a regimental officer. He was totally unprepared for Staff College and initially worked himself into a state. Then, after agonizing, he decided to put his new philosophy into action and allow himself time for relaxing. He did very well, graduating first in his class. He was offered staff posts but declined them and was then offered CO of the Seaforths, which he eagerly took.

Vokes and Simonds in Italy

Harry Salmon was the 1st Division's GOC. Hoffmeister saw him only twice. Chris Vokes was brigade commander, and when Hoffmeister reported to him on his return from Kingston, Vokes said the Seaforths were the poor third battalion in the brigade, and he wanted them to be first. After the

....

5 Hoffmeister's breakdown *was* on his personnel file. See the account in Granatstein, *The Generals*, 191-92.
6 Staff Learners were, as the name suggests, attached to an HQ to learn the duties of a staff officer.
7 On Montgomery, see the first two volumes of Nigel Hamilton's *Monty* (London: Hamish Hamilton, 1981, 1986).

Seaforths trained in Inverary, Scotland (where they were told they were the best ever to go through), and after changes in officers and NCOs, they were fit to fight. The officers and NCOs took courses, they had done battle drill and been given full equipment, and they were happy. The original members of the unit were still largely there and most bad apples, despite begging to stay, had been returned to unit (sent back to Canada). Hoffmeister himself now felt prepared for war: thanks to Major P.H. LaBouchere, a British Eighth Army officer who had brought new ideas to Kingston, his Staff College training had given him confidence.

Hoffmeister said he got on well with Vokes and had confidence in him. He was a good guy who never stopped trying (he even set up a brothel for his soldiers in Sicily!).[8] He threw challenges at Hoffmeister with confidence and worked hard to equip himself for command. The troops trusted him, and he was honest. Moreover, in Sicily and Italy, all senior officers benefitted from being part of the British Eighth Army – their way of doing things was effective, and the army commanders treated corps commanders like friends and so on down the line. They watched, patted you on the back, and never let you feel alone.

Hoffmeister considered Guy Simonds, who took command of the 1st Division after Salmon died in an air crash of late April 1943, to be cold-blooded, and he clearly did not like him. He'd summon his COs to see him and coldly give orders. "Any questions?" Unlike the Brits, he paid no attention to the psychology of the situation. On one operation when Hoffmeister was brigade commander, Lieutenant-General Miles Dempsey, the Eighth Army's XIII Corps commander, popped in – "Have you got a moment?" – and gave him an extra battalion. When Hoffmeister asked about artillery, Dempsey told an aide, "Get Bert some guns." He even got him air support. This Simonds wouldn't do. Hoffmeister said that Simonds's tactical skills

....

8   Although establishing medically supervised brothels made sense as a way to control venereal disease, rampant in Sicily and mainland Italy, the idea did not go far. Canadian official prudery and fears about the concerns of those at home made such initiatives impossible. With the exception of Paul Jackson's *One of the Boys: Homosexuality in the Military during World War II* (Montreal and Kingston: McGill-Queen's University Press, 2010), there are no fully researched examinations of wartime sexual activity in the Canadian military. One useful American study is Mary Louise Roberts, *What Soldiers Do: Sex and the American GI in World War II France* (Chicago: University of Chicago Press, 2013).

were bad at the Arielli River operation of January 1944,[9] and he resented Simonds telling him at the German surrender in 1945 to turn his back on the defeated enemy. He refused to do this and returned their salutes. "The bastard" Simonds was later a representative for German companies and said that their owners were the finest people. He was the kind of man who liked to kick people when they were down, Hoffmeister stated.[10]

Hoffmeister remembered that Vokes called him in Sicily to say that Brigadier M.H.S. Penhale, marked by Montgomery for return to England, was in line for a decoration. Could he dream up a Distinguished Service Order citation for him? Hoffmeister made clear that he was out of sympathy with this. Penhale was unfit to be a brigade commander, and he himself was surprised that Simonds even took him to Sicily. He thought PFers such as Penhale drank too much and that some were too old and too fat. He himself never drank his rum ration, except behind the lines.

On the way to Sicily, Hoffmeister personally briefed every platoon in the Seaforths. He had friends in the ranks; for example, he used to row with one sergeant. He knew that other COs didn't brief every platoon, but the Seaforths saw him as a friend. This also meant that in action he had to put his neck out too. Morale would fall if he didn't show himself. He had to know the men's situation if they were to have confidence in him.

When he became Acting Brigadier of the 2nd Brigade on 1 November 1943, a Royal Artillery lieutenant-colonel was unhappy at following his orders because he looked too young to be in such a position. Hoffmeister then pushed him hard, and after that there was no problem, that artillery unit even switching to the 5th Armoured Division when Hoffmeister became its GOC and staying with it throughout the war.

On Crerar, Burns, and Foulkes

Vokes was completely different from Simonds as GOC.[11] Vokes was determined to make it work with Simonds, but he hated Harry Crerar, "that little yellow man," as he called him. But Hoffmeister said he liked Crerar. He

9 In the Arielli River operation, a brainchild of Simonds and George Kitching, the 11th Brigade made a daylight attack on the 1st German Parachute Division but was repulsed and retreated in disarray.

10 On Simonds, see Granatstein, *The Generals*; and Dominick Graham, *The Price of Command: A Biography of General Guy Simonds* (Toronto: Stoddart, 1993).

11 Vokes wrote a tape-recorded memoir: *Vokes: My Story* (Ottawa: Gallery Books, 1985).

didn't rate with British commanders who had battle experience and who were always better than Crerar, E.L.M. Burns, or Charles Foulkes.

No senior officer tried harder than Burns, Hoffmeister estimated, but he had the unfortunate knack of doing stupid things.[12] For example, when Hoffmeister was GOC of the 5th Armoured Division, he went to see Brigadier Ian Johnston of his 11th Brigade and discovered Burns there. "I've just been going over the operation with the Brigadier," Burns said. Hoffmeister was furious, that being his job, and Burns tried to settle him down. Hoffmeister threatened to complain to the army commander, their mutual superior, and Burns, repentant, asked him to overlook his blunder, which he did. But again when a New Zealand Division was attached to the Canadian Corps, Burns (who, he said, had guts and always went forward) declared that an operation would proceed even though the muddiness of the terrain advised against it. Hoffmeister and the New Zealand GOC disagreed. Burns insisted, and Hoffmeister again asked to see the army commander. Only then did Burns back down.

This made it very hard when Lieutenant-General Ken Stuart came from England to the 5th Armoured Division to ask Hoffmeister what he thought of Burns as corps commander. The British Eighth Army commander was trying to get rid of Burns. Hoffmeister decided that he wouldn't say anything against Burns and avoided answering his questions. He believed that Stuart should have had the guts to interview him in Burns's presence. He didn't know whether Vokes spoke truthfully to Stuart, though there was real animosity between Vokes and Burns. Hoffmeister wondered if he could have helped Burns, but he repeatedly did silly things. He was wound up too tight, didn't enjoy a drink, and didn't much care for the company of women. Evidently, he had been lined up with an Italian countess who asked him what he liked, only to be told that he was a man's man. Hoffmeister had heard this story and said that it was true.[13]

In November 1944, Vokes wrote to Brigadier M.H.S. Penhale, saying that he and Hoffmeister were planning to resign because they were fed up with Burns.[14] Hoffmeister absolutely denied the truth of this. Sure, he and Vokes

....

12   Burns wrote *General Mud: Memoirs of Two World Wars* (Toronto: Clarke Irwin, 1970).
13   For more on the "man's man" anecdote, see the interview with Major-General Desmond Smith, page 89.

had spoken of Burns's weaknesses, and Brigadier Pres Gilbride, the Deputy Adjutant and Quartermaster General of the I Canadian Corps, who could be devious and who had the ear of important people, probably played a role in the escalating complaints against Burns.[15] Nonetheless, Hoffmeister said he never threatened to resign.[16]

He thought Vokes would have been beyond his ability if he'd replaced Burns. He himself never gave a thought to the possibility that he might get command of the corps; he was so junior. Still, in Northwest Europe, Crerar told him there was a letter on file saying that he was to get the next corps vacancy.

Hoffmeister made clear that he disliked Charles Foulkes, the successor to Burns as I Canadian Corps GOC, this "vain, egotistical" man who spent his time determining what was good for Charles Foulkes.[17] He bristled at "that bastard" recalling him from leave at Positano to watch the 5th Division's move to Northwest Europe. Its staff was so good that it could do this by itself. "The silly bugger," he called Foulkes. Still, when Brigadier Graeme "Grimy" Gibson wanted Lieutenant-Colonel Syd Thomson, the Seaforths CO, sacked and Hoffmeister protested, Foulkes backed him up. When asked if any PFers showed courage in the field, he said, "I wished you hadn't asked that."

Going to the 5th Canadian Armoured Division
When Hoffmeister was 2nd Brigade commander in Italy, Crerar, the corps GOC, called him to meet at a bridge and offered him the 5th Canadian Armoured Division.

"How would you like to command 5th Armoured?" asked Crerar.

"Very much," said Hoffmeister. "When can I start?"

---

14 See the account in Granatstein, *The Generals,* 141-42, and Chap. 6.
15 The Deputy Adjutant and Quartermaster General directed and co-ordinated the Adjutant and Quartermaster matters, or the personnel and logistics matters, on behalf of a corps commander. He was assisted by the Deputy Assistant Adjutant and Quartermaster General as his deputy. At division, the Assistant Adjutant and Quartermaster General did this job. Gilbride had held this position for the 1st Division; as a brigadier, he became Deputy Adjutant and Quartermaster General of I Canadian Corps.
16 I believed Hoffmeister's statement. See the discussion of problems with Burns as I Canadian Corps GOC in Granatstein, *The Generals,* 132-43.
17 There is no biography of Foulkes, but see Douglas Delaney, *Corps Commanders: Five British and Canadian Generals at War, 1939-45* (Vancouver: UBC Press, 2011), Chap. 5.

"Well, you're a cool one, aren't you?" replied Crerar.

As GOC, Hoffmeister said, he exerted his personality on the 5th Division. For example, after the debacle of the Arielli River, the 11th Brigade was low in morale. Hoffmeister, who had just taken over the division, visited each unit and worked on them. The Perths, a regiment of the 11th Brigade that had also participated in the Arielli operation, had been hard hit, so he spoke to representatives from each platoon and got them talking about the problems with the regiment. The men revealed that four officers had performed badly on the Arielli. "That," Hoffmeister said, "was the reason for the low morale in the regiment." He sacked majors and captains and moved some others around. The Perths performed very well thereafter and led the way at the Gothic Line.[18]

He also said he organized division exercises so that all the infantry could get a sense of the firepower behind them, and to show that there was little threat from friendly fire, he personally went with every infantry company on field firing exercises so they would see there was nothing to fear. One day, a round fell short, and he remembered the troops looking at him – "What do you say now, wise guy?" The men realized that he had new ideas and would look after them. He also visited the quarters of every man and was appalled at the conditions of some. He made clear to the officers that there was more to command than the drill square or tactics. As a result of his approach, he stated, the division was completely transformed overnight.

Hoffmeister had no recollection of complaints from the Eighth Army about the 5th Armoured Division's staff work at the Hitler Line battles in May 1944 (the army had blamed the division for clogging the roads through the Liri Valley). He then talked of how Eric Snow was forced on him as a brigadier. Burns told him that this decision came from higher up, that Snow was PF and had to have his chance. In battle, Snow disappeared, and Hoffmeister had to track him down and force him into command.

Hoffy's Mighty Maroon Machine
After V-E Day in May 1945, Hoffmeister said that he was determined to thank every man in the 5th Canadian Armoured Division. Thus, he arranged to get

....

18 A graduate student paper written for me in 2003 at the University of Western Ontario by Lieutenant-Colonel (Ret'd) Richard Holt carefully checked unit war diaries and argued that Hoffmeister was not at the Perth Regiment at the time of this recollection.

every fighting vehicle on parade so that all could see Hoffy's Mighty Maroon Machine of which they were part. He ensured that all the men were on the parade ground twenty minutes beforehand and arranged for trucks to take them there. He also brought in the Royal Canadian Army Service Corps and Royal Canadian Ordnance Corps because, as he said, they too were fighting troops in the 5th Division. Hoffmeister got tears in his eyes when he talked about men stopping him on the street in Vancouver to say they'd served under him. That, he said, was all the thanks he ever wanted.

He spoke quite frankly about the difficulty of giving orders that sent men to die. After making several hospital visits to see the wounded, he could no longer bear to continue for fear that such visits would weaken his resolve as a commander.

MAJOR-GENERAL GEORGE KITCHING (1910-99)

INTERVIEW | VICTORIA, BC, 25 FEBRUARY 1992

A junior officer in the British Army, Kitching moved to Canada in 1938 and joined the Royal Canadian Regiment at the outbreak of war. He was a staff officer under Guy Simonds in the 1st Canadian Division and became GOC of the 4th Canadian Armoured Division until Simonds fired him during the Falaise Gap battle in August 1944. He then served as Brigadier General Staff for the I Canadian Corps. Kitching remained in the army after the war.[19]

We began by talking of the PF officers with whom he served.

The PF had no officers of quality, he said, nothing to work with. Major-General Harry Salmon was one of the best trainers, but he couldn't make up his mind under stress. (**Bruce Matthews**, Kitching said, had mentioned that to him, adding that Salmon was as good a teacher as Guy Simonds.) He wondered whether the 1st Division would have been as good under Salmon as it was under Simonds. He thought the inability to make decisions was general among those who'd been in the Great War, and he added that he often sat up at night for hours while Salmon dithered, doing things that he himself could have completed in twenty minutes.

....

19 Kitching's memoir is *Mud and Green Fields: The Memoirs of General George Kitching* (Langley, BC: Battleline Books, 1986).

He said he had gone from a junior officer to general in a few years and did the job. One day in 1934, when he was in the British Army officers' mess in India, his CO talked about generals and asked what the officers thought of them. In reply, Kitching said that everyone over thirty-five should get out of the infantry and everyone over fifty should drop dead. In other words, war was a young man's game; his confidence in himself was enormous, or so he claimed. And 1st Division in Sicily was so well trained in 1943 that there was confidence all down the line, though possibly the division had been wobbly during its 1942-43 training in Scotland. It had not participated in Exercise Spartan in 1943, which was a shambles, simply providing ammunition for those who wanted Andy McNaughton sacked.[20] The Brits didn't want anyone who would argue with them, which McNaughton was prepared to do. With his warm smile, McNaughton was loved by the men, especially the 1st Division. In Sicily, Kitching said, they were thrilled when he visited.[21]

On Simonds

Kitching liked Major-General Dan Spry, who had an open mind, a sense of humour, and the ability to argue. RMC closed minds – Simonds was the example of that. He wouldn't change his mind, wouldn't realize that divisions were affected by their casualties. Kitching thought that Operation Veritable in February 1945 had finally taught Simonds that a battalion of a hundred men couldn't be given the same orders as one of five hundred.[22] He would go forward to the front lines, and in Veritable he suddenly realized the effect of casualties. Simonds had never commanded an infantry battalion and knew little about infantry. He knew, however, what it should be able to do. He wouldn't go to hospitals until the battle was over; Kitching too hated visiting

....

20 Intended as a dress rehearsal for the invasion of Europe, Exercise Spartan was staged in southern England. Plagued by rushed decisions and muddled planning, it did not go well. McNaughton commanded the two corps of the First Canadian Army, which participated in the exercise, and badly mishandled his troops. This simply confirmed the suspicions of senior British generals that he was unfit to command in battle.

21 See the discussion of McNaughton in Granatstein, *The Generals*, 53-82. More favourable accounts can be found in Swettenham, *McNaughton*; and Rickard, *The Politics of Command*.

22 Operation Veritable in February 1945 pitted Simonds's corps against German defences in the Reichswald between the Rhine and Maas Rivers. Defending their homeland, the Germans fought fiercely from prepared defences, and the Canadian casualties were very heavy, the sometimes hasty attacks launched without sufficient support. Stacey, *The Victory Campaign*, Chap. 18.

hospitals. You knew you were sending men to their deaths, but you needed to focus on their mission, such as taking a hill, and remember that not all of them would die.

Kitching then spoke about his August 1944 firing by Simonds, a subject that clearly obsessed him. He suggested that he might have been sacked because he was not PF. After Operations Totalize and Tractable had failed to close the Falaise Gap as quickly as Montgomery had demanded,[23] someone had to go, and as he wasn't PF –. Foulkes had been nearly sacked before, but they'd decided to keep him in place, which meant that Kitching was the only remaining target. And since he was green –.

In Operation Totalize of August 1944, Kitching said he was done in by the Germans' 88-mm guns, which he'd never seen before and on which he'd never been briefed.[24] He thought his 4th Armoured Division's frontage (eight hundred yards) in the attack was too small – the cemetery there now takes almost all that frontage! Later, the Germans told him how astonished they were that the Canadians didn't keep going. General Harry Crerar had said they were to push on, but Simonds ordered a halt until after the second Royal Air Force bombing. That frustrated Kitching. To Simonds, concentration and surprise were the key principles of war. But by putting two armoured divisions on one mile of front, you had only four tanks up front with the rest behind.

Kitching argued that the Canadians were as well trained as the Wehrmacht in Normandy, but not the SS. The SS men were fanatics, trained to die.[25]

On Brits and Canadians

He thought the British generals largely disliked their Canadian counterparts. Field Marshal Montgomery did, except for Simonds. After his indiscreet

....

23 Operations Totalize and Tractable in August 1944 aimed to close the Falaise Gap and trap the retreating Germans between the eastward advancing US forces and the British and Canadians who were moving south from Caen. Stacey, *The Victory Campaign,* Chaps. 9-10. Simonds's plans were bold and initially broke through the defences but faltered, perhaps because they were beyond the capacities of his relatively untried troops and commanders, including Kitching and his 4th Armoured Division.

24 That Kitching had not been briefed on the 88-mm anti-tank gun seems unlikely. The Germans had certainly used it in the Spanish Civil War, in the 1940 campaign in France, in North Africa, and against Canadian troops in Italy's Liri Valley in May 1944. Reid's *No Holding Back* is excellent on Operation Totalize.

25 On the SS, see John A. English, *Surrender Invites Death: Fighting the Waffen SS in Normandy* (Mechanicsburg, PA: Stackpole, 2011).

letters of 1941 came to light, E.L.M. Burns had blotted his copybook with
them.[26] Kitching used to listen to Brits in their clubs, griping about "what
would Rod Keller, etc., know?" Monty led the crusade against them, and
he sneered at Chris Vokes, dismissing him as someone who would never
be anything more than a "good plain cook." Kitching remembered that the
Chief of Staff of the Eighth Army told him to "keep his generals awake" upon
finding out that Harry Foster liked to take a twenty-minute nap after lunch.
He claimed that the British generals who were bluff and hearty with Canadians were much stiffer with their own troops. He said that the British
Generals J.T. Crocker, Miles Dempsey, and Monty – all abstainers – reported
unfavourably on Keller, who was a drinker. Keller would have been unnerved
by these people. (Kitching added that he was with him on the night that the
4th Armoured Division took over from Keller's 3rd Division in Normandy.
Keller had had one Scotch. And though he'd lost some of his previous fire,
he seemed in good shape.) Kitching said he'd also objected to Monty telling
George Pearkes to go away when he was talking to Pearkes's officers. In 1953,
Monty told Kitching that Pearkes would have led the final charge against
the Germans and fought with a bayonet. Kitching thought Pearkes was a
good soldier with a brain (though one a bit warped).

Dan Spry's sacking from the 3rd Canadian Division in early 1945 came,
Kitching said, when Simonds asked him to do something and he replied,
"No, Sir, I don't think the division can handle that."[27] Then Holley Keefler
took over as GOC. He had as much personality as a dead dog, and the 3rd
Division went downhill.

E.L.M. Burns, Kitching said, got no credit because of his absolute lack of
personality. He couldn't relate to troops and couldn't praise them. When the
Irish Regiment came out of the line after fighting at Orsogna in 1944, Burns
detained it in the rain for twenty minutes while he gave it a lecture about
proper dress. Kitching's attitude was "Up the Irish," for which Burns criticized
him, probably pressured to do so by Crerar.

Crerar, Kitching said, was a good schoolteacher who rehearsed every word
he uttered to two or more people. A month before D-Day, when Simonds

....

26 Burns had written to his mistress in Canada, talking out of turn about generals and
     politicians, and his letters were intercepted by the censors. See Granatstein, *The
     Generals*, 128-30.
27 There are many versions of Spry's sacking. Others appear below.

did a sand table demonstration of the Seine crossing, Crerar said, "Gentlemen, I not only commend what Simonds has said but I command you to do it."[28] He was a ham actor with alliterative prepared spiels. After this, Simonds said, "I hope he's not there" when we do cross the Seine.

At Dieppe in August 1942, Crerar wanted action for the troops and, because he was a gunner officer, not an infantryman more accustomed to evaluating risky operations, accepted a plan for landing on a shore dominated by cliffs. Kitching said that Crerar had asked Pearkes to land at Dieppe with the 1st Division, but Pearkes had refused; that was why he was sacked, or so Pearkes told him.[29] The brigadiers in the 2nd Division saw their GOC, Hamilton Roberts, to complain about the plan, and Roberts wrote Crerar. "Roberts, if you don't want to do it, I'll find someone else who will," was the answer. Roberts was a damn good soldier, Kitching said. He thought the Brits weren't honest with the Canadians in connection with Dieppe, especially about the stoniness of the beach, which fatally impeded the Canadian tanks.[30] He blamed Royal Navy Captain John Hughes-Hallett, the Dieppe Naval Force commander during the raid, for the debacle.

Simonds became human after the war. He was always kind to Kitching and never gave him the back of his hand. Even his 1944 sacking was not done in anger. Kitching mentioned the Simonds-Crerar letters of January 1944.[31]

Simonds had also complained to Defence Minister J.L. Ralston that neither he nor Montgomery had been informed about Corps HQ coming into the Italian campaign. Ralston pretended to be annoyed that Simonds hadn't been advised. Then Simonds complained about the I Canadian Corps taking

....

28 On Crerar, see Dickson, *A Thoroughly Canadian General*; and Granatstein, *The Generals*, Chap. 4.

29 Pearkes told a different story to his biographer: "I was thankful my division wasn't asked to go. My views [opposing raids] were well known." Reginald H. Roy, *For Most Conspicuous Bravery: A Biography of Major-General George R. Pearkes, V.C., through Two World Wars* (Vancouver: UBC Press, 1977), 173.

30 There are many studies of Dieppe. See Denis Whitaker and Shelagh Whitaker, *Dieppe: Tragedy to Triumph* (Toronto: McGraw-Hill Ryerson, 1992). Whitaker was a junior officer in the Royal Hamilton Light Infantry at Dieppe, one of the very few to return to England.

31 When Crerar dispatched an officer to take measurements of Simonds's caravan, Simonds objected because he had not received advance notice. The subsequent dispute, conducted by an exchange of letters, was so bitter that Crerar wondered whether Simonds had gone mad. See Granatstein, *The Generals*, 161-63.

the vehicles intended for the 5th Armoured Division and told Ralston that he didn't want Crerar as a corps commander. Montgomery used to talk to Simonds about the strategic issues because he knew he'd absorb the information, but he wouldn't do so with Crerar. As far as Kitching was concerned, Simonds was fit in January 1944 (at the time that Crerar thought he had snapped). They'd spent a week on leave in Naples, and after Simonds rescued Prince Umberto from a car breakdown (the Prince was soon to become the last king of Italy), they enjoyed a day in Capri at the prince's expense. Still, dealing with Crerar might have unhinged Simonds. They'd not got on when he was his Brigadier General Staff in England. In mid-January 1944, however, Simonds was fine, and there was far greater strain around the time of Operation Veritable, when he'd been under stress for a year.

The Canadian Reinforcement Unit

The Canadian reinforcements situation was a shambles, Kitching stated. After he was sacked from the 4th Armoured Division, he went to the 13th Brigade, a training formation in the United Kingdom. It gave twenty-three days of so-called infantry training to Ordnance Corps men and other soldiers who were being remustered to the infantry. He found that General Roberts's Canadian Reinforcement Unit staff was full of washouts, and Roberts was morose. Perhaps Dan Spry was sent to the unit after he was fired the next year because he really was needed there.

On Charles Foulkes and senior officers

As Chairman of the Chiefs of Staff in Ottawa during the 1950s, Charles Foulkes was well into the booze, Kitching maintained, but he didn't drink much during the war, at least until the liberation of Holland. Vokes said, "One drink and Charles Foulkes will fall down." Kitching saw Foulkes at Operation Spring in Normandy in July 1944, when he was terrified of Simonds, fearful of being sacked and obsequious with him. He saw him next in Italy, where he discussed plans with **Bert Hoffmeister** and Harry Foster, the division commanders. Still, Foulkes didn't show to advantage by pretending that Italy was a second-rate show. Nonetheless, his plans were effective there and in Holland. In fact, sending the 5th Armoured Division to the Zuiderzee in April 1945 was classic. Kitching and Harry Salmon also saw Foulkes as Brigadier General Staff of the First Canadian Army to discuss the planning for Sicily; he knew his job and was on the ball. Socially, however, he was a problem, and Kitching recalled that he was plastered when he opened a soldiers' club at Ravenna, Italy. His evil genius was Brigadier Pres Gilbride, the Deputy Adjutant and Quartermaster General. When George Pearkes took over as Defence Minister in 1957, Kitching told him that Foulkes – who'd called Pearkes "that stupid fool" when Prime Minister Diefenbaker appointed him to the position – should be sacked. Later, Pearkes said that Kitching was right.

Foulkes got his revenge on Simonds for the way he'd been treated during the war. When Monty wrote to Canada in the 1950s, asking for Simonds as ground commander of NATO's Central Front, Foulkes quashed it. As Monty told Kitching, he'd been advised that Defence Minister Ralph Campney wouldn't permit it, and the Chiefs of Staff didn't like the idea.

General Basil Price, Kitching said, would have led a damn good platoon.

The 4th Armoured Division was not in good shape when Kitching took it over from F.F. Worthington in early 1944. Worthy was a bit like McNaughton in his technical bent. He had two jeeps – one to drive and one to sleep in – and two drivers, one fast and one for parades. He would have been a good leader, Kitching said, but Simonds sacked him in early 1944, believing it was wrong for someone of his age to plunge into fighting.

MAJOR-GENERAL HARRY F.G. LETSON (1896-1992)
INTERVIEW | OTTAWA, 21 MAY 1991

A badly wounded Great War veteran, Letson was an engineer, a professor at the University of British Columbia, and a Militia stalwart. During the Second World War, he served as Military Attaché in Washington and then in Ottawa as Adjutant General; he later returned to Washington to head the Canadian Joint Staff Mission. After the war, he was secretary to the Governor-General, Field Marshal Viscount Alexander. Letson was in his mid-nineties, ill, and very deaf when we spoke. Major-General N. Elliot Rodger was with me when he was interviewed.

General Letson began by speaking of the PF and RMC.

Letson noted that he was in command of the Vancouver–New Westminster Militia area when war broke out in 1939. His Non-Permanent Active Militia career had been long, despite his Great War wounds, and he played a major role in the Conference of Defence Associations, whose first meeting he attended in 1932.[32] (General **Elliot Rodger** interjected that he took notes there for Maurice Pope.)[33] He never saw difficulty between PF and Militia officers, and he didn't feel that RMC ex-cadets had a special "in." Overseas, it was always the best man for the job.

Pope, Letson said, carried out his duties well. Lieutenant-General Ken Stuart was "one of our top chaps," and, as he was an engineer too, he liked him. Letson knew him from an Advanced Militia Staff Course that Stuart ran. Lieutenant-General J.C. Murchie was a good chap, whom he had met when he came to British Columbia to inspect defences.

Major-General George Pearkes was no great administrator.

Dieppe

Dieppe was a "stupid" move for which Admiral Lord Louis Mountbatten was to blame, Letson said bluntly. Generals McNaughton or Roberts couldn't be faulted here; they didn't do the planning.

His time as Adjutant General

Letson took over as Adjutant General in February 1942. The biggest job, he said, was reorganizing the medical services. The senior Medical Officer was a Great War man, and the corps was starved to death, not that this was his fault. The air force and the navy were getting the doctors, and the army, held in low regard, was shortchanged. He got the Dean of Medicine at McGill to be Chief. Many people thought that Brock Chisholm was the right man for the job, but Letson said that Chisholm was thinking only of women's heads, by which he meant that Chisholm was too focused on psychiatry, his area of expertise, and thus he became second-in-command.[34]

Letson said that after serving in Ottawa, he was offered the choice of High Commissioner to India or chief of the Canadian Joint Staff Mission in Washington; he took Washington.

He said he admired Defence Minister J.L. Ralston and never forgave Prime Minister Mackenzie King for the way he'd treated him, firing him during

32 The Conference of Defence Associations, which began as a Militia lobby group, now devotes itself to defence advocacy.

33 Pope's memoir, *Soldiers and Politicians: The Memoirs of Lt.-Gen. Maurice A. Pope, C.B., M.C.* (Toronto: University of Toronto Press, 1962), is very useful.

34 In fact, Major-General Brock Chisholm became Director General of Medical Services in September 1942.

the 1944 conscription crisis.[35] He did say that Ralston was inclined to go into detail too much and to nitpick. Rodger added here that he'd once drafted a telegram for Ralston at Canadian Military Headquarters in London. Ralston edited it; he had to revise everything that was drafted for him.

MAJOR-GENERAL A. BRUCE MATTHEWS (1909-91)

INTERVIEW 1 | TORONTO, 25 APRIL 1991

A Militia gunner from a prominent Toronto family, Matthews commanded a regiment in England, was Commander, Royal Artillery (CRA), in the 1st Division in Sicily and Italy, Guy Simonds's senior artillery commander (CCRA) in the II Canadian Corps, and then the GOC of the 2nd Canadian Infantry Division.

Matthews was ill and frail when I saw him at his Toronto condo, but he was very clear-headed, and his memory was sharp. He began by talking of the Militia, the PF, and RMC.

Matthews had been in the artillery Militia in Toronto. The unit was terribly understrength, and many men and all the officers assigned their pay to the regiment. As it was, regimental funds had to be used to buy boots for the unit during the Depression because the Department of National Defence couldn't provide them. Serving in the Militia was time consuming – at least one night a week normally and an extra night or two if teaching a course or taking one. There was, he thought, good work done on theoretical training and at camp, though ammunition was in short supply, and one year there were literally no rounds to fire. Things began to change in about 1938, with Military District No. 2, headquartered in Toronto, becoming more attentive to the unit. The practice camps in 1938 and 1939 were well conducted, with

....

35 There are many studies of the conscription crisis. See Granatstein and Hitsman, *Broken Promises.* Letson was unwilling to forgive Andrew McNaughton for joining King's Cabinet: "I shall go to my grave wondering at the unbelievable arrogance of Andy in thinking that he could solve a problem [i.e., conscription] which so many able men had attempted to do without avail." Quoted in Richard J. Walker, "The Revolt of the Canadian Generals, 1944: The Case for the Prosecution," in *The Insubordinate and the Noncompliant: Case Studies of Canadian Mutiny and Disobedience, 1920 to Present,* ed. H.G. Coombs (Toronto: Dundurn, 2007), 78.

good instructors who put the men through their paces. He said he enjoyed the company of PF officers after hours and that there was a lot of talk about his unit's potential. However, there was some tension between PF and Militia, though less so in artillery than in other corps. "They embraced us," Matthews recalled. Gunners stuck together. Many gunner generals served in the war, so many that others complained of the "gunners' union."

Matthews said he saw a lot of PF instructors such as C.F. Constantine, Guy Simonds, H.O.N. Brownfield, T.V. Anderson, and **W.A.B. Anderson**. He did the long course at Kingston to qualify as a first lieutenant, and because he lived in quarters for a couple of months he got to know the artillery PFers there. He also did the Militia Staff Course, which gave him a good sense of appreciations, orders, and staff duties. The PF officers who taught this course, on one or two nights a week, were good; he thought they had passed the Staff College course in Britain.[36]

Matthews said his unit sought out RMC ex-cadets and that eight to ten a year usually came back from RMC to Toronto Militia units. He saw no resentment toward them, perhaps because they were good at whipping recruits into shape or preparing a grave-side party for funerals, etc. There was no resentment of RMC ex-cadets overseas either; at least he saw none. The army depended heavily on them during its first few years in the United Kingdom.

He did add that there was some grumbling in the Armoured Corps at PFers, perhaps because the corps was new, and there were few guidelines or set practices. He himself served under H.O.N. Brownfield, a PF officer from the Royal Canadian Horse Artillery, without problem. But the PF itself did have a problem when it came to promotion.

On promotion

Promotion struck him as mysterious, he claimed. The Military Secretary in Ottawa and at Canadian Military Headquarters in London moved in strange ways, and if seniority didn't govern promotion, he couldn't tell how it worked. He spent some time with Brownfield, who was the first CRA in the 1st Division, and they discussed the men who might potentially be promoted; those

....

36   The British Army's Staff College at Camberley trained selected captains from across the empire on a two-year course. The Staff College at Quetta in India had equal status. Getting the post-nominal "psc," or "passed staff college," was the route to high command. A military appreciation, routinely produced before an operation, followed a set approach, covering standard categories: Aim, Factors, Courses Open, and Plan.

with adverse comments on file went back to Canada. The problem was the huge expansion of the army, the scramble for talent. There was experimentation and many failed.

As for himself, he had come into the Militia after taking the long course, and he was promoted reasonably quickly to Captain. He served as Adjutant of his unit, which was mobilized in September 1939 – a tribute to its good results at camp and in competition, and to its very near complete strength. In Britain, his battery was merged with another, and he became superfluous. He thought he might be sent home, but instead he was posted to the 1st Medium Regiment. Then in 1941, when a new Medium Regiment was formed, General Andy McNaughton called him in and offered him command. He was allowed to hand-pick forty men from his old regiment and forty more from another. He admitted to a certain nervousness about taking over a unit of that size, but more from fear of artillery accidents than anything else. As it was, the Brits were very helpful – "They were damn glad to see us." He did say that his regiment initially had old steel-wheeled 60-pounder guns, but it devised a way of carrying them on tank transporters and found that they could be moved into action almost as quickly as rubber-tired guns. He worried too about the lack of opportunity to train with the other arms, and when exercises of that sort began, he was frustrated that the other units weren't ready. Later, as the Canadian Corps' Counter-Battery Officer, he roamed around as eyes and ears for the CCRA, being under-employed at the time, and found that some artillery regiments were slack. This tended to confirm the complaints about the low standard of training. When Major-General Harry Salmon was the 1st Division commander, Matthews recalled, he'd get the whole HQ out for physical training (PT), and Salmon would do the exercises along with the men; in his own Medium Regiment, Matthews said, there was vigorous PT five days a week.

Andy McNaughton

McNaughton, Matthews said, was revered during the first year, especially by gunners. But his charm diminished considerably. Matthews used to hear senior people bemoaning him. Andy was a dragon about equipment and would happily get his hands dirty, sometimes scrambling under a vehicle to repair it. He had a difficult role because of Cabinet orders to keep Canada first – looking after Canadian interests trumped everything else. He wasn't an eloquent man and didn't try to persuade the Brits of this – he would just say these are my orders. There was a sense about him of refighting the Great War, and the Chief of the Imperial General Staff Alan Brooke and General Bernard Montgomery found him tiresome, lacking in spirit and drive.[37] Matthews said he remembered going to a conference at Corps HQ and finding McNaughton under a truck, looking for the source of transmission problems.

Eighth Army influence

In Sicily and Italy, he admired British Eighth Army procedures: there were no frills, but everyone was kept informed. Verbal orders were only occasionally followed by a memo. The Canadian practice was more formal, so when he became CCRA in Northwest Europe, he found that much of his time was now taken up with procedure, and he attended constant meetings to work out fire plans. Corps or Army HQ Orders Groups could be unfocused, and senior commanders sometimes had difficulty in figuring out what their superiors wanted, but because he'd watched the Eighth Army operate, he knew what to do.[38]

Simonds, Matthews said, had frequent Orders Groups and even more frequent meetings of his small executive.

2nd Division GOC

Matthews talked about his own role as a division commander. The responsibility did not awe him. As a CRA and CCRA, he had worked closely with the infantry and armoured commanders, watched attacks with them, and thought he knew their minds better than they did. The turnover in infantry commanders was such that he'd been involved longer than many of them, such as **George Kitching**, Rod Keller, and Dan Spry. (Kitching, he added, was very able and found himself caught in a difficult situation between the Poles and Canadians in Normandy.[39] As it was, he made a good comeback after being fired.) Matthews had gained much experience in Sicily and Italy,

....

37 On Brooke, see A. Danchev and D. Todman, eds., *Alanbrooke War Diaries, 1939-1945* (London: Weidenfeld and Nicolson, 2001). Brooke and McNaughton had served together in the Canadian Corps' artillery during the Great War.

38 Fire plans lay out what the artillery is to do where and when in an operation. Orders Groups occurred when a commander issued his orders to his subordinates. The term could apply at all levels from platoon to army.

39 In the Falaise Gap battle in August 1944, the green 4th Armoured and the Polish Armoured Division were operating alongside each in a fluid battle, facing heavy fighting and casualties. Inevitably, command and control suffered, and Kitching was sacked from his post as GOC.

but even so it was difficult to command. He gave his brigadiers a free run, and his job was to allocate support to them. He had trouble with Brigadier **W.J. Megill**, the one PFer who may have resented serving under a Militia GOC, but it was too late in the war to do anything about this.

Matthews recalled that Simonds came frequently to his HQ, as did Harry Crerar and Monty. Simonds drew up the overall plan for operations, allocating areas to his divisions. He'd go over Matthews's plan, asking pointed questions. But most discussion/negotiation was through the General Staff Officers, Grade 1 (GSO1s), who argued over supplies, road use, and so on.[40] As a GOC, Matthews said, he modelled himself on Simonds. He would go forward to brigades, as he was constantly urged to do. And when an attack was under way, he'd try to go to the battalions near the start line to sense whether the company and platoon commanders had a grip on their objectives. There was never enough time to conduct reconnaissance before the attack, which meant that the advancing Canadian troops commonly stumbled onto mines or obstacles that no one knew about. Of course, because the Allies had air superiority and could thus protect their troops, battalions could be trucked very close to the start lines.

His 2nd Division had had a hard time at Dieppe and then during the July 1944 attack on the Normandy village of Carpiquet and its airfield. Its morale had been badly dented. When he took over in November 1944, he was told that the division needed careful handling, a boost in morale, and more training. Fortunately, he had six to eight weeks to achieve this, and he ran company schools, training, and so on. He also gave reassurance, reasoned with the troops, and encouraged their questions.

He tried to avoid hospital visits, something that was easy to do because wounded men were evacuated so quickly. Appalled by the casualties, he tried

....

40 The General Staff Officers, Grades 1, 2, and 3, were the key planners at brigade and division level, handling intelligence, operations, and monitoring of the battle. In a division, the GSO1 was a lieutenant-colonel, the GSO2 his deputy, and the GSO3 the deputy's assistant. Additional GSO3s handled intelligence and other areas. In a brigade, the Brigade Major was the de facto GSO1, with several GSO3 captains covering various functions. In a corps, the General Staff, or G branch, was led by the Brigadier General Staff, later renamed Chief of Staff. In an army, the Colonel GS was replaced in early 1944 by the Chief of Staff in brigadier rank. The Adjutant General, or A branch staff, had responsibility for personnel – training, discipline, and replacements. The Quartermaster General – or Q staff – dealt with logistics, the stockpiling of ammunitions and weaponry, and the movement of troops and supplies.

to assure the troops that he was doing everything possible to minimize them. He also spoke of this with Simonds and his Chief of Staff, **Elliot Rodger** – was everything being done to minimize casualties? When they were high in a particular operation, had something gone seriously wrong? The reinforcement situation and the cold, wet winter of 1944-45 made the whole situation that much harder.

On Crerar and Simonds

Harry Crerar was a professional, but his approach was too academic and he always did things by the book. He could be charming to talk to, but his Orders Groups weren't inspiring, as he monotonously outlined his plans. There wasn't much vigour there, not much aggression, though he wasn't incompetent. Matthews said he didn't resent this, but he was clearly no admirer of Crerar. Nor did he admire Brigadier Churchill Mann, the Chief of Staff, First Canadian Army. Mann was too eccentric for the GOCs' taste: he seemed to feel he had to polish up Crerar's plans to make them more dynamic.

Simonds lived up to his reputation. He was brusque and demanding but reasonable. If you stated that a plan wouldn't work, he'd hear you out, though he might insist on sticking to it. He had a reputation for being ruthless with people, but Matthews saw no signs of this. As CRA of the 1st Division, he was close to Simonds; of course, as an artillery officer Simonds understood the problems of gunners. For example, Matthews's HQ ship was sunk en route to Sicily, leaving him with no other office support than a typewriter and a clerk. He was obliged to borrow help from the British forces, and when the first divisional shoot was laid on, he had to tell Simonds that because he was so understaffed, it couldn't start when scheduled.

"When will it be ready?" asked Simonds.

"Three hours later," Matthews replied.

"Then make it so." Simonds trusted Matthews.

Still, as a commander, Simonds kept the pressure on, which contributed to casualties and waste. He regularly got annoyed at the armour, which wouldn't go far enough forward for him, Matthews said. He pioneered night armour attacks in Normandy with Operation Totalize, and Matthews did the fire plan, using tracers and smoke to guide the advance. There were significant problems with supplies, the red smoke shells arrived only at the last minute, and the Normandy bridgehead was chaos. The real difficulty was that everything had to be done at once, that there was never enough time for proper planning.[41] For example, the old idea of registering artillery targets was scrapped, and they shot by the map, a real problem as the maps weren't very accurate. The pressure, the magnitude of the operations, was unbelievable. Simonds was genuinely innovative, though he had limited success. At Caen and on the road to Falaise, he had the 4th Armoured Division, which was semi-trained, and the 2nd and 3rd Divisions, which had had a hard time.

Keller and Vokes

Generals Rod Keller and Chris Vokes were close friends. Matthews knew Vokes well, but not Keller. He never felt confident that either really grasped things. Vokes was likeable and full of energy but very nervous at times. He could ring up Matthews as CRA in the middle of the night, worried because he'd heard guns firing. In fact, he was an ideal brigade commander, comfortable lying in the mud, looking through binoculars. But he didn't meet the standards of either the Eighth Army or Simonds. Keller wasn't up to snuff either, and his artillery commanders had a hard time with him. It was difficult to find him in action. Vokes was very critical of everyone from the Prime Minister on down and didn't think much of the higher echelons.

Harry Foster was a better brigadier than GOC, a tough fighter. Matthews thought he didn't enjoy being a division commander. But when Foster (or Vokes, with whom he traded divisions) was on his division's flank, he did all that was asked. (In a subsequent telephone conversation on 14 May 1991, Matthews said he'd been too harsh on Vokes and Foster. Both were good brigade commanders, and he was incorrect if he suggested they were a bit edgy as GOCs. He had no right to say that, and, he added, he'd served under Vokes for seven to eight months without difficulty.)

Foulkes and senior officers

Matthews liked Charles Foulkes as an individual, but he wasn't popular with his commanders or with the Eighth Army. He'd had a difficult time with the 2nd Division and got really smeared during the attack on Carpiquet. It wasn't his fault that he had trouble with his brigade commanders, Matthews said, as he hadn't had the division for long. Foulkes and Simonds tolerated one

....

41 For a good account of the time pressures on commanders, see Ben Kite, *Stout Hearts: The British and Canadians in Normandy, 1944* (Solihull, UK: Helion, 2014), Chap. 8.

another, though he thought Foulkes was envious of Simonds. Still, Foulkes proved to be a better corps commander than a division GOC.

Clearly, Matthews couldn't quite understand why the 2nd Division was given to Foulkes; others could have done better with it, such as Brigadier Sherwood Lett. He repeated that Foulkes was unpopular up and down the ranks, and concluded that he probably rose because his seniority as a PFer meant that he couldn't be overlooked.

Holley Keefler was ambitious and able, though Matthews didn't like the way he instantly adopted Highland dress when he took over the 3rd Division. He thought he looked down on other senior officers because of his education. Still, he was a good brigade commander, and he himself got on well with him.

Dan Spry was dreadfully young, he said, about a month or two younger than he was! Their first action in Italy, when Spry got a brigade, had a complex plan requiring two barrages and a change of axis in between. It didn't work and Matthews, as CRA, had to stop the barrage in mid-shoot, something that was never done. But Spry learned. Then the strain got too much for him (when he had the 3rd Division), and he had to be relieved.

On manpower and reinforcements

Matthews thought that Canada, for political reasons, took on too much in the war. The country couldn't support an army, with all its specialist units, and was always begging for assistance. Having just two corps and serving under UK command would have been better.

On reinforcements, he said, there were problems, especially with French Canadian units, but he didn't seem to see the difficulties as darkly as Ottawa did. Still, he had to put anglophone officers who couldn't speak French into the Régiment de Maisonneuve. He blamed the manpower crisis on Canada's too numerous military commitments, though he didn't criticize Defence Minister Ralston, who worked hard.

MAJOR-GENERAL A. BRUCE MATTHEWS

INTERVIEW 2 | TORONTO, 10 JUNE 1991

This second interview took place over lunch at Matthews's residence. His wife was present.

He began with his early youth.

He described himself as a dropout. He spent ten years at Upper Canada College and then applied for RMC in 1926-27 but failed the entrance examinations, though narrowly. He was urged to sit them again, but refused and went to Europe, taking French lessons in Switzerland and sitting in on lectures at Geneva. Then it was back to Canada and into business with his father's brokerage. He worked in New York City from 1929 to 1930 and was supposed to go to London, but he came home because of the Depression. He then passed his time in the Militia almost as a hobby, but he'd wanted to be in the service. He wanted to join the Naval Reserve, but when he was turned down because of colour-blindness, a neighbour, the Adjutant of an artillery regiment, hooked him instead. He found he could do reasonably well in the Militia and took the officers' long course at Kingston. He knew a lot of RMC graduates and got them into his 7th (Toronto) Regiment, where they were a boon to it.

Sophistication in the artillery
He said he'd heard that his battery was to be mobilized in 1939. This was for geographical reasons – Toronto had to be represented – but it was also based on some crude assessments of readiness. He thought there were differences between Toronto and Prairie or Maritime artillery units in sophistication. The Prairie and Maritime officers were a bit crude but competent – he called his Toronto-centric attitude schoolboyish – and there was no fraternization for a time. But postings broke this down. There was an element of snobbery here and of class, he said.

With his wife in England
Matthews's first wife was an American whom he met in Canada. Her mother was Canadian, and she was visiting her sister, who had married a Canadian. They married in 1937, and she came to the United Kingdom in 1940 to be with him. At the time, American citizens were not permitted to travel to a war zone, but his father, then the Lieutenant-Governor of Ontario, arranged a passport for her in forty-eight hours, and she came over. She had left one child at home, and she returned to Canada in August 1940, when wives had to be sent home. In 1941, when she gave birth to twins, acquaintances gossiped and counted the months, not knowing she'd been in Britain with her husband. Matthews did not get back to Canada for the entire six years of war – every time he was scheduled to return, he'd be promoted or posted. And when he did get back in late 1945, one of his twins, then five years old, said, "Mommy, who is that man?"

Matthews added that what he missed postwar was his batman and two good Aides de Camp. It also took time for him to learn that business didn't work quite the way the army did. Nor did the church when he was involved in fundraising.

When he sailed to Britain in 1939, Matthews shared a cabin with **Frank Lace**, who had worked in his father's firm and was his battery captain. After that, they saw little of each other until Lace was made CRA of the 2nd Division. And then, curiously, they shared a cabin again, upon returning to Canada in the fall of 1945.

Matthews claimed to be puzzled by his own rise. He obviously kept track of his rank – he knew he was the senior artillery major in 1941, for example, but he never got the call to command a regiment. He wasn't bypassed; it was just that he didn't get a regiment. Then McNaughton called him in, gave him command of a Medium Artillery Regiment, and told him to take it over the next day. He had forty NCOs and gunners, and his pick of officers.[42]

Matthews had heard rumours that he'd been promoted because his father was Lieutenant-Governor of Ontario. But this was patently untrue, he maintained; and anyway, his father wasn't in a position to pull strings. People shot down this story effectively. He mentioned that his parents came from Lindsay, Ontario, and that his father had switched to the Liberals after the Great War, though he was friendly with Conservative leader Arthur Meighen.

In Italy and Northwest Europe

Matthews spoke warmly of the Brits' generosity in helping the Canadians learn. But they used to rib him – how could he, a militiaman, be a CRA? How could someone so young have this job? As he said, the army's sudden growth meant that positions had to be filled, and someone had to be found to do the job. In Sicily, after his HQ ship had been sunk and a British Eighth Army Group Royal Artillery came to help out, he noted its helpfulness. Its members gave advice with good grace. The armoured units received similar help, but not the infantry – it was too big.

Matthews spoke of the freedom a GOC had in Italy, where you were more on your own. In Northwest Europe, however, the operations were so big that you were just a cog, and there was little a GOC could do about tactical

----

42 A Medium Regiment had sixteen 5.5-inch (or 4.5-inch) guns and was ordinarily under army command, able to support any brigade, division, or corps as required.

requirements. It was a rushed, difficult atmosphere in which to command. After the Normandy breakthrough in August 1944, and after the Rhine crossings in March 1945, there were periods of relative freedom, however.

Matthews recalled that he had enough French to talk to the francophone units in the 2nd Division (two infantry battalions and one Medium Artillery Regiment). He got on well with them, but the lack of French-speaking officer reinforcements was a big problem. He was obliged to use English-speaking officers in the francophone units.

Kitching, Matthews said, was a professional who made a good comeback after he was sacked. Matthews doubted that even a highly trained 4th Canadian Armoured Division could have done better at Falaise, where Kitching was fired – the fog of war there was terrific. He was surprised when Kitching was sacked so quickly but didn't think that Simonds had fired him to save his own job. Certainly, there were no rumours to that effect. He felt sorry for Kitching.

He noted that the Canadians never fought a rear-guard action or a retreat and wondered whether they'd have done well. Their aggressive nature and desire to be on the move might have made it difficult.

Harry Salmon, as GOC of the 1st Division, was a conventional commander, no innovator.[43] He wasn't easy to serve under, though he was pleasant enough. But his instructions in training exercises weren't always clear, and it was hard for officers to know what to do. Still, even if he was no Simonds, he knew his way around. Matthews mentioned an order from Montgomery that all officers were to do PT for thirty minutes a day and remembered that Salmon always arrived late for the HQ's awkward squad exercises.

On the way to Sicily, Matthews was on the command ship with Simonds when they ran into a storm the day before the landing. He was retching and ill but had to do his job.

He recalled that he went on leave to Cairo with Vokes, and as they travelled south by train they were told that their carriage had to be fumigated. When Vokes demurred, the conductor zapped him full in the face with a flit gun to kill the bugs. Later, Vokes had a snake charmer wrap a python around him as part of some fortune-telling ritual.

....

43 Major-General H.L.N. Salmon was a decorated Great War veteran and PF officer who commanded the 1st Division. In late April 1943, on his way to North Africa to be briefed on the division's role in the invasion of Sicily, he died in an airplane crash. Guy Simonds replaced him.

Postwar

After Simonds married the ex-wife of G.G. Sinclair, a lawyer, the two of them spent a few vacations in Jamaica with Matthews and his wife. Simonds decided to take up golf and spent hours practising. He wanted to be good at anything he did, and his wife would ask Matthews how well he'd played, knowing that there'd be trouble if things had gone badly. Simonds, he said, became a good player.

2 | THE FIGHTERS

IN THIS CHAPTER, I grouped alphabetically the twelve officers whom I characterized as fighters. Four came from the Permanent Force, and the rest were from the Militia. Bell-Irving, Bennett, Calder, Moncel, Rowley, Smith, and Whitaker came from comfortable family circumstances; the others did not. Four graduated from RMC – Bogert, Smith, and Ware joining the PF, and Whitaker the Militia. Most of the twelve held staff positions at one time or another, ranging from Aide de Camp to General Staff Officer, Grade 1, but their primary wartime role was to lead troops in battle at levels ranging from the platoon to battalion to brigade. Some knew their division, corps, and army commanders well; others had only limited contact with them, often from a distance. Their job was to carry out their orders and to issue them to their subordinates. If the orders made sense, the battle sometimes went as planned; if the orders were misguided, the battle could turn into a debacle. In that case, the subordinates were more likely to be sacked than the senior commander. Naturally enough, all held strong views on the Canadian Army's leaders, and it ought to come as no surprise that these views differed, sometimes very sharply.

Andrew McNaughton was just the first army leader to be praised highly by some and viewed askance by many. So were Harry Crerar, Guy Simonds, E.L.M. Burns, and Charles Foulkes, and the fighters' comments on other leaders are often scathing but must be judged against the stress and pressures of war and the complexity of command; in times of such extraordinary difficulty and challenge, harsh or intemperate language must be put into context. The officers whose interviews are presented in this chapter were nevertheless especially riled by the "dugouts" – the senior officers with Great War experience who led the army during the first two or three years of the war. It is also fair to say that virtually no one had a good word for General Charles Foulkes, whose rise to command of the 2nd Canadian Division and then of the I Canadian Corps seemed mysterious to those who served under him or watched his wartime and postwar career arc. Similarly, Rod Keller, the

3rd Division GOC who led the Canadians in the invasion of Normandy, had few defenders, though Roger Rowley, who became a battalion Commanding Officer in Normandy, spoke highly of him.

Several of the interviews are particularly useful, notably those of Generals Bogert, Megill, Moncel, and Tellier, who remained in the army after the war. Generals Bogert and Megill were successful brigade commanders, Megill in the 2nd Division under Foulkes and Matthews, and Bogert in the 1st Division, commanded by Generals Vokes and Foster. Both were PF officers, and Megill, who had a reputation for being "difficult," was said to resent GOCs who came from the Militia. His time with Bruce Matthews, however, went reasonably smoothly, a sharp contrast to his stint in Normandy, when the 2nd Division was led by PF officer Charles Foulkes, for whom Megill had little or no regard.

Moncel had a certain natural hauteur, but his interview was also first-rate, not only because he served under and observed Guy Simonds for a substantial period as a staff officer, but also because he took command of the 4th Armoured Brigade in the 4th Canadian Armoured Division during the last stages of the Falaise Gap battles in August 1944 and led it successfully through to the end of the war under Harry Foster and Chris Vokes as GOCs. His comments on the time it took to build the First Canadian Army into a first-class fighting force were very suggestive, as were his remarks on how leaders could act to minimize casualties in action.

Henri Tellier's interview was one of two that I conducted with francophone officers, the other being with Ernest Côté in the next chapter. Tellier was Aide de Camp to Crerar in England and then fought in Italy with the Royal 22e Régiment. His remarks on Canadiens in the army, on reinforcements, and on leadership were very useful to me in my research for *The Generals*.[1]

All these interviews offer the perspective of officers at "the sharp end" of military life. They trusted – or sometimes mistrusted – their superiors, and they sometimes earned or lost their leaders' trust, and occasionally that of their subordinates. They appreciated kind words from senior officers, and they deeply resented slurs; they fretted over promotions and demotions. They knew that fighting the war was their primary role, but they struggled for place and prestige much as people in civilian life did and do in peacetime.

....

1   And also for my book *Canada's Army: Waging War and Keeping the Peace* (Toronto: University of Toronto Press, 2002).

BRIGADIER H.P. BELL-IRVING (1913-2002)

INTERVIEW | VANCOUVER, BC, 4 MARCH 1992

Bell-Irving was a Militia officer in the Seaforth Highlanders before the war, commanded the Loyal Edmonton Regiment, rose to Brigadier by 1945, and served on SS commander Kurt Meyer's military trial for war crimes. He was later Lieutenant-Governor of British Columbia.

He began by talking about General Hoffmeister.

Bert Hoffmeister was already in the Seaforth Highlanders when Bell-Irving joined in 1933. At the time, Hoffmeister was too young for Bell-Irving to suspect that he might one day be a great man, though overseas he did deliberately transfer into Hoffmeister's company because he disliked his own Company Sergeant Major. In Vancouver before the war, Bell-Irving had dated the daughter of timber baron H.R. MacMillan, and the old man told him that he had a young employee in Pine Company, one Bert Hoffmeister, who was about to leave the production line. "In twenty years," predicted MacMillan, "he'll be president of the company." Hoffmeister's father was a low-rank worker/manager of little consequence. Hoffmeister was a good Commanding Officer in the United Kingdom, and under him the regiment tended to respond positively to requests to send officers on courses. He had to fire a few people. Bell-Irving recalled that when he was Support Company Officer Commanding and had to discipline a sergeant, Hoffmeister then received an anonymous letter threatening to have the Seaforths boo the king and queen on a forthcoming visit unless Bell-Irving were sacked. That frightened Hoffmeister, but nothing came of it.

He thought there was PF resentment when Hoffmeister got command of the Pacific Force in 1945.[2] Hoffmeister had taken the 5th Armoured Division and transformed it into the Mighty Maroon Machine, with every man conscious of the tag. He made the esprit division-wide and did wonders for a latecomer, makeshift division such as the 5th Armoured. It was rare for a division to have this spirit – the 1st Division really didn't, in part because Guy Simonds was always dreaming of a corps whenever he commanded it.

....

2 Canada had agreed to provide an infantry division, organized and equipped on American lines, for the invasion of Japan in 1945. Japan's surrender after the atomic bombings of August 1945 cancelled the planning.

As far as Bell-Irving was concerned, he was a Seaforth, a 1st Division and, an Eighth Army man – and a Canadian.

Hoffmeister's working-class origins didn't matter in the Seaforths. They had no class consciousness; instead, they were peers, largely from the professional class in the city. They took no pay, Bell-Irving stated, assigning it all to the regiment.

Militia training

The Militia gave useful training, or at least made the Seaforths into a regiment with esprit. The Seaforth Warrant Officers and NCOs were first class; they all worked together and enjoyed each other. But of things military they knew little. They did drill, and in their field exercises a section was two men holding a ten-foot pole. Still, they produced their own COs overseas and provided them to other units. What made no sense was that when they went to the United Kingdom, they were taught from useless 1917 texts.

On the PF

Bell-Irving maintained that he'd had a poor opinion of the PF in the 1930s. PFers had too little to do, and they spent too much time in the bar, which upset the "working professionals" in the Seaforths. They were lazy and sloppy, and they didn't think or work like Militia officers. Certainly, overseas he thought the Seaforths were better than the three PF regiments in the 1st Division. According to him, Militia officers thought that PFers received more promotions than they did; he knew nothing about the political links of Militia officers.

On senior officers

He remembered hearing Victor Odlum described overseas as "a silly old political general who knew nothing," a remark that prompted one officer to get up and walk out of a meeting.

George Pearkes was a splendid brigadier, a tremendous man who believed that if his brigade had been in France during 1940, the country would never have fallen. That was nonsense, Bell-Irving said, but soldiers are happy to believe comments like that.[3]

....

3   Reginald Roy covers Pearkes's life in *For Most Conspicuous Bravery.*

Bell-Irving described Andy McNaughton as a scholar and a gentleman who was too much a technician to be a senior commander. When he came to see the Seaforths in Scotland before they went to Sicily, his interests were in ballistics, entirely unlike those of Simonds. Still, when Bell-Irving was running the Battle Drill School, he redesigned the two-inch mortar, and the result greatly interested McNaughton, even if the War Office disliked Bell-Irving's innovation.

He said he didn't know Simonds in Sicily and didn't like his aping Montgomery. In Amsterdam after the war, when the Brigadier J.F.A. Lister scandal blew up, Simonds had people arrested very fast.[4] To Bell-Irving, this was to ensure that he wasn't blamed. Still, he deserved his military reputation.

Chris Vokes was something special, and Bell-Irving claimed he liked but didn't have great respect for him. He worked well with him because he stood up to him. At Catania, Sicily, Vokes invited him to dinner and then forgot about the invitation. But when he showed up, Vokes was unfazed and sat down with him anyhow. His humour was coarse and crude but not really dirty or nasty. He was no great man. When Bell-Irving was CO of the Loyal Edmonton Regiment, he was ordered to take an objective by a set route, but he diverted from it and got to the objective. Vokes had been furious at the diversion but then was pleased. When he had the 4th Canadian Armoured Division, Vokes asked for him and made him a brigadier because he was lonely: "I'm 1st Division and I know how to do it," Vokes said, and the 4th Armoured didn't like that.

Kurt Meyer

Bell-Irving, who sat on the Kurt Meyer military trial, described Meyer as a splendid man and fine soldier.[5] He approved when Vokes commuted Meyer's sentence to life imprisonment – and said that the original sentence of death by firing squad was intended to be a step up from hanging.

....

4　Lister was the senior administrative officer of the Canadian forces in the Netherlands after V-E Day and was court-martialled, essentially for living too well in Holland's straitened economy.

5　On Kurt Meyer, the commander in Normandy of the 12th SS Hitler Jugend, judged guilty of ordering the murder of Canadian POWs in June 1944, see especially P.W. Lackenbauer and C.M.V. Madsen, eds., *Kurt Meyer on Trial: A Documentary Record* (Kingston: Canadian Defence Academy, 2007).

LIEUTENANT-COLONEL PETER BENNETT (1917-96)

INTERVIEW | LONDON, UK, 6 SEPTEMBER 1991

*Bennett came from the Toronto elite (he attended Upper Canada College)
and was in the 48th Highlanders before the war. He went overseas in 1939
with the 48th Highlanders, was Brigade Major to Harry Foster on D-Day,
CO of the Essex Scottish at Falaise in August 1944, and General Staff
Officer, Grade 1, to Bruce Matthews in the 2nd Division.*

Bennett opened the interview by talking about the PF and RMC.

PF officers were seen as poseurs by the Militia, and RMC graduates were
scorned and resented, not least on the dance floor, where they cut a swath
in the 1930s. But once the war was on, this didn't matter; moreover, there
were very few from RMC in the infantry by 1944, the officers being Militia
or those who enlisted during the war.

Training in England with the 48th Highlanders

Bennett thought that the Canadian Army was ill-trained in 1939-40 and that
the 1st Division was ill-equipped. There was no sense of readiness, though
the troops were keen enough. He gave the example of going on a Bren gun
course in Britain, the 48th having none, and on his return giving a lecture
on how not to do fieldcraft in the 48th. He had the feeling that, despite their
defeats, the Brits were good and the Canadians not. From his point of view,
training in the corps began only when General Montgomery arrived, and he
still remembered the rigours of Monty's big Exercise Tiger in May 1942. He
recalled that the 48th's CO in early 1942, Lieutenant-Colonel W.B. Hendrie,
persisted in using his own training program after Monty had ordered all units
to follow a set program – that is to say, his. When Monty arrived and discovered that the 48th was still using the old program, Hendrie was gone in
forty-eight hours. Bennett thought that many Canadian generals were Brits,
but upon reflection he concluded that they just acted as if they were.

On senior officers

As a General Staff Officer, Grade 3, Bennett went riding with George Pearkes,
who had won the opportunity to go hunting by supplying a Home Guard
cavalry unit with hay.

Although Bennett never met Harry Crerar, he did speak with him on the
phone at one point. During the winter of 1944-45, when Bennett was a staff

officer in the 3rd Division at Nijmegen, Holland, Crerar called and asked him for a patrol report. Bennett invented a report on the spot and was astonished when he later got kudos for it. He didn't feel that Crerar made any impact on the troops, though Guy Simonds, who had presence, did. The soldiers knew who **Bruce Matthews** was, but they didn't know Harry Crerar, who wasn't seen as a commander.

He agreed with the widespread suspicion that General Rod Keller "was yeller." Though he was popular with the troops, Keller stayed in a slit trench at a D-Day or D-Day+1 Orders Group, giving his orders while everyone else stood up top around the trench. Harry Foster scorned Keller, though he said little; Bennett had never heard of a plot by 3rd Division brigadiers to get rid of him.

For his part, Foster was very brave, going forward with a fag in hand and his elbow held high, although there were snipers about. He was also a very heavy drinker, though he wasn't ever drunk. Acquiring enough alcohol was a problem when they went to France, where liquor was rationed. Bennett told the mess sergeant to see that Foster got his Scotch first but then weaned him onto the powerful Norman Armagnac in a day or two.

Chris Vokes wasn't bright, Bennett said, but he was seen as a leader.

He mentioned a dinner that he'd attended before the end of the war. Guy Simonds, who was present as well, was asked if he expected or wanted to be Chief of the General Staff. "Yes," said Simonds, "if it wasn't for those damn politicians."

Bennett hadn't known **Bruce Matthews** in Toronto before the war. He recalled that Matthews and **Frank Lace**, another Toronto gunner, brought their wives to Britain in 1940 and rented a villa in the south of France on the assumption that they themselves would be fighting in France while their wives were on the Mediterranean and that they could join them there during leaves. That showed the unrealism of the day. Matthews came from a strict background, which made him disciplined and organized. It helped him rise, as he always did what he was supposed to do and on time.

Bennett couldn't explain why Charles Foulkes rose. Foulkes was always good to him, but he remained an enigma. Was it the "old boy" net? PF favouritism? Bennett couldn't say.

Dan Spry was a natural staff officer, not a commander. Bennett had heard the story that Spry was sacked for being drunk or asleep before an attack, but he blamed his GSO1, Lieutenant-Colonel N.L.C. Mather, for the problem, and had Monty, not Guy Simonds, doing the deed.

Bennett thought that the Germans were better soldiers than the Canadians. The Hitler Jugend in the 12th SS were "animals" whose attitude to dying differed from that of the Canadians. And he said that the Allies won only because of material superiority and artillery. Still, the Canadians didn't let down the side and, unlike the Americans, didn't waste men.

Bennett took the Essex Scottish into the Falaise battle in August 1944. He claimed that when he became CO, he tore up forty court-martial files for desertion. But, he said, in one August battle he had to park his jeep in a strategic spot and stand on top with a Sten gun to discourage the faint-hearted from deserting. He also said that at one point his battalion was slowed in its advance by trucks on the road. He went forward, whipped back a tarpaulin, and discovered that the truck was full of Germans fleeing the Falaise battle.

MAJOR-GENERAL M.P. BOGERT (1908-99)
INTERVIEW | DONNINGTON, UK, 8 SEPTEMBER 1991

Bogert graduated from RMC in 1930 and served in the PF with the Royal Canadian Regiment. He then held posts as a staff officer and a battalion commander in Italy; he led the 2nd Canadian Infantry Brigade from 7 October 1944 to 4 June 1945 in Italy and Northwest Europe. He remained in the army after the war and commanded a brigade in Korea.

Quite vigorous in his eighties, General Bogert began with the mobilization of the 1st Division.

In 1939, he was a lieutenant and the senior subaltern in the PF, stationed at Military District No. 1 as General Staff Officer, Grade 3 (GSO3). He was charged with working out the mobilization scheme in the district. Each district did this and sent in its proposals to Ottawa, which then produced a plan. He was pleased that the blank forms he'd designed for unit commanders were included in the plan, but at mobilization, typically, there weren't enough of the forms to go around.

That wasn't the only problem. Most of the COs were too old or not very proficient and not all were replaced. Some, though unsuited to take units into the field, were adequate for mobilization purposes. Some division and brigade commanders weren't competent. The units that were picked from the Militia for the 1st Division were all understrength and had had little infantry training. Only the Engineers, Supply and Transport, and Signals were good because they were made up of people who largely did the same kind of work in civvy street. Even so, the Militia battalions had esprit, they could handle small arms, and they were an organization. As far as Bogert was concerned, the 1st Division was the crème de la crème.

The PF, Militia, and RMC

Bogert thought there was some difficulty between the PF and the Militia. The Militia officers were infuriated that PFers, who weren't rich stockbrokers as some of them were, knew more about the army than they did. He didn't see much resentment against RMC ex-cadets. They were pretty good on the whole, though they knew little about tactics. But they were disciplined, and they filled the posts because they deserved them. They'd also been trained not to question orders; at the universities, questioning authority was taught.

Senior officers in the 1st Division

At the beginning of the war, Major-General Andrew McNaughton and the 1st Division's staff officers, such as Ernest Sansom and Guy R. Turner, were totally incompetent. Andy liked them as they'd been in the Great War with him. Sansom was the most incompetent general in the army. McNaughton once asked him to write up a report on the division's transport. Sansom stayed up all night preparing it, and Bogert accompanied him to deliver it to McNaughton. After scanning it, McNaughton handed it back to him, saying that he could have done a better job if he'd written it from memory. The problem was that McNaughton was bad at selecting people. He was able, but he couldn't combine the roles of general and politician. There was never a sign that he was popular with the troops. He wanted to soft-peddle regimental distinctions and have shoulder flashes that simply said "Canada."

When Bogert arrived in Ottawa to become the 1st Division's GSO3, he wasn't shown in to meet McNaughton. Andy wouldn't say hello to people in the elevator; he wasn't friendly. He wasn't interested in war, but only in the instruments of war. He liked gadgets; for example, he once sent someone to Oxford to study Greek fire.

Training in the United Kingdom

On the training side, the Great War was a problem because it lingered in the memory. During that war, the infantry needed courage and endurance but little by way of tactics. The dominating factors had been barbed wire and the machine gun. In the Second World War, however, mortars and mines were the keys, and tactical skill was necessary.

Training was slow, Bogert stated, because there was little ammunition, especially after Dunkirk. There were few instructors for weapons training. What the senior officers should have done was send the PF training cadre overseas on a one-per-unit basis, but they didn't. They didn't send enough officers on course initially, but a retired British officer was attached to each battalion, and that worked. The generals did conduct a few exercises, such as battalion exercises with a British tank brigade. The problem was that officers and men weren't well enough trained to actually benefit from training. Thus, when McNaughton proclaimed that the Canadians were "a dagger pointing at the heart of Berlin," the men laughed. Bogert went to a battle drill course, which was pretty good. What didn't work were the efforts to make men hate the enemy – every time, the Canadians just laughed.

Guy Simonds was GSO2 when Bogert was GSO3. Everyone thought he was first-rate; even if he wasn't, people thought he was. You could talk to him if you knew him; if not, you couldn't. Certainly, he was the only one in 1st Division HQ who knew anything (though A.E. Walford and J.F.A. Lister on the administrative side were good). "If Simonds hadn't been there," Bogert said, "I don't know what we would have done." The three Brigade Majors in the 1st Division (Harry Foster, Rod Keller, and Charles Foulkes) held their brigadiers' hands and coddled them. They didn't get training going, but there was little to train with in any case.

Bogert was in the 1st Division as GSO3 for a long time. When the VII Corps formed under McNaughton in the summer of 1940, everyone at Division HQ moved up a rank and went to the VII Corps – except Bogert.[6] One day, when he was left in charge, a message arrived saying that German paratroops had landed but that he wasn't to inform anyone of this. Bogert decided he had to tell at least the brigade commanders, and did. But Guy Turner blasted him for breaking security, even though Simonds, the sole competent staff officer at HQ, said he'd have done the same thing.

Bogert knew that reinforcements received poor training. Men would be tested for vision but never taught how to fire a mortar. Also, there just weren't

....

6 Established in July 1940, the VII Corps incorporated the 1st Canadian Division and a British armoured division under McNaughton as GOC. The Canadian Corps, incorporating the 1st and 2nd Divisions, came into being on 25 December 1940.

enough men. He remembered how upset Defence Minister J.L. Ralston was when he discovered companies that consisted of only forty-nine men. He also said that the X List, which recorded who was absent on courses, in hospital, or in detention, was cooked to make it look as if the strength were greater. The list was massaged in the United Kingdom, possibly by Brigadier Warwick Beament, the Officer in Charge, Canadian Section, 21st Army Group.[7] Whoever was to blame, it was very demoralizing to the troops.

On more senior officers

Guy Turner had a nebulous job at the VII Corps. At one point, he complained that too much use was made of transport, with gasoline wasted as a result, and pointed to a nearby staff car as an example. This turned out to be his own car. The driver said that he'd used all the gas in question when Turner and a blonde had been sitting in the car with the heater on, out on Leatherhead Common, a secluded spot in the Surrey countryside.

If McNaughton contributed anything, it was that the politicians thought he was great. This may have helped the division. Brigadier George Pearkes, on the other hand, was an energetic trainer who made everyone in the division think that it was the best. His enthusiasm was important. Bogert remembered an exercise where Pearkes, acting as umpire, declared that a reconnaissance troop had been eliminated and told the lieutenant to draft next-of-kin letters to the wives of the "deceased" troop members. The lieutenant asked Harry Foster, his CO, what to do. "You'd better start writing," was the reply. On another exercise, a Seaforth Highlanders Bren gun carrier platoon was declared to have been wiped out. In summarizing the exercise, Pearkes blasted all involved for their lack of dash – except the carrier platoon.

Pearkes could be vicious. F.F. Worthington, who, like Pearkes, was an officer in Princess Patricia's Canadian Light Infantry, visited the division when Pearkes was giving a rundown on an exercise. Pearkes pointed to Worthington, said there was an outsider present, and insisted that he had to leave. He must have been thinking that only 1st Division people mattered, and there was no room for outsiders. Pearkes did something similar to Major-General Harry Crerar, who had just arrived from Canada. Assuming that Crerar had come to replace him, Pearkes told officers at an exercise, "I want you to picture

---

7 There were two Beament brothers, G.E. (Ted) and Warwick, both Ottawa lawyers and brigadiers by war's end.

yourself as an officer just arrived from Canada and knowing nothing –." That greatly embarrassed everyone and probably contributed, Bogert said, to Pearkes's recall.

Major-General Harry Salmon was a good trainer and an officer who might have been as good as Simonds had he not been killed in an air crash before he could lead the 1st Division into Sicily. He was a Royal Canadian Regiment officer and was given the Hastings and Prince Edward Regiment to take overseas in 1939. When he met the regiment, he said, "In my opinion this is the worst regiment in the history of the empire. It is going to be the best."

Major-General Victor Odlum, GOC of the 2nd Division, was a joke, and people were "ashamed of him." Major-General Price Montague at Canadian Military Headquarters (CMHQ) in London said that PF people shouldn't be decorated; they were simply doing their duty.

On the 1st Division
The 1st Division personnel were very good, even the ones who'd been on the dole or worse. By 1945, they were like Peninsular War veterans, they'd been away from Canada for so long. At the end of 1944, when the home leave scheme came in, Bogert said, there were five thousand original members left in the division.

It was very hard to get rid of a bad soldier. Before the invasion of Sicily in July 1943, Bogert made up a list of twenty to thirty problem cases in his battalion, the West Nova Scotia Regiment (WNSR), and got rid of ten or so. On his first reinforcements draft, one of them was returned to him.

Throughout the whole war, there was a tendency to sack people who failed once. Anyone who fought the Germans would be bound to lose at some juncture. If he were replaced with someone who knew even less, the benefit of his experience was lost. Simonds, he said, did this too much.

Bogert was Acting Brigadier of the 3rd Brigade as a lieutenant-colonel. (He didn't get promoted, he said, due to politics: his brother was a Tory in Liberal MP Brooke Claxton's Montreal riding.) He'd been sent out to the Middle East to fight with the Eighth Army, and in June 1942 took over the WNSR. In December, he became GSO1, 1st Division. Then he was sent to Lieutenant-General Sansom's II Canadian Corps, his most unpleasant experience of the war. After that, he worked at CMHQ on the training side, where Brigadier **Elliot Rodger** – "the only general we had who wasn't a shit" – was good. Then he went back to the WNSR in Scotland in 1943, the regiment already loading for Sicily. There'd been an officer mutiny in the regiment, where most had lost confidence in the CO. Brigadier M.H.S. Penhale saw each officer individually, heard that they'd willingly serve under Bogert, and put him back in.

Sicily and Italy

Bogert thought the 1st Division was lucky because it didn't go into action under McNaughton, because its PF units set a standard of discipline to which other battalions aspired, and because its first taste of real combat was the comparatively gentle campaign in Sicily. On the other hand, the 2nd Division never recovered from Dieppe. The 1st Division was also lucky in its GOCs – Simonds, Chris Vokes, and Harry Foster. Foster was better and braver than Vokes. Vokes, in fact, was gun-shy, quick to leap into a slit trench. He had no great tactical sense, but he was good enough.

Foster was a very good GOC, a man with guts who stood up while others dove for cover. He backed up his officers, didn't like Foulkes, and drank a lot but could hold it. (His brother Gil was brilliant, Bogert said, but drank himself out of the PF. He enlisted in the Buffs, the Royal East Kent Regiment, in the British Army.)

Then there was Simonds, who was as good as his reputation suggested. He was shy, he'd fire you for one offence, but he had knowledge and self-confidence that inspired others to trust him. The Howard Graham case showed his tendency to sack people, but General Bernard Montgomery, commanding the Eighth Army, saved Graham.[8] Simonds got better the higher he went. He was better at strategy than tactics, and his problem was dealing with people. His small circle of friends included RMC classmates such as Vokes. Basically, he liked to keep people at arm's length, though at the National Defence College after the war he mixed with people.

The Royal 22e Régiment (R22eR, also called the Van Doos) couldn't be compared to any other regiment, Bogert claimed. Most battalions had platoons full of average chaps, but the Van Doos were likely to have twenty-nine cowards and one hero who carried the rest. This was a gross exaggeration, he admitted, but certainly the temperament of the R22eR differed from that of the English Canadian battalions. At the beginning of the war, its officers

....

8 Graham commanded a brigade in Simonds's 1st Division in Sicily, and after a dispute over the brigade's role in an early action, Simonds sacked him. Montgomery persuaded Simonds that he had been rash, and Graham returned to his command. See Granatstein, *The Generals*, 158.

were terrible except for "Paulo" (Paul) Bernatchez, whose leadership saved the regiment.

In Sicily, the 1st Division worked with the 1st Canadian Army Tank Brigade, and each disliked the other.[9] The brigade liked being part of a British corps and disliked being part of the I Canadian Corps in Italy. The I Canadian Corps didn't know what it was doing.

Lieutenant-General E.L.M. Burns was really clever but lacked the ability to convey his personality. He always seemed to be criticizing. Bogert thought it was OK for Vokes and **Bert Hoffmeister**, both division GOCs, to criticize Burns; but it wasn't acceptable for **Des Smith**, his Brigadier General Staff. Smith owed Burns loyalty, but he always was a suck. Still, Burns was the coldest of cold fish, though a nice man underneath. He was sacked in late 1944 as I Canadian Corps commander for a combination of operational and personality reasons. If he'd been popular, the operational problems would have been played down; but he wasn't.

Lieutenant-General Charles Foulkes did better as a corps commander than as a brigade commander or division GOC. He was quite able and certainly not stupid, though his personality wasn't very attractive. When Bogert succeeded him as Brigade Major of 3rd Brigade, things were in good shape. Foulkes disliked the PF and RMC, apparently because Brigadier C.F. Constantine, the RMC Commandant, had tried to steer him away from the infantry and to the Ordnance Corps. His demeanour was such that people felt he wasn't suitable for command. As a result, many bent over backward not to show prejudice against him. He had few friends and had little to do with his family. He drank.

Bogert thought that staff work in the 1st Division was very good, the credit belonging to **George Kitching**, who was GSO1 and who had set up the system his successors used. Kitching had been Salmon's GSO1, and Simonds inherited him. Salmon and Kitching had not got on. They went to see the GOC of the 3rd British Division that they replaced for Sicily, and the GOC, perceiving the tension between them, said they had to make up, as it was bad for a division to go into action when a GOC and his GSO1 were fighting.

Chris Vokes was stubborn and didn't like to be crossed. At his Orders Groups, for example, Brigadier T. Graeme Gibson of the 2nd Brigade would

....

9   The brigade's name was soon changed to the 1st Canadian Armoured Brigade. It worked infrequently with the I Canadian Corps after the initial months of 1944. See Nicholson, *The Canadians in Italy*.

ask for changes in a plan, and Vokes would snarl. What Gibson should have done was to see him privately. Still, Vokes got on well with the troops, even if he wasn't as keen on going to the front as Foster was.

The Canadians got on well with the British in Italy. Monty didn't care what the officers thought, but he liked to charm the troops. Bogert remembered him coming to the West Nova Scotia Regiment and saying, with mock seriousness, "Let's see, WNSR, that's Western Canada." Loud groans, equally theatrical, erupted from all the men. Then he'd say, "We're going into battle and we're going to win because you know I wouldn't put you into a battle that we couldn't win." The troops loved this. Few Canadians could compare with Monty – Simonds was shy and so was Salmon.

More on senior officers

Bogert spoke with great bluntness about Canadian senior officers. He was at RMC when C.F. Constantine was there as Commandant and remembered him on the Halifax docks, waving when the 1st Division left for England. He was almost sentimental, a strange response from a Commandant whom Bogert thought of as almost exalted.

Lieutenant-General Maurice Pope was a brilliant staff officer.

Major-General T.V. Anderson, who had just one arm, was Chief of the General Staff at the beginning of the war. But he was past it by that time.

Major-General Rod Keller was a nice fellow, nicer than Vokes. He got on well at RMC, where his "Captain Blood" moniker came from a movie character of the same name. His wife was as crude and foul-mouthed as he was.

Major-General **Bruce Matthews**, Bogert said, was a nice, conscientious chap, who learnt his trade through application. He got on well with Simonds.

Major-General **Bert Hoffmeister** was another nice chap who was lucky to get a division and did a fair job. Bogert thought the politicians wanted a Militia general, which partially accounted for Hoffmeister's rise.

Lieutenant-General Price Montague was OK and efficient but an out-and-out political appointee.

Lieutenant-General Ken Stuart was hopeless. In his CMHQ job as Chief of Staff in 1944, he was responsible for reinforcements. There were enough reinforcements, Bogert stated, except for French Canadians. Faced with the choice of breaking up one French Canadian regiment or adding English-speaking reinforcements to it, Stuart did nothing. He was a nice fellow but not much good.

Major-General E.J.C. Schmidlin, the Quartermaster General in Ottawa from 1940 to 1942, blotted his copybook over Hong Kong.[10] He'd been Director of Studies at RMC, a brilliant mechanical engineer who knew so much that he couldn't understand why others couldn't understand.

General Harry Crerar was an acceptable army commander, intelligent but with no great military skills.

Major-General Hugh Young was no good, a petty man.

Major-General C.R.S. "Bud" Stein was a nice chap who was sacked after a corps exercise. He told his 4th Armoured Division officers that the exercise had two aims: "One was attained: to sack me; the other was to put Young in command."

Bogert didn't think that Canadian generals tried to emulate their British equivalents. The PF and Militia both thought of themselves as part of an Imperial army and their dress and organization matched those of the Brits. Andy McNaughton didn't like this, but it was sensible and saved money. The problem was that Canada had generals who'd never been in action at a battalion level. They didn't know what they were asking men to do.

There were no French Canadian generals, because it was hard enough to find a French Canadian brigadier who was any good. Bernatchez was the best, Bogert claimed.

COLONEL J. ALLAN ("DING") CALDER (1908-95)

INTERVIEW | MONTREAL, 4 MAY 1992

Calder was a Royal Montreal Regiment Militia officer who commanded his regiment in the United Kingdom, the Saskatoon Light Infantry, a machine-gun battalion, in Italy, and the 1st Canadian Infantry Brigade until he was relieved by Charles Foulkes after the disastrous action on the Lamone River in December 1944.

Colonel Calder, still bitter over being fired as a brigade commander in Italy, opened by talking about the Montreal regiment.

....

10   The vehicles that were to accompany the Hong Kong–bound force failed to arrive at the docks in time, and the Canadians arrived in Hong Kong without them. Schmidlin took the rap for this failing.

Calder joined the Royal Montreal Regiment (RMR) after serving as a cadet at Lower Canada College. He and a friend had done a "frat rush" on the local regiments, had rated them on a ten-point scale, and decided that RMR was best. He thought the training was great and said that Basil Price, a Great War hero and the RMR CO until 1929, was the heart of the regiment. Price was sincere, hardworking, and friendly. Calder thought he was a first-class soldier. He was relieved as 2nd Division GOC, the story went, after he learned during a big exercise that his son had been killed in the RCAF, and Charles Foulkes, his General Staff Officer, Grade 1, did nothing to pick up the reins so he could grieve.

On general officers

Calder served under Major-General Hamilton Roberts at the Canadian Reinforcement Unit in Britain. He saw him infrequently, and though Roberts didn't impose himself, he could deliver a real chewing out if necessary.

Calder was clearly no fan of Charles Foulkes, who sacked him in 1944. They'd already had a run-in during December 1939, when they sailed with the 1st Division to Britain. Foulkes radiated PF know-everything, but his uniform, in which the holes from his captain's pips were still visible under his new major's crown, showed just how recently he'd been promoted. At the Lamone River, Italy, in December 1944, Chris Vokes had drawn up the plan of attack several days in advance. Foulkes arrived to take the corps, Vokes departed, and the Royal Canadian Regiment threw a dinner for Foulkes. He got drunk, made a stupid speech in which he declared that Italy was a second-class show compared to Northwest Europe, and then turned up at Calder's HQ, had a few more drinks, and stumbled around. This created a bad first impression of the new GOC. And this, Calder felt, explained his sacking.[11] He thought Foulkes's 3rd Brigade had been the worst in the 1st Division (or at least, Vokes claimed it was). And moreover, Foulkes had no friends.

McNaughton had inspected the RMR in Montreal in October 1939. The CO, unable to draw boots from stores for the unit, had bought them at Eaton's and the army had refused the bill. When he told this to McNaughton, he

....

11 A textbook example of how not to wage war, the attempt to cross the rain-swollen Lamone River, part of the push toward Bologna, was hastily planned and badly co-ordinated. It came under heavy fire from the enemy and ended in failure. For more on the Lamone River setback, see Nicholson, *The Canadians in Italy,* 616ff.

approved the purchase on the spot. That immediately created the impression that he'd do the sensible thing and that he thought first of the men. McNaughton also barred bands from going overseas, but the RMR got around this by taking its drummers and buglers into its anti-aircraft platoon. When McNaughton saw them practising in the United Kingdom, he quickly borrowed them for an inspection.

Calder saw E.L.M. Burns in Italy as I Canadian Corps GOC only a few times – perhaps his bad relations with Vokes kept him away from the 1st Division. Calder thought Generals Oliver Leese and Richard McCreery were a terrible comedown from Montgomery as Eighth Army Commanders.

He liked Vokes, though he was crude. He gave good orders, always ending with the admonition to "get out there and kick them in the fork." You knew where you stood with him. Vokes was concerned with the numbers of soldiers who had self-inflicted wounds, and he got Calder to look at creating a new detention campsite closer to the front and within artillery range – "Then fewer would be interested in going there."

When Calder was in Italy, Corps HQ was near the Saskatoon Light Infantry. Calder bumped into Harry Crerar one night and invited him for a drink. Crerar declined, saying that he never took a drink when there was a possibility he'd have to make a decision concerning troops in action. Calder admired that.

He recalled that when the Saskatoon Light Infantry was on ship to Britain with the RMR, George Pearkes, the senior officer, ordered everyone to stay aboard in Halifax. A.E. Potts, the Saskatoons' CO, disobeyed, and Calder said he had to detail an RMR major to put him under arrest.

As a brigade commander, Calder saw Defence Minister Ralston when he came to Italy in the fall of 1944 about reinforcements. He arranged for him to talk with soldiers and knew they'd speak their mind. Ralston asked leading questions and was forthright about what he wanted to hear.

MAJOR-GENERAL W.J. MEGILL (1907-93)

INTERVIEW | KINGSTON, ON, 18 JANUARY 1992

A Permanent Force Signal Corps officer, Megill went to Staff College at Quetta, India, and served in staff positions and with the 3rd Division. He then commanded the 5th Infantry Brigade in the 2nd Division from February 1944 to the war's end and remained in the army afterward.

He was military advisor to the Canadian members of the International Control Commission in Indochina during the 1950s.

Still vigorous in his mid-eighties and living in a retirement home when he was interviewed, General Megill started by talking about his career in the interwar PF.

Megill joined the PF as a signaller in 1923, becoming the seventy-seventh member of the new Royal Canadian Corps of Signals (RC Sigs). The government was improving communications in the North West Territories, and the army took over the project, with the result that there were chances of promotion. Thus Megill, still only in his teens, was given relatively rapid promotion to Sergeant and Staff Sergeant, though without pay for a time. There was a living allowance of $1,000 for Northern service, a messing allowance of 50 cents a day, and pay of about 75 cents a day. He took a commission in 1930 and was sent to university. PF officers were required to have a degree, but not enough Canadians did, so the PF had to borrow officers from the United Kingdom for a time. He stayed in the PF during the grim period of the Great Depression. The peacetime establishment for RC Sigs was only thirty officers, but the Depression made it look good, and because he'd been posted in the North, he was able to save money. He said there was no prejudice against officers who were commissioned from the ranks except for classified commission officers such as quartermasters, who couldn't command troops. They were looked down on.

He thought it was all bull that RMC officers were snobs.

Major-General E.C. Ashton, Chief of the General Staff from 1935 to 1938, was politically connected and was allowed to stay on past normal retirement age so he could get a larger pension. This irked the whole officer corps.

Megill said there were frequent Tactical Exercises Without Troops.[12] When he was District Signals Officer in Toronto, he was always out on these exercises. The District Officer Commanding was W.H.P. Elkins, a good, capable officer of high reputation.

Staff College

Megill attended the Staff College preparatory course at RMC. Ken Stuart had prepared the instructional material, but he was taught by G.C. Bucknall, a

---

12 Tactical Exercises Without Troops, or TEWTs, were instructor-led exercises for officers to practise battlefield tactics.

British officer who later commanded a corps. He said most Canadians took correspondence courses with Brits who helped them cram for two years prior to trying the Staff College exams. You had to be recommended and had to prepare on your own. You also had to pass the Militia Staff Course examinations. Churchill Mann and Eric Snow were among the six to eight officers who were taking the prep course, all competing for three vacancies. The course was run on the tutorial method. Yes, he said, passing Staff College was the key to promotion.

The Militia Staff Course and the Advanced Militia Staff Course were no breeze. Most Militia officers couldn't get the time away from their jobs, but those who'd taken the courses found them enormously beneficial during the war. They caught on quickly after mobilization. Harry Crerar once said that if he had to choose between a Militia and a PF officer of equal ability, he'd opt for the Militia officer. If he were as good as the PFer, he still had to be even more on the ball. Nonetheless, Militia standards were low because militiamen simply couldn't get the training. But they had esprit, their officers came from the local elites, and they threw the best parties in Canada at their armouries. The rural units were less well trained than urban ones due to lack of opportunity.

Megill opted to go to Staff College at Quetta, India, not Camberley in England. It had the same status, and he thought India might be interesting. In his assessment, if the Advanced Militia Staff Course was first-year university, Quetta was fourth year. Megill found it hard at Quetta. Coming from an army that lacked real units, he'd had no collective training above company level.[13] There was also some Imperial snobbishness, though directed more at Indian Army officers than those from the dominions. Oliver Leese, who later commanded the Eighth Army in Italy, was the Chief Instructor at Quetta, an odd bird but clever. His difficulties with people were personal, and he was definitely a Guardsman.

National Defence Headquarters at the war's outset

After the war began, Megill came back to Canada and went to National Defence Headquarters, into the Directorate of Military Operations and

....

13   The interwar PF, scattered across the country, had no full-strength units, and even company-level training (involving, say, 120 officers and men in infantry units) was rare except in summer training. Unless they had served in the Great War, most PF officers – and all Militia officers – had never seen a full-strength unit in the field.

Intelligence under J.C. Murchie. Murchie had a very good brain, but he harboured no illusions that he was a field soldier. Years of deskwork had made him sedentary. Megill worked on the operations side, where there were only three officers. One, W.H.S. Macklin, had written all the memos for the mobilization of the 1st and 2nd Divisions. His choice of which Militia units would be mobilized was determined by their geographical location. Some battalions had to be included: the 48th Highlanders, for example, were good, and their officers were keen. The original plan was to have the Black Watch replace the R22eR in the 1st Division and then form a French Canadian brigade in the 2nd Division. In the end, due to advice from senior francophone officers, this wasn't done – it would give the impression that only one brigadier had to be a francophone. There was also the problem of a shortage of supporting French Canadian units.

Overseas in England

Megill went to the 3rd Division when it was being set up. He liked Basil Price, the GOC, a good man and a nice fellow, though he couldn't have commanded in the field. Still, he did no harm at the stage of mobilization in which the country found itself. Sure, Megill said bluntly, George Pearkes and Victor Odlum were stupid too, but in 1940-41, while others learned, no one better was available to command. He thought, moreover, that they'd have acquitted themselves well if the Germans had invaded: they'd have sat in their slit trenches and been brave.

He then went to Canadian Military Headquarters (CMHQ) as General Staff Officer (Staff Duties). He dealt with technical people, again under Murchie. He was no admirer of General Price Montague, who couldn't have been a GOC, and who was something of a cipher in an equally irrelevant office. CMHQ just carried out Ottawa policy. Montague was a figurehead who took few decisions, but his staff was good. Still, he did little harm or good, Megill recalled. Andy McNaughton ran the show, and Montague didn't try to buck him. The CMHQ staff would never pick a fight with McNaughton's people.

On senior officers

Megill remembered McNaughton coming to talk at the 1938 Militia Staff Course at the Connaught Ranges near Ottawa. Although McNaughton was at the National Research Council, he made it obvious that he was still a serving officer in the PF and would be in command when war came. There were looks of horror at that, for even then Andy was seen as more of a scientist than a soldier. He was a very ambitious man, a strong nationalist who resented any attempt to get the army into action except under him. None of the troops overseas knew him. Clearly, he wasn't in the Montgomery class. The troops didn't see him or care about him, Megill claimed. He made no impact.

Harry Crerar was a first-class brain but a difficult personality. He couldn't raise any more enthusiasm than a turnip, was completely cold, and almost useless in a discussion. But he could write a beautifully organized paper on that discussion. He was a natural staff officer or Chief of the General Staff, but he wasn't a natural commander.

Rod Keller was first class. Megill knew him from PF days in Toronto and was his GSO1 overseas. Although Megill begged him not to, Keller had recommended him to be Crerar's Brigadier General Staff. Keller did nothing wildly exciting on exercises, but he was as good as anyone else, and his orders were sensible. Megill knew nothing of his private life but knew he drank heavily, though he never saw him drunk. His COs liked him too, and he was helpful to them.

Chris Vokes was first class, Megill stated, though he saw him only in the Occupation Force in Germany.

F.F. Worthington was also a first-class man, and Megill regretted that **George Kitching** replaced him at the 4th Armoured Division. He himself was on just one exercise with Worthy, who had a clear understanding of military tactics and gave his officers good instructions. He'd have been delighted to fight under him. He was uncertain about Kitching, whom he thought no commander, hesitant, and lacking grip. Worthy wouldn't have been indecisive, Megill believed. Guy Simonds liked Kitching from their time together in Italy.

Fighting in France

In February 1944, Megill took over the 5th Brigade in the 2nd Division and took it to France. He thought Operation Spring in July 1944 should not have gone ahead.[14] The battlefield was overlooked by a hill that the British had failed to take, and the start line was in German hands. He went to Charles

....

14   Operation Spring pitted the II Canadian Corps against the Germans on Verrières Ridge, just south of Caen. It was a near-disaster with heavy casualties, not least in the green 2nd Canadian Division.

Foulkes, the GOC of the 2nd Division, to ask that the Régiment de Maison-neuve take the start line, but Foulkes refused. Megill simply couldn't understand why Foulkes had risen the way he did. He was a politician, not a commander. When he commanded the 3rd Brigade, he'd failed to make a good job of it, and Megill couldn't figure out why he was given a division. Megill should have asked to be paraded to the corps commander about Spring, but he knew he'd have been replaced, and who could have done his job any better?

He thought Guy Simonds learned as he went along. He was quite good though definitely unapproachable. He was under pressure throughout the war. Like Foulkes, he had little confidence in his underlings: he gave his orders and didn't ask for opinions. So, when **Bruce Matthews** as GOC took over the 2nd Division, it was a banner day, because he asked for opinions as Foulkes never did. Megill liked Matthews, who looked for advice and either took it or explained why he couldn't. He understood all about infantry-artillery co-operation, and he trusted his commanders and listened. In any event, he couldn't have been worse than Foulkes, who got all his advice from his staff.

Simonds was hard and had to be. Operation Totalize on 8 August 1944 was a mess, not the glorious victory it ought to have been. The early advance wasn't exploited, and there was no reason to use bombers (Churchill Mann, Chief of Staff at the First Canadian Army, was the instigator of the air attack, said Megill). In addition, the 4th Canadian Armoured Division units didn't get their orders prior to the attack. That was Kitching's fault.

Megill thought Canadian commanders were generally weak. They had little experience, and though no great brain was required, they failed to stick to essentials. Firings were sometimes wrong – the sacking of Brigadier Blackader in late September 1944, for example.[15] The problem was that Simonds never listened to what his juniors said. Nor was he much at the front in Normandy, though later he was. If Simonds had seen the lay of the land at Operation Spring, it would not have proceeded. The real problem until the winter of 1944 was that everyone was green. There were shortages of good COs once the originals were wounded. It all went back to the formation of

....

15   In fact, Brigadier K.G. Blackader, commander of the 8th Brigade, had to be hospital-ized in September 1944 during the struggle to clear the Channel ports; he was replaced by J.A. Roberts in October.

the First Canadian Army. It was too big, its requirements too large for Canada to fill. This caused the reinforcement problem and created large staffs that absorbed good lieutenant-colonels.

Infantry reinforcements generally were OK, Megill maintained, though some were untrained. Holding units, after all, didn't get good trainers – all the duds were there. When he'd been at CMHQ, he'd tried and failed to get five hundred duds returned to Canada, but Ottawa wouldn't play. There were hundreds who were suitable only for pioneer units, he claimed, and the units themselves were unneeded anyway. Thus, by 1944, infantry battalions were short of men. In his brigade, the units in two battalions were one hundred men short, and the Régiment de Maisonneuve was 50 percent undermanned. Still, the conscript Zombies were no better or worse than general service volunteers, and, he said, the troops didn't give them too hard a time.

LIEUTENANT-GENERAL ROBERT MONCEL (1917-2007)
INTERVIEW | MAHONE BAY, NS, 6 OCTOBER 1991

Born in Montreal, Moncel served in the Militia there and joined the Royal Canadian Regiment at the outbreak of war. He commanded the 12th Manitoba Dragoons, then became General Staff Officer, Grade 1, at the II Canadian Corps until he was made a brigade commander in the 4th Canadian Armoured Division during the Falaise Gap battle of August 1944. He stayed in the army after the war and served with the International Control Commission in Indochina and as Vice Chief of the Defence Staff.

At his seaside home, Moncel began by talking bluntly and fluently about the PF and RMC graduates.

Moncel was no admirer of the PF, remarking on the "miserable performance" of many PFers and RMC graduates in the war. They had everything going for them technically, including Staff College, much more than the Militia, but after four years of war a lot ended up as captains or majors and as drunks. They were like the English, either very good or bloody awful. Of course, the Militia wasn't much different, with the good and the bad. Moncel apologized for sounding like a snob, but those Militia and RMC officers who had gone to private schools and had responsibility as prefects and who joined good

– that is, urban – Militia regiments did well. They knew what responsibility was, they could take and give orders, and they had good minds – **Bruce Matthews**, for example. The Militia officers from rural regiments were much less good, and in many cases, outsiders had to be brought in to run those regiments. The Royal Canadian Regiment (RCR), he said, stocked large numbers of these outsiders.

He mentioned the 12th Manitoba Dragoons (18th Armoured Car Regiment), which he was sent to whip into line. The CO, J.S. McMahon, was Simonds's RMC classmate, and the second-in-command was Gordon Churchill, later a minister in the Diefenbaker government. They had to get the chop, hadn't a clue, and had done no trades training. The squadron leaders were drunk in the afternoon. They had to go, and he got new officers and a Regimental Sergeant Major from the RCR, created new badges and shoulder flashes, broke the regiment into training squadrons, and worked them hard for five months. No one told him how to do this.

At the onset of war, the Militia generals were terrible, Moncel said, but there was no one else. Mind you, the PF also had problems in 1939. He joined the RCR, where companies had a strength of forty and had one light machine gun. The officers were drunks – he poured his company commander into bed every night. The RCR CO, Lieutenant-Colonel Vernon Hodson, hated the staff – he said Staff College was "a forcing ground for shits" – and believed that decorations or praise shouldn't be offered. But the drunks and incompetents were soon weeded out. Moncel said that when he had the RCR's Bren gun carrier platoon, a UK officer told him his men should be drawing trades pay. So he spoke with Dan Spry, a lifelong friend who was the Adjutant, and asked to see the war establishment.[16] This shocked Spry and the CO because the war establishment was secret, they said. But eventually these regulars agreed that trades pay was permitted. Astonishingly, they'd not known this.

Moncel took the RCR Bren gun carrier platoon to France in June 1940, and after the Canadians' retreat to Brest, a British officer told him to destroy the scarce armoured vehicles. He flatly refused and got them loaded on a ship as ballast after ordering his platoon sergeant to shoot the officer if necessary. When they finally landed in Southampton, it was to the sound of a

....

16 The war establishment was the full wartime complement of the men, equipment, and vehicles of a military unit.

band playing – for a tea dance. He was told to turn over his carriers to the general pool, refused, and managed to keep them due to the intervention of "Boy" Browning, later Lieutenant-General Sir Frederick Browning, whom he'd met on a course. When he got back to the RCR mess, two weeks after everyone else, the CO chased him out for looking scruffy.

On Simonds

Despite its flaws, the PF did produce Guy Simonds. He was just a baby in 1939, a captain, but he loved the business. He was Moncel's idol and mentor – the only one of the whole bunch with talent, brains, and guts. After the war, the government, frightened of him and fearing he could be a loose cannon, treated him badly; indeed, it was mean to all the generals postwar. He had met Simonds when he was sent to the first Canadian Junior War Staff Course, which Simonds ran in Britain, and he stood first in the course. Simonds was then a lieutenant-colonel; dapper and smartly turned out, he knew what he was doing. Moncel didn't see him again for some time.

On Worthington

Moncel's posting after Staff College was as GSO3 at Corps HQ, where he never saw General Andy McNaughton. He hated this job and was rescued from it by F.F. Worthington, who made him a GSO3, then Brigade Major, and finally GSO1 of his division. Worthington was the kindest, nicest man, the most enthusiastic, and the most divorced from reality. He regularly proclaimed that his 1st Canadian Army Tank Brigade and eventually his 4th Armoured Division were ready for action when in fact they were nowhere near ready – they had no gunnery and no tradesmen. That was his weakness, an inability to see reality. Even though Worthington understood armoured tactics and was the only one who believed in the tank, Moncel doubted that he could have commanded in action: he'd have been out at the front, waving his sword. He wanted to see blood on the tracks.

He remembered an exercise that Worthington's brigade had to put on for Monty. Worthy wouldn't make a plan for the exercise or let Moncel create one. When the day arrived, he told Moncel to simply say, "How would you proceed, Brigadier?" and turn it over to him. Moncel complied, and Worthy blew the exercise, which made Monty restless and angry. Worthy left in a huff. To Moncel, this cock-up was typical of the PF. He said Worthington and General McNaughton got on well because both liked gadgetry. McNaughton was fascinated by Worthy's workshop.

On Sansom

Moncel said that Lieutenant-General Ernest Sansom was incompetent. Sansom had read a book about a desert corps commander who travelled with a truck full of cable, which he unrolled as he went so that he could stay in contact wherever he was. While Sansom was in the United Kingdom, he decided to try this for himself, and he got **Fin Clark**, his Chief Signal Officer, to put the corps' entire cable reserve on a truck. It was a disaster – the cable was cut everywhere. The problem with Sansom, as II Canadian Corps commander, was that he gave no direction. He told Moncel to produce a plan for a big exercise, and when he did so, Sansom flipped through it and said it looked great. That was all. But he was fun in the mess, and it was a party every night. Moncel was once asked to get Sansom drunk so he could be fired for drunkenness. He refused to do it. But Sansom was ultimately sacked anyhow. He and McNaughton lived in another world.

Simonds as II Canadian Corps GOC

When Simonds took over the II Canadian Corps in early 1944, things changed. Simonds wrote out a plan in longhand and gave it to Moncel, who was GSO1, for distribution. Moncel changed a few things and sent it out. When Simonds discovered that, he called him and reamed him out: "Don't you ever do that again." He had the palest blue eyes and looked just like a hawk. He gave direction; he knew what he wanted; and the British generals respected him, which wasn't the case for other Canadian senior officers.

Simonds had come from Italy to take over the corps, and Moncel was the junior member in A Mess.[17] Each morning at breakfast, another staff officer would be gone until finally only Moncel was left. Simonds smiled and said, "You're staying."[18] He brought in his own people from Italy, and his decision to can certain corps staff was right. His people performed well.

He was great to work for. He knew what he wanted, and he had enough confidence in his people to leave them alone to do their job. He knew they'd break their necks to carry out his wishes. Many were frightened of him, but

....

17 The senior staff officers of a division, corps, or army ate in A Mess. Moncel's memory is slightly faulty here: Simonds's Aides de Camp would also have been in the mess and junior to Moncel, a lieutenant-colonel.

18 This too is incorrect. Others who stayed were the Chief Signal Officer, Brigadier S.F. Clark (see his interview on page 152), and Brigadier Darrel Laing, the Deputy Adjutant and Quartermaster General.

not Moncel. He travelled with him at the front and saw him in all kinds of circumstances. They became good friends.

Simonds and Foulkes

Simonds didn't like Charles Foulkes. When Foulkes's 2nd Division was to stage an early morning attack in Normandy, Simonds got up at 0500 and was just behind Division HQ, waiting for the scheduled attack to go in at 0600. The barrage was twenty minutes late, and Simonds said, "I'm going over to relieve the division commander." Moncel urged delay, as it wouldn't help the battle. Simonds fixed him with his hawk-like glare but agreed: "You owe me one." The battle was a disaster, like everything Foulkes touched. To Moncel, his rise was inexplicable. His staff were poor – he attracted poor officers. When Foulkes had the 4th Armoured Brigade under command, his HQ was cut off by the Germans, and one of Moncel's own officers rescued him. Moncel couldn't forgive the officer for that.

In battle

Moncel talked about courage in battle. When he took over his brigade, he visited his artillery regiment, commanded by an RMC graduate. The second-in-command was at the gun lines, and the CO was back with the transport. This happened twice, and finally the second-in-command said that the CO wouldn't come forward. Moncel went to see him, begged him to go up to the gun lines, failed, and had to fire him. The CO had run a good regiment in Britain, but he couldn't stand up to action. There was no way of predicting who would do well in battle and who didn't. You were often wrong. Who'd have expected the druggist Fred Tilston of the Essex Scottish or the mechanic David Currie of the South Alberta Regiment to get Victoria Crosses for courage in battle?

When **George Kitching** was sacked in August 1944, it was because he'd been let down by his brigadiers. Brigadier E.L. Booth was brave and experienced, but he put his HQ in three tanks during Operation Totalize in August 1944, and when he was killed, there was no communication to 4th Armoured Division HQ. Kitching couldn't find out what was going on, and the attack ground to a halt. The key was, as Simonds said, to have HQ in a safe place with good communications; then the CO could go forward while his HQ stayed in touch.

Five days passed before Moncel was told that he'd be taking over Booth's brigade. He said he'd learned of a promotion once before, just prior to D-Day.

When Brigadier R.A. Wyman of the 2nd Canadian Armoured Brigade foolishly blabbed the plans for D-Day, Monty was furious and wanted him canned. Moncel was tapped to replace him, but Simonds said it was wrong to change commanders at that point, so Wyman led the brigade on D-Day and got wounded before he could be sacked.

Operation Totalize was Simonds's own plan. In Moncel's opinion, Simonds hadn't asked too much of green regiments. The troops reached their objectives – he mentioned Major Ned Amy of the Canadian Grenadier Guards – so the operation would have worked if the communication problem hadn't stopped the orders from coming through. The brigadiers were inexperienced. Possibly, Simonds ought to have taken that into account.

Simonds had charisma and the troops saw it. Perhaps he aped Monty too much with his black beret, which helped make some hate him. The British tolerated idiosyncrasy better than the Canadians did. Still, he was charming and great fun, a challenge at all times. At a Cabinet Defence Committee meeting after the war, Simonds tried to get the government to authorize creation of the Canadian Guards. One minister queried this, and Simonds responded, "When the mobs storm Parliament Hill, you will be glad to have two loyal battalions."

Problems with officers

Moncel talked about how a commander couldn't believe a CO who claimed that his men were tired. Too often it was the commander who was tired. Simonds was once informed that troops were "pinned to the ground," but on going forward, he found the men lounging in the sun. He fired all the commanders. They ought to have been going forward to see things for themselves. A brigadier should go down to company level to see what was happening. Moreover, good brigadiers had gone to Staff College and had a sense of inter-arms co-operation and of the resources available. He recalled sitting in on a brigadier's Orders Group when, on being offered extra artillery and armour support, the brigadier refused. The attack was a disaster and two hundred men died. Like this brigadier, officers got tired and sometimes stopped caring. They ought to have been relieved of command – with honour.

The problem wasn't the men, Moncel maintained – they were splendid. It was the officers. Still, by the end of the war, the First Canadian Army was superb. It had taken five years to build, could move instantly, and was magnificent. His own brigade was superb, tough, and efficient. A bad brigadier could lose in a day what his 4th Armoured Brigade lost in all of Northwest Europe – 350 men killed in action. The Germans, he added, were a ragtag lot at war's end, though their good units were excellent. And the Canadians had equipment in such quantity that it was extravagant to the point of immorality.

On senior officers

Moncel was obviously no great admirer of Chris Vokes, who ended the war as his 4th Armoured Division GOC, though they had riotous times post-war and were friends. Vokes knew nothing about armour and wasn't a happy camper in Northwest Europe. He rarely came to see Moncel's brigade – just two or three times – and left him on his own. This was because the orders came from Corps HQ, and the GOC had little to do. One day, Vokes came to Moncel's HQ as they were being shelled, and Vokes jumped into a trench with his tin hat on, while Moncel's officers walked around. One saluted Vokes every time he passed his trench. Moncel had insisted that staff officers wore caps, not tin hats. Vokes, he said, ran the Occupation Force in Germany as if he were a warlord.

He remembered being in a doorway with Harry Foster at Caen under fire when two privates jumped in for shelter.

"You're a general?" one of them asked.

"Yes."

"You can do what you want?"

"Yes."

"Well, if I was a general I'd get the hell out of here."

He saw little of Harry Crerar. He was a gentleman with a lovely wife, and he liked to have RMC boys around. Moncel mentioned **Bill Anderson** especially, saying it was terrible that he wasn't allowed to command a unit in action but was kept at First Canadian Army HQ as a staff officer.

George Pearkes was like Worthington, who'd have had his sword in hand during an attack. He actually travelled with a trumpeter and once introduced Mrs. Churchill as Labour leader Clement Attlee's wife. Whatever brains he'd once possessed had been blown out in the Great War.

Dan Spry recovered from being canned and did well. Rod Keller left Moncel cold – like Vokes, too much blood and guts.

To Moncel, Ottawa wasn't the enemy; Canadian Military HQ in London was, though this ceased once the troops got into action.

He had no sense that reinforcements were short. Certainly, they weren't in the 4th Armoured Brigade's armoured regiments and not in his motorized infantry.

MAJOR-GENERAL ROGER ROWLEY (1914-2007)

INTERVIEW | OTTAWA, 23 MAY 1991

A bond trader, Rowley was a militiaman with the Cameron Highlanders of Ottawa. He served in Iceland and in the United Kingdom, commanded the Stormont, Dundas, and Glengarry Highlanders in Northwest Europe, and won two Distinguished Service Orders. He remained in the army after the war, served as Director of Military Training in Ottawa, and commanded the brigade group in NATO and the Canadian Army Staff College.

General Rowley began by talking of the Militia and the PF.

As a Militia officer in the Cameron Highlanders of Ottawa, Rowley met Harry Salmon and General R.O. Alexander, who taught him much about being an officer. In his view, his unit was well trained, perhaps because the Militia was a refuge from the Depression, a way of keeping up pride in hard times. At mobilization in September 1939, there were about three hundred men in the Camerons, and the CO and company commanders, with two exceptions, were Great War veterans who soon retired.

In Iceland and England

His unit spent the winter of 1939-40 in Ottawa and then went to Camp Borden, north of Toronto (under Alexander, a short man who was neat, sensible, and firm). They went to Iceland to work with the British 49th Division, the Canadians under Brigadier L.F. Page, a good man who knew what he was doing. They remained in Iceland until May 1941, when they went to the United Kingdom, initially as corps troops in the I Canadian Corps.

In England, Rowley dealt with E.L.M. Burns, the Brigadier General Staff to Andy McNaughton. Rowley wrote a paper in which he argued that machine guns had to be mounted on tracked vehicles to keep up with mechanized infantry. He sent it to Corps HQ, and Burns, a brilliant technical soldier, saw it and offered careful comments. Soon after, Rowley said, Burns's indiscreet letters to his girlfriend hit the censors, and he was returned to Canada for revealing military secrets. Eventually, the machine-gun battalions, including the Camerons, were mechanized.

Rowley grew up in Ottawa with McNaughton's sons, and he saw McNaughton himself in the United Kingdom through his Aide de Camp, Alistair Buchan, the son of John Buchan, Lord Tweedsmuir, who was Governor-General until his death in 1940. Andy wanted a machine gun, a thousand rounds, and a new sight so that he could see how well the gun worked. Rowley provided these but couldn't get them back; they were needed for training in Wales. He saw McNaughton at Leatherhead, the Canadian HQ in England, and at one end of his office was a cot and work-shop table, with the machine gun and other stuff disassembled. Another story: McNaughton was the man who invented air burst ranging for artillery. His son, Ted, was on the Commander, Corps Royal Artillery staff and was handed a problem that he couldn't resolve. During Sunday lunch with his father, he showed him the problem, and Andy resolved the question, which, as it turned out, he himself had assigned to the CCRA.

Rowley wasn't impressed with the performance of the generals during the endless exercises. Most exercises were screwed up. The generals hadn't fought since 1918, they'd seen no service on the frontiers, unlike British of-ficers, and though most division GOCs had passed Staff College, they weren't pros and it showed. Still, the Militia officers in units did better than their PF counterparts, though they couldn't be generals as they were too young. He thought RMC graduates were a disappointment, though they were well ahead of everyone else.

Basil Price, GOC of the 3rd Division, was a delightful man but too old and too heavy. He was good on exercises and knew what he was doing. The men liked him.

Rowley ran the Battle School in Yorkshire in 1943. The school had been established soon after Dunkirk, when the Brits realized the Germans fought better than they did. The point of its training was to develop a simple word-of-mouth tactical manoeuvre plan for use at platoon level. The Yorkshire school was tough – the men were made to crawl through sewers, abattoir offal, and other unpleasant things. It taught platoon officers and NCOs, and it also worked with carrier platoons. McNaughton stressed night fighting, so Rowley instituted a day-night reversal, sought advice from specialists, and added carotene to the men's rations to improve their vision. The results were dramatic, as people learned to use their senses.

In battle in Northwest Europe

Guy Simonds was a brilliant, innovative officer who designed and executed the tactical profile for deep penetration assault at night – and it worked. He went on doing that kind of thing and was admired and spoiled by Montgomery. In battle, he was relentless (Vokes was too). In July 1944, after the terrible Operation Spring, the 9th Brigade, which had done badly, was housecleaned, and Rowley was summoned to Simonds's caravan. There he found Lieutenant-Colonel J.M. Rockingham and Major D.F. Forbes. Thirty seconds later, Rocky was a brigadier and the others were battalion COs. Simonds was always up at the front in his "goddamned white scout car." The units had full confidence in him; he knew what he was doing and told them what to expect during an operation.

At the Rhine crossing in March 1945, Rowley was worn out, one of the few COs who hadn't been killed or wounded in action. Crerar, who was a family friend, came over to Rowley, put him in charge of the Battle School for a rest, and offered condolences on the death of Rowley's brother. "I want you to go home and pick up your sister-in-law," who was a friend of Crerar's daughter, Peggy, "and there will be a job for you in the Pacific Force." This was very understanding and kind.

Years after the war, when he was Director of Military Training at Army HQ in Ottawa, Rowley got a handwritten paper by Kurt Meyer on the Caen-Falaise battle that was very critical of the Canadians. Meyer said Simonds's initial assault was brilliant, but the initiative was lost when there was no follow-up, and he had time to reorganize his anti-tank defences. Rowley took it to Simonds, who decided there was no benefit in publishing it. Rowley said he thought historian Carlo D'Este's account of the Normandy campaign was exactly right.[19]

On senior officers

Rowley called Rod Keller "old carrot top." He was a wild one but competent, a real infanteer, and he whipped the division into shape with his bare hands. Rowley disagreed with the stories about Keller in Normandy: he didn't stay in his caravan but was at Division HQ, where he was supposed to be. He ran

....

19 Carlo D'Este, *Decision in Normandy* (Old Saybrook, CT: Konecky and Konecky, 2001).

things – Rowley had attended his Orders Groups – and there was no sign of his being yellow. Remember, urged Rowley, the 3rd Division achieved its D-Day objectives, and this was no accident. Remember too that brigadiers always elbowed each other for status.

Dan Spry was GOC of the 3rd Division, a first-class general. He and Rockingham were the two best bosses Rowley had. He did a fantastic job fighting his division at the Scheldt.[20] Simonds fired Spry because he hadn't been forward for an attack. Rowley disagreed with the firing: a GOC needed to stay back so that he could deal with the unexpected – the only certainty during an attack was that some surprising event would occur. He couldn't do anything useful until it did, and then he had to be at his communications centre to handle it. Spry had been very good in the terrible winter at Nijmegen, making special arrangements for the troops and dominating No Man's Land. The story was that, at Nijmegen, the 3rd Division drank more rum for the cold than an entire UK corps, or so a British quartermaster general said. That was a sign Spry looked after his troops.

Rowley always had a funny feeling about **George Kitching**. He found him tricky, and wondered if he'd left the Gloucestershire Regiment in the British Army during the 1930s under a cloud. But he was capable and bright.

Vokes was unrelenting in battle and fun to be with. Down deep, he was soft, cared about people, and was stereotypically Irish. He could laugh, curse, and cry within the space of ten minutes. In appraising Simonds's postwar policies as Chief of the General Staff, which sent him to Ottawa to raise hell, he was very knowledgeable and sensible.[21]

Charles Foulkes was a great politician. But two badly planned divisional exercises – Bluebird and Swallow, he thought – were the two worst ever held in the United Kingdom, and both were done by Foulkes as General Staff Officer, Grade 1. As the 2nd Division GOC, Foulkes didn't do well, and Rowley said he couldn't understand his rise. He seemed humble and had no self-aggrandizement, but he couldn't exercise his authority. Still, he did well as Chairman of the Chiefs of Staff.

....

20   On the 3rd Division in the Scheldt battle, see Stacey, *The Victory Campaign*, Chaps. 15-16.
21   See the account in Bercuson, *True Patriot*, Chaps. 11-12.

MAJOR-GENERAL J. DESMOND B. SMITH (1911-91)

INTERVIEW | LONDON, UK, 14 SEPTEMBER 1991

> *An RMC graduate and a PF officer in the Royal Canadian Dragoons, Smith*
> *served on staff in Britain and led the 5th Armoured Brigade in the 5th*
> *Canadian Armoured Division in early 1944 and the 1st Infantry Brigade*
> *in the 1st Division from December 1944 to the war's end. He remained in*
> *the army after the war and served with NATO and as Adjutant General.*
> *Smith began with his thoughts on RMC and the PF.*

Smith never saw any sign of resentment to RMC or the PF. He himself didn't even know who was from RMC.

In 1939, he was in Ottawa, working under E.G. (Bunny) Weeks, who was Director of Organization. Between them, with one NCO, they mobilized the army.

On McNaughton

He greatly admired Andy McNaughton, a wonderful guy, an intellect with a real brain, and a very human man. When the planning was on to send troops to Norway in early 1940, Ernest Sansom was Assistant Adjutant and Quartermaster General of the 1st Division, and Smith was two or three slots under him. Instructed to acquire winter kit for 1,500 troops, he discovered there was none in British stocks. So he phoned Lilywhite's, a sports clothing store where his father used to shop before the war, and arranged for it to make fleece-lined jackets. They duly arrived, but the Norway operation was cancelled, and the girlfriends of the soldiers ended up with nice coats. Then Smith was summoned to see Andy, who showed him an invoice for a large sum. He very sternly waved it at him and said that if it were taken from his pay, he'd need his entire service career to recover. Then McNaughton's expression changed, and he said, "To hell with rules, get it done, that's the kind of young officer we want." McNaughton sent him to Staff College at Camberley and called him personally every time he was promoted.

"Is that Major Smith?" he would ask.

"No, Sir, Captain Smith."

"It's Major now."

McNaughton was damned by the British for the debacle of Exercise Spartan in 1943, but he had political responsibilities as well as military ones. The Brits wanted to use Canadians as cannon fodder, just as in the Great War, but Andy wouldn't permit this. He also produced the "snake," a device for clearing mines, and he worked on the flail tank with General Percy Hobart, who commanded the 79th Division – the "funnies," or specialized armoured vehicles.

Smith was supportive of the old brigade – Generals Odlum, Price, and others had held the Militia together in the face of government neglect. They formed the nucleus on which recruiting could begin, and you couldn't just dismiss them after their efforts. For his part, he had spent the 1930s holding a yellow flag to represent a machine gun on exercises.

On Burns

E.L.M. Burns was such a prissy man that no one could believe he had a girl-friend until the censors picked up his love letters. Had anyone else written them, he would have been court-martialled for his comments on operations and planning.

Smith was concerned with Burns because he took over the 4th Armoured Brigade from him. When he arrived at the brigade, he discovered that four COs from three of the armoured regiments and one motorized infantry battalion were Great War colleagues of his own father. They couldn't possibly lead troops into action, and as Burns hadn't sacked them, Smith had to. F.F. Worthington, as division GOC, couldn't really be expected to concern himself with such matters. The next thing Smith discovered was that Burns had slapped governors on the tanks, which limited their speed to six miles per hour. Those had to be removed so proper training could be carried on.

After that, he saw nothing of Burns until the Italian campaign, when Smith got command of the 5th Armoured Brigade in the 5th Armoured Division and Burns "became God" as GOC of the I Canadian Corps after Harry Crerar left for England in early 1944.

After Ortona

The situation was terrible in January 1944 after the Ortona battle, the troops and tanks frozen in the mud. Ammunition was short for the 25-pounder guns, and Smith worked out ways to use the guns of his Sherman tanks for artillery purposes. With the aid of aerial spotters, he could concentrate the fire of 168 tanks on a spot. When word got around that he was doing this, the Brigadier General Staff Armour at the Eighth Army and the Commander, Royal Artillery, ripped into him. He was summoned to meet General Harold

Alexander, the Army Group commander, who arranged a target-practice shoot-out between tank guns and artillery – which the tanks won. This made Smith a favourite of Alex's.

Then the Canadians moved to the Naples area for six weeks of training prior to the Liri Valley battles of May 1944. In the Hitler Line battle, the corps failed. No instructions had been given regarding what to do if they did break through the line. Burns was a great man with a pencil and as a planner, but when plans went awry, he lost control. He could tell Chris Vokes or **Bert Hoffmeister** to do X or Y, but they would say it wouldn't work. Burns could have fired them, but they were experienced, and he wasn't. It wasn't his fault that he was put in command when he was green. Nor did his personality help. He would see battle-weary troops with their jackets open and give them hell for improper dress.

After the Liri Valley battles, General Oliver Leese called Smith to British Eighth Army HQ and told him he had to become Chief of Staff at Corps HQ. He replied, "Oh, no, I'm happy with my brigade." But Leese insisted: "Corps isn't doing what it should, and the corps commander needs help as he's not doing a good job." Smith said that the traffic mess after the Hitler Line wasn't the fault of the Canadian Corps. The single road (Highway 6) was within the Canadian boundary, but British and Polish divisions also used it. The mess was the fault of Army HQ. When he went to Corps HQ to work for Burns, Vokes and Hoffmeister, no admirers of the corps GOC, stopped talking to him and called him a traitor. This was hard because when Burns wanted to urge one of the divisions to push on, he wouldn't drive out by jeep and speak face-to-face with Vokes or Hoffmeister. Instead, he'd send Smith, who had to try to interpret his wishes.

More on Burns

An effort was made to loosen Burns up. Smith saw Brigadier Bunny Weeks, who was the Officer-in-Charge, Canadian Section 1st Echelon, Allied Forces HQ in Naples. Weeks volunteered to stage a dinner with some duchessas and contessas, with a view to getting Burns laid. During the affair, a beauty asked Burns, "What do they call you back in Canada, General?" His answer, which came during a sudden lull in the conversation, was "a man's man." That, said the lady, explained everything.

Burns never changed as commander. He had difficulty telling people that they'd done well. The corners of his mouth were always turned down, it was hard to get a laugh out of him, and his whole attitude suggested he was a know-it-all, which annoyed many. He seemed to assume that everyone had read his 1930s articles in the *Canadian Defence Quarterly*. He was a meticulous planner, but a successful commander is one who inserts his personality into the action. He simply did not have the military respect of his division GOCs.

When Defence Minister J.L. Ralston came to Italy in the fall of 1944, he spoke privately to Smith after dinner and spent forty-five minutes trying to get him to talk about Burns, but Smith refused to answer questions about him. Ralston had already talked to Eighth Army GOC-in-C General Richard McCreery and General Alexander, and possibly to Vokes and Hoffmeister.

On Vokes and Crerar

Vokes was no great planner, but he co-ordinated his staff well, Smith said. He was a bit of a Schwarzenegger type – rough and tough, and he looked the part and used lurid language. He could talk to the troops, and they loved him. But he cried when his brother, a regimental CO in Smith's brigade, was killed, the first crack in his armour that Smith saw. If a battalion's men wouldn't follow his orders as he wished, he tried to win their compliance by explaining what he wanted in careful detail and with his usual expressive terms. He would have been corps commander except for army politics.

Although Vokes disliked Foulkes, he laid on a great reception for him at an airfield, but unfortunately Foulkes was left by mistake at another field and had to scrounge a lift from someone. To add insult to injury, the driver insisted that Vokes, not Foulkes, was the corps commander.[22] As it happened, Smith claimed, Foulkes did all right as corps GOC, even if he was hated in the army.

Crerar hated Simonds and wanted to build up Foulkes to be postwar Chief of the General Staff; hence, Foulkes got the job. Crerar had been very correct as corps commander, a man with the ability to stand off and to see the big picture.

On Hoffmeister

Smith never thought staff work in the 5th Canadian Armoured Division was as weak as General Leese claimed after the Liri Valley battles against the

....

22 Perhaps the driver had misheard: the two surnames, Vokes and Foulkes, could sound similar.

Gustav and Hitler Lines south of Rome in May 1944.[23] Sending the division into the mountains had been a mistake. It had arrived without equipment and inherited the "falling apart" tanks of the British 7th Division, the "Desert Rats." The 5th went from Ram tanks in the United Kingdom to old British junk and then to new Shermans. The men had to learn how to operate their new tanks, almost from scratch. In any case, he thought Hoffmeister had good staff, notably Pres Gilbride, the Assistant Adjutant and Quartermaster General.[24]

Smith did not know Hoffmeister until he took over the 5th Armoured Division. Some people thought that Smith, as senior brigadier, would get the command, but Hoffmeister won over Smith at once: "Des, I know sweet-bugger-all about armour, and I'm going to depend on you." That started a great relationship. His ability to win people over helped him succeed. He also had a great appearance, was built like a brick shithouse, and had personality. He was technically competent, though the tactical skills required for armoured divisions in Italy were limited. He studied the ground, worked out a fire plan, and didn't get overwhelmed by it all. And he was innovative: he and Smith found that by welding old no. 9 wireless headsets on the back of a tank, they could greatly improve infantry-armour co-operation. Unlike **Bruce Matthews**, he had been no business leader prewar, just a mid-level management person.

On Harry Foster

Harry Foster was brought out to Italy to take over the 1st Division, as Vokes didn't want to stay on with Foulkes in command. Before the war, there had been only six potential leaders in the PF (Vokes, Foulkes, Simonds, Keller, and the two Foster brothers, Harry and Gil), and there was a lot of jealousy in a small army.

Foster could drink more than anyone else and would get a glow but never be drunk. Smith didn't like him much because he put his brigade into two or three river crossings where they'd make a bridgehead that was subsequently lost by another brigade. As a result, Smith's brigade would have to

----

23 On the May 1944 battles, see Nicholson, *The Canadians in Italy,* Chaps. 13-14.
24 The Assistant Adjutant and Quartermaster General of the 5th Armoured Division was Lieutenant-Colonel C.M. Drury, not Gilbride, who was Deputy Adjutant and Quartermaster General at the I Canadian Corps.

do it over again. He threatened to resign over this. It was a hard time, with some troops in the line for ninety days and no reinforcements. He thought that because of their experience in Northwest Europe, Foulkes and Foster believed that whenever they got into a tight corner they need only push a button to call up air support. Italy was a sideshow to them and the other Normandy generals.

On Simonds

Before the war, Smith's first wife had been very friendly with Simonds and his wife, Kay. Simonds was unbelievably ambitious. He lost his personal friendships when he began to emulate Monty, although he was still admired as a soldier. His first wife was a mousy lady, and Simonds's own background was humble. But his wartime mistress brought him into contact with the UK notables, and he began to move only in those circles.

Still, he was good, Smith said. As GSO2 in the 1st Division, Simonds was a sand table expert and very quick to voice his opinion. He often made Sansom and Turner look ridiculous in front of other officers, but they at least had heard guns in action, unlike Simonds. At that point, he was just a theorist.

Then he was put in charge of the Canadian Junior War Staff Course, and George Pearkes, GOC of the 1st Division, was asked to lecture. For the benefit of college visitors, Simonds had produced a simple form that explained its administrative details. Pearkes blustered in, and Simonds introduced him to the class. Pearkes began by saying that "staff officers are useless and know nothing about battle." He then held up Simonds's form as an example, and he went on to talk about infantry and tanks – "Tanks are stupid; can a tank go up a staircase to clear a house?" This was the first time Simonds had really been hit between the eyes, and Pearkes didn't even stay for lunch. His lecture set the course back for a week.

Many admired Simonds for Operation Totalize of August 1944, but Smith thought it was crazy. Later Conservative Party stalwart Eddie Goodman in the Fort Garry Horse called Totalize murder; none of the troops knew where they were. It was a failure, but Simonds wasn't blamed for it. Smith's lovely 4th Armoured Brigade was chewed to pieces in Totalize, and it took more casualties than it should have.

Matthews was a good Militia soldier who did well, trained his men, and kept up his equipment. That was the role of a Commander, Royal Artillery. He was a business leader, a mathematics expert in plotting fire.

MAJOR-GENERAL JAMES TEDLIE (1916-2008)

INTERVIEW | SIDNEY, BC, 25 FEBRUARY 1992

*A Montrealer, Tedlie served in the army from 1939 in the 17th Hussars and
the Royal Montreal Regiment. He then fought with the British Columbia
Regiment in the 4th Armoured Division through the Northwest Europe
campaign. He remained in the army and, after service in Indochina,
Germany, and Cyprus, ended his career as a major-general.*

*Tedlie started talking about Major-General Basil Price, the father of one
of his neighbours in Sidney.*

He greatly admired Price but realized he was "too nice to be a general in the
Second World War." As the president of a dairy between the wars, Price gave
jobs to vets and even eliminated the automatic bottle-washing machines so
as not to cut employment. He'd been the Regimental Sergeant Major of the
Royal Montreal Regiment and reverted to Company Sergeant Major when
he went overseas in the Great War. He won the Distinguished Conduct Medal
and ended the war as a lieutenant-colonel. A bit long in the tooth in 1939, he
was a conscientious Militia officer and went overseas. When Price was sacked,
he stayed in Britain with the Red Cross, also becoming a lance-bombardier
in the Home Guard. One of his sons was killed on RCAF training; another
became a drunk. He couldn't have commanded in action.

Worthington

F.F. Worthington was a wonderful but difficult man, and he was the bane of
all Armoured Corps personnel because he revelled in his role as the founder
of the corps. Long after the war, he still expected all the perks due him. He
was a devious old devil. He went to the training camps in 1940-41 to try to
persuade officers to join armoured units. "Fearless Frank" had a charming
wife, but his son, the columnist **Peter Worthington**, was a prick. His burial
at Camp Borden in 1967, right in the water table, was hard to arrange, and
the padre insisted that if he could be buried there, so could others.

Worthy trained the 4th Armoured Division from February 1942 to March
1944. The British Columbia Regiment was pretty poor mechanically, and
Tedlie thought **George Kitching** didn't deserve his sacking in Normandy,
given the little time he had as GOC of the 4th Armoured. He wondered if
perhaps the cause of Kitching's troubles could ultimately be laid at Worthy's

door, as Worthy could have done a better job of training the division. Still, in the 1930s, Worthy could see what the battlefield of the future was going to be like.

Armoured losses

During the war, Tedlie said, the British Columbia Regiment lost 105 Shermans, 44 Stuarts, and 1 Crusader in action. The regiment's establishment tank strength was 44.

On senior officers

Tedlie noted that when he was awarded his Distinguished Service Order, he received congratulatory calls or letters from Chris Vokes, Harry Crerar, and Vincent Massey, the High Commissioner in the United Kingdom – but nothing from Guy Simonds. That was the difference between the generals. You rarely saw Simonds at the front, unlike Lieutenant-General Brian Horrocks, GOC of British XXX Corps, who was visible.

He recalled that he once had to parade a junior officer before Andy McNaughton for passing bad cheques. Andy bawled him out and said, "Remember, young man, no one ever comes before me twice."

"Oh, no, Sir," replied the guilty party, "you've given me a severe reprimand before."

"March him out," Andy said, which Tedlie did, barely closing the door before Andy's peals of laughter rang out. The troops liked his fatherly approach.

Tedlie said he met Vokes when he took over the 4th Armoured Division in December 1944. He approved of his person and persona. He was direct and to the point in battle management, and his bluffness concealed a caring nature. He could shriek one minute and cry the next. He was soft as a baby's bottom, a showman who loved to party, and he was too outspoken to reach the highest levels in peacetime. He handled the division well – he was a thruster. That made him different from gunner generals who tended to handle battle as a stately pavanne – even when they had self-propelled artillery, they still hung back, Tedlie said. Vokes's favourite word was "shit," and he didn't go forward much. He was a great trainer and was interested in training junior leaders. He started schools in the Canadian Army Occupation Force in Germany, and during the no-fraternization period, he set up leave centres in Denmark so that officers and men "could get fucked."

Tedlie thought some brigadiers made their generals: Paul Bernatchez, the finest fighting soldier he ever saw; **Geoffrey Walsh**, who went forward; **Elliot Rodger**; and **Robert Moncel**, who came from the DeVilbiss Company fortune. He thought **Bruce Matthews** was a genius.

Tedlie felt there was a sense that giving an English-speaking division to a French Canadian GOC would cause difficulties, as much as putting all francophone regiments together.

RMC, the PF, and Kitching

Tedlie thought the RMC net was stronger than the PF net. He'd tried to sack a drunken ex-cadet major and was blocked by his classmates.

In the British Columbia Regiment, you were dead if you didn't get a promotion. As for how captains rose to become generals, he said there was a vacuum that needed to be filled and no one else to fill it. Only a few rose and did well. On the subject of the PF cavalry, he jokingly said that the PF shot the horses but kept the horses' asses.

Over lunch, Mrs. Tedlie remarked that **George Kitching** had married his first wife in the United Kingdom after he found he couldn't pay his Gloucestershire Regiment mess bills; she could. He then went to Canada.

LIEUTENANT-GENERAL HENRI TELLIER (1919-2009)

INTERVIEW | STITTSVILLE, ON, 22 MAY 1991

> *Born in Montreal, Tellier served in the Régiment de la Chaudière, as Aide de Camp to General Crerar, and in Italy and Northwest Europe with the Royal 22e Régiment. He remained in the army after the war, serving in Ottawa, Cyprus, and in Brussels with NATO.*
>
> *General Tellier started by talking of his time working for Harry Crerar.*

In December 1941, while still a lieutenant in the Régiment de la Chaudière, Tellier was doing a stint as Liaison Officer at Brigade HQ. Harry Crerar interviewed him and two others as possible Aides de Camp (ADCs) and picked him. He wanted a French-speaker to go with his English-speaking ADC.

Crerar had a certificate as a translator, but he spoke what Tellier called "Diefenbaker French," after the Prime Minister's stumbling mispronunciation. He talked to himself when looking at a map, Tellier recalled. He said it helped him to think, and if he were killed in action, his ADC could relay his thoughts to his successor; moreover, it might teach the ADC something. He smoked horrible tobacco (Picobac), was very frugal, and had regular habits about meals and drink. At the table in A Mess at Canadian Corps HQ were Simonds, the Brigadier General Staff; A.E. Walford, the Deputy Assistant Adjutant and Quartermaster General; H.O.N. Brownfield, the Commander, Corps Royal Artillery; J.A. Linton, the Deputy Director of Medical Services; J.L. Melville, the Chief Engineer; and a Colonel Westrup, a British officer in charge of exercises. At breakfast, there was no talk. Lunch was at 1230, sometimes out of Crerar's car, a Buick. At 1945 hours, he'd have a Scotch and go to eat at 2000. He might have one more drink after dinner. He didn't drink wine. He had sayings: "The staff officer is the servant of his troops, not the master, and don't forget it." "Lead always, drive seldom, but when you drive, drive hard." He would test Tellier's knowledge of platoon organization or of the tactical signs on vehicles. He was always properly dressed and carried a steel helmet in the car for use when necessary on exercises. On balance, he appeared to have as good a relationship with Monty as a subordinate could have with a senior. They were on a first-name basis.

Tellier saw Montgomery perhaps twenty times during the four months he was ADC. On one occasion, Brigadier Blackader was with them and offered a cigarette to Monty, who declined it.

"Do you mind if I smoke?" asked Blackader.

"No," replied Monty, "but not in my car."

At one lunch at Monty's house, Tellier was shown the great man's bedroom. On the table were two books – the Bible and a cowboy story.

Crerar's relationship with McNaughton, Tellier claimed, was also good and they used first names. McNaughton couldn't function without the aid of his wife – his mess kit was a shambles. Tellier recalled attending at the Royal 22e Régiment on Saint Jean Baptiste Day, 24 June 1942, where Mrs. McNaughton was present, sobbing a bit – their son in the RCAF had been shot down and killed.

He remembered George Pearkes running a Tactical Exercise Without Troops in a theatre, with Crerar, as corps commander, in the audience. The scenario of the exercise included a witless staff officer just out from Canada who screwed everything up. Tellier thought this a deliberate affront. In his opinion, Pearkes was a lousy general, a relic who fought in Boer War terms. He simply didn't understand the "don't give a shit" attitude of Canadians.

Tellier accompanied Crerar to the Netherlands as his ADC for the enthronement of Queen Juliana in 1948. At one ceremony, they drove into a packed stadium, and Crerar drew a standing ovation.

Crerar was a man of duty (he surprised Lloyds Bank when, after being made a director, he actually showed up for meetings). Perhaps that was why he was so upset by his drunk driving charge after the war. He called Tellier and said he'd been made to walk a line in the station, something he probably couldn't do when sober. This episode may have dashed his ambassadorial hopes.

Crerar's public relations people wanted to dub him the Hamilton Tiger (because he came from Hamilton) and to use PR photographs in which he held a submachine gun. This idea didn't take, Tellier said. Crerar wrote well but couldn't appeal to human passions. The troops scarcely knew him. But he was concerned about them and insisted on plastering the enemy's defence lines with artillery to save lives, even though artillery doctrine called for counter-battery work. He also told Tellier that if a Militia lieutenant-colonel and one from the PF were up for the same job, he'd take the Militia officer – if someone could become a lieutenant-colonel after just one night of training a week, he must be good.

On Simonds

Tellier remembered an exercise in which Guy Simonds moved a brigade flag from point A to B on the map. The staff and the artillery in vehicles would be OK, but he forgot that the troops would have to march an extra 345 miles because he'd moved the flag. Tellier liked the story of Simonds's morning orders – that there were no desks in the room, no coffee, and the whole thing was over in just a few moments. But he thought Simonds took advantage of junior officers – you can ask an officer to do something that you can't order him to do. Moreover, at table he'd talk harshly to mess staff. Still, as Brigadier General Staff, he got on well with Crerar.

Francophone generals and soldiers

When Rome was liberated in June 1944, the Royal 22e Régiment (R22eR) arranged an audience with the pope, and Georges Vanier came from Algiers to attend it. There was one Protestant and one Jew in the R22eR. Vanier's son said his father expressed himself best in English. He played tennis and always won – no one wanted to lose to him because he had a wooden leg from the Great War. And in Quebec City, he once went for a horseback ride, Tellier recounted. At some point, he fell off, the horse returned with only the wooden leg in the stirrup, and a search party had to be sent out to find him. In the Quebec Military District, Vanier had to get on with the English community, look the part, see that recruiting went well, send staff officers out to training centres, and get on with the church, the press, and the politicians. He was good at it, Tellier said. So were Generals E. de B. Panet and E.J. Renaud. General Leclerc from Quebec had been an R22eR corporal in the Great War and a janitor in Joliette during the 1930s. This prompted the comment that if the Anglos had to promote a French Canadian to the rank of general, they'd make a point of choosing a stupid one.[25]

In francophone regiments, everything was in English, even disciplinary charges. This bothered people, but that was how it was. Promotion was slow for French Canadians – the francophone PF officers were too young to expect promotion, and their Militia counterparts were too old. Paul Bernatchez didn't want his good people to go to staff. There were various reasons why francophones weren't promoted: Brigadier Gauvreau was wounded; Jean Allard didn't have time to make major-general; Bernatchez may not have had the staff capacity; the other regiments didn't have the people. He remembered a sketch from the play *Tit-Coq*, in which a French Canadian came onstage with a ladder and put it under a banner inscribed with the word "Success." An Anglo entered and easily climbed the ladder. Then a Jew followed suit, mounting the ladder with a helpful boost from a French Canadian. But when a French Canadian tried to reach the top, he was pulled down by other French Canadians.

Major-General T.L. Tremblay was an engineer, the R22eR CO in the Great War who shot a deserter in front of the regiment. He became a brigadier in his twenties. He chaired the court-martial review board at the end of the Second World War. He was tough, without humour, but highly respected.

Tellier had served on court-martials of infantry, and the R22eR had the highest rate. Reinforcements were second-raters by 1944 – one draft of one hundred to the R22eR from the Chaudières consisted entirely of bums. The best in early 1945 were home defence conscripts – at least they didn't have criminal records! If the conscripts had been sent earlier, he would have welcomed it.[26]

....

25 Leclerc wasn't stupid. See Granatstein, *The Generals*, 249-51.
26 On the conscripts who were recruited under the National Resources Mobilization Act, see Byers, *Zombie Army*; and Granatstein and Hitsman, *Broken Promises*.

On senior officers

Charles Foulkes was a bit of a tippler.

Chris Vokes would stand on his head in the mess and drink a whisky at the same time, Tellier recalled.

E.W. Sansom: "Sammy" was a good officer.

Basil Price was a gentleman, president of Elmhurst Dairy, but too old mentally, too kind. He injured himself during an exercise: "I'm the booby who detonated the booby trap," he said. During the 1945 election, he ran in the Westmount riding as a Progressive Conservative against Liberal Defence Minister Douglas Abbott. Price was a Militia officer, promoted one rank too high and ten years too old.

F.F. Worthington had limited formal education but was well educated, a patriot, conscientious, and courageous. Technology was a bit beyond him, but he was a good trainer, and troops respected him. He couldn't give a formal speech, Tellier remembered.

Kitching's father was a British Army lieutenant who got rich on gold bars at the looting of Peking in 1900. Kitching and Simonds looked and acted alike – both Brits.

E.L.M. Burns had a mistress. He was no defeatist. "Picklepuss" was tough.

Tellier envied **Bert Hoffmeister** his Mighty Maroon Machine. After the Gothic Line battles in August-September 1944, the 5th Armoured Division received fifty decorations – to encourage it. In Tellier's view, Vokes was a better GOC than Hoffmeister – the 5th's tanks could be used only when everything was in their favour; the 1st Division had to fight even when conditions were unfavourable. But Hoffmeister had everything going for him.

General A.E. Walford was an accountant and thought like one, but he was a superb administrator. Quiet, soft-spoken, and respected, he understood the political process, and he moderated Crerar in some ways.

MAJOR-GENERAL C.B. WARE (1913-99)

INTERVIEW | VICTORIA, BC, 24 FEBRUARY 1992

An RMC graduate who went into the Princess Patricia's Canadian Light Infantry (PPCLI), Ware led the regiment in fierce actions in Italy and rose to Colonel during the war. He remained in the army after the war, serving in the Far East, as brigade commander in Germany, and as Commandant of the National Defence College.

General Ware spoke at length on the prewar PPCLI, PF, RMC, and
Militia.

Ware was on attachment to the Rifle Brigade in the United Kingdom when
the war started and was sent back to Canada. As a PPCLI officer, he had never
seen B Company, based in the West, until he got back, his service being with
the company based in the East.

Ware said that drink was the curse of the PF – if a bottle was there, you
finished it. The District Officer Commanding in Regina, Jumbo Russell, was
a drunk, and when Rod Keller, the General Staff Officer, Grade 2, ordered
the booze to be removed, Jumbo crawled into the mess pleading, "Where's
my bottle?" The PF was full of incompetents as well. The PPCLI CO, Jimmy
Edgar, repeatedly failed his promotion exams but was CO nonetheless. Still,
the PF trained, trained, and trained. The Militia, he thought, was full of duds
and retreads, but the good ones stood out. During his first posting, he did
the Militia Staff Course in Winnipeg, and he came first in the class. He sweated
blood on promotion exams, and preparing for the lieutenant-to-captain exams
took two years. If you wished to proceed to Staff College, you had to be recommended in three confidential reports. Studying was a lieutenant's lot.

Ware said he didn't believe in the PF old boy network. He recalled an order
from the interwar years, which stated that there were too many RMC officers and that others had to be commissioned. His father, Colonel C.B. Ware,
brought in Charles Foulkes, and Dan Spry came in from the Militia too. But
RMC grads, he said, did stick together.

Senior officers
Andy McNaughton was a friend of his father, but Ware saw nothing of him.
Certainly, he didn't believe the stories of Andy's great reputation. He was
aloof, neither visiting troops nor appearing on exercises. Still, a friend on
McNaughton's staff said he loved him.

He recalled Hardy Ganong, when CO of the Carleton and Yorks, in an
anxious state before undergoing a McNaughton inspection. A member of
the Ganong chocolatier family, he said, "I'm just a poor chocolate maker
from New Brunswick – if anyone wants this command he can have her."

George Pearkes, however, Ware adored. He knew him from before the
war, and he was a good teacher. He could have commanded a brigade in action and a division, and Ware hoped he'd get the corps. His orders were clear,
and he knew what he was doing. He appealed to troops and commanders,

yet he could have a vicious tongue. Ware added that Pearkes once demonstrated night patrol movement on a mess table and put Rod Keller up on the table to perform too. Like British generals, he had a nice personality. Most Canadian generals, such as E.L.M. Burns, had none. One day, Ware was on a hill with Burns and Chris Vokes, watching his PPCLI do a demonstration attack. All Burns said was, "Why do they have no entrenching tools?" At that, Vokes winked at him. The commander's personality mattered because troops were prone to criticize and complain if he was lacking in that department.

Rod Keller, who was Pearkes's Brigade Major, drank a lot. He'd been the PT man at RMC and was adored by cadets. He was great fun in a blustery way, and he commanded the PPCLI when Ware was a company commander. He had passed Staff College – he had his psc – and was seen to be rising.

A.E. Potts was a joke. He always referred to Keller for aid whenever he was giving his orders. A drinker, he was invisible most times, hoping he wouldn't screw up. Ware's father had picked him to head the University of Saskatchewan Canadian Officers Training Corps. After the war ended, his son, Sam, was in the Royal Canadian Engineers and was killed in a level crossing accident. Another son, who was the twin brother of **Joe Potts**, shot himself. Of Potts himself, Hammy Gault, the founder of the PPCLI, said he was one of the finest sergeants and worst subalterns in the Great War.

Bert Hoffmeister was the best brigade commander Ware ever had. The "War Lord" Vokes left when Hoffmeister took the brigade, and he was a breath of fresh air. He gave precise orders, was always up front, and knew what was happening at the height of the battle. He created confidence, and there was no sign in him of PF-Militia tension. One officer said of Hoffmeister, "He's German, he's good."

The Foulkeses lived next door to the Wares in London, Ontario. Foulkes married money, and Ware's father thought him a comer. Ware was briefly Foulkes's Brigade Major in 1942, and he believed that Foulkes grasped things quickly.

When Ware went on leave to London, he became friends with Dan Spry, who was there with the Royal Canadian Regiment. He had a great sense of humour and shone among the regiment's subalterns.

When **George Kitching**'s child by his first wife died, Spry had to arrange to bury it and never forgave Kitching. Ware remembered that Simonds, who'd sacked Kitching in Northwest Europe, would never promote him afterward, and that Howard Graham as Chief of the General Staff did so after he succeeded Simonds.

Worthington was a great trainer, Ware stated, who had no use for hangers-on in the mess.

On Simonds

When Simonds sacked Graham as a brigade commander in Sicily, Montgomery (according to his ADC) told Simonds, "Now Guy, take him back."[27] At the start, Simonds was a bit hyper, but Monty urged him to adopt a more human approach. As a result, astonished soldiers were handed cigarettes from Simonds's jeep. He was brilliant, and you had confidence in him in battle. Ware knew him from his prewar articles in the *Canadian Defence Quarterly,* and he was regarded as a comer.

When Simonds took over the 1st Division from Harry Salmon in 1943, he called in the officers. Projecting confidence, he mentioned the gossip that he was the only staff officer without regimental training. The story wasn't true, he said: "I have had twelve years regimental training since RMC." Unlike Salmon, he impressed people, even if he wasn't gregarious. You liked working for him – you knew what he wanted, and you didn't screw it up. His briefings were good, even if he wasn't a great success at bantering with troops around his jeep. Simonds was pretty tense and maybe a shade unhinged in the 5th Armoured Division when he had his run-in with Crerar about his caravan, but certainly not psycho. Mrs. Ware said he "liked women" and described his first wife as "prissy."

Simonds and Vokes as classmates got on well. Simonds probably thought Vokes crude, but they were friends, and Vokes never said a word against him. He had no difficulty in speaking against Burns or Foulkes, whom he hated, dating back from before the war. Vokes was easygoing and good to work for, no deep thinker but clear on the things he understood. He would huff and puff, though, Ware recalled. He was thought to be a bit gun-shy, and his orders usually went along the lines of "take that hill and fix the details with the gunners."

Vokes disliked Burns because of professional jealousy or perhaps because they were just so different. How did the natives receive you? Burns asked him in Italy. "With open arms and legs," Vokes replied.

....

27   The ADC was probably Trumball Warren. See page 210 for Warren's comments on this episode.

BRIGADIER-GENERAL DENIS WHITAKER (1915-2001)

INTERVIEW | TORONTO, 19 MARCH 1991

An RMC graduate and a well-known football player, Whitaker served in the Militia with the Royal Hamilton Light Infantry (or Rileys) and went overseas with the regiment. He fought at Dieppe and as CO of the Rileys in Normandy, participating in heavy fighting in Northwest Europe and winning two Distinguished Service Orders. He was the author of several very good books on the war and had a successful business career.[28]

Whitaker started by talking of the RMC old boy network and its impact.

There were many captains and majors at RMC when he was there from 1933 to 1937 who rose to high command. Most of the top commanders were ex-cadets, which was only natural as they had the background that the Militia lacked. It was also only natural that camaraderie should keep ex-cadets together. Even so, Whitaker didn't think he received any favouritism because of his ex-cadet status.

The Militia and the PF

For the most part, the Militia had poor training before the war, and the officers lacked education and training. The PF was better, though not great. There was also tension between the PF and the Militia, and Whitaker recalled the fear in the Militia units when they were to be inspected by PF officers. There wasn't a solid relationship before the war, though this problem largely disappeared after 1939.

On senior officers

Whitaker talked of various generals, mainly 2nd Division GOCs. Victor Odlum was for the birds, a peculiar, slightly sissified individual who was a stickler for fine points – he gave the Royal Hamilton Light Infantry (RHLI) a bad report for having mud on its trucks, for example. Whitaker couldn't comment on his tactical ability.

....

28 Whitaker's four war histories, co-authored with his wife, Shelagh Whitaker, include studies of the Dieppe raid and the Canadian campaigns in Normandy, the Scheldt estuary, and the Rhineland.

Hamilton Roberts he liked – a damn fine soldier who was put into a no-win situation when he led the 2nd Division at Dieppe. In June 1940, he had saved his guns from destruction in France and was promoted as a reward. But Roberts had never commanded infantry before he became 2nd Division GOC; nor had he attended Staff College. And there were, Whitaker said, no divisional exercises under him. Training was generally poor at all levels – platoon, company, battalion, and occasionally at brigade.

Dieppe

He got to know Roberts well after 1945, when both were at Aldershot, in southern England. The media crucified Roberts because of Dieppe, which was too bad, largely because he had referred to the upcoming raid as a "piece of cake." Roberts claimed that he never said this, but Whitaker himself and at least one other officer heard him do so at a 27 June 1942 briefing.[29] Whitaker felt that the plan for the Dieppe operation was "outrageous," with objectives that were impossible to achieve, and he blamed Churchill Mann, Roberts's key staff planner, for this. Neither he nor Roberts had any sense of what troops could do, of what could be done. But then, Harry Crerar, Andy McNaughton, and General Alan Brooke, the Chief of the Imperial General Staff (all artillery officers), ought to have known how much firepower was needed to get the troops ashore. Roberts could have refused to carry out the plan, but he told Whitaker that if he had, someone else would have taken over and done it. He was the scapegoat and had a rough ride.

More on senior officers

Whitaker was sent off to senior officers' (battalion commander) school in late 1943, where the instructors were top-notch Brits. This was the first time he learned the requirements of the job and how to get the best use of the available equipment. According to him, most COs had no idea of their jobs (he mentioned Lieutenant-Colonel R.R. Labatt of the RHLI as an example).

Simonds, however, was a knowledgeable and professional soldier, though he did make a mistake in the Hochwald battles of 1945.[30] When Simonds met

....

29   Long after the war, when Roberts was living in England, he was apparently still receiving pieces of cake in the mail, sent by survivors of Dieppe.

30   Fighting in heavily forested terrain against well-dug-in troops, Simonds's Canadians battered themselves nearly senseless in February and March 1945. For more on the Hochwald fighting, see Stacey, *The Victory Campaign,* 503-8.

Whitaker, he called him by his first name. He had drive and enthusiasm; he wanted to be the "compleat" soldier and had done well at Staff College. He was tough and cold, and his underlings were careful not to make stupid mistakes. Soldiers respected him. He was prepared to take casualties to achieve an objective and thus save lives overall. Whitaker saw nothing wrong with this.

E.L.M. Burns was called "the smiler" because he never did. Whitaker had no sense of his tactical skills.

Charles Foulkes was a diplomat and pretty good at diplomacy. But few thought him a good tactician, and everyone was happy when he went to Italy from Northwest Europe. He was very good to Whitaker – on one occasion after Whitaker had been wounded, Foulkes wanted to put him in command of the South Saskatchewan Regiment, but Whitaker argued that he should go back to the Rileys. Foulkes agreed. Whitaker had some sense of the bad feeling between Foulkes and Simonds.

Bruce Matthews came from the Militia. He worked out because he was very intelligent and had an excellent personality. He could delegate. He was solid and thoughtful, had the men's best interest in mind, and was level-headed. He wasn't a driver like Simonds, though he got on well with him. He rose because of luck, ability, and being in the right place at the right time. By contrast, **Stan Todd**, as good a gunner as there was, stayed a brigadier – it was just the luck of the draw. Whitaker doubted that Matthews would have done any better than Roberts at Dieppe.

He'd met McNaughton a few times, and though everyone considered him clever, Whitaker had no sense of his charisma or of his tactical skills. Nor was there any sense at battalion level that McNaughton had screwed up big exercises like Spartan. The exercises were always a mess because of the umpires, who judged units' performance by their own rules.

Whitaker liked Crerar, who was a warm person. Moreover, he came from Hamilton, so he was very good to the RHLI. He was a courageous commander who came to the front, which was not the norm in an army where most operated solely on the basis of the map. In this respect, Crerar was like the legendary Brigadier John Rockingham, who was always at the front.

Rod Keller had been the infantry and drill instructor at RMC, where he was known as "Blood." The men in his division had no high regard for him, and he was also thought to be a drinker.

Whitaker liked Ken Stuart, whom he had known at RMC. He recalled a Canada-US football game that Stuart organized. It was held in London on

13 February 1944, and Stuart was the driving force behind it, even getting the team a barracks and six weeks to prepare for the event.[31] He liked Stuart for this, but he still blamed him for the conscription mess.[32]

On command

Essentially, Whitaker believed that a battalion was the largest unit that could be motivated by one man. A good CO could move the men in the battalion and develop loyalty and pride. Some brigadiers, such as Rockingham and F.N. Cabeldu of the 4th Brigade, could also do this.

He knew of no generals who suffered from battle exhaustion, though Dan Spry possibly did. He thought Brigadier J.G. Spragge might have been sent away because of battle fatigue. In a sense, the fact that so few senior officers cracked was surprising, given the pressures. But all a commander could do, and here he was referring to himself, was attempt everything possible to ensure success – plan, get support, and use the equipment to best advantage. You knew there would be casualties, but you had to make yourself go ahead.

....

31 Played before an audience of forty thousand, the game followed Canadian rules during its first half and US rules thereafter. It was won by the Canadians at a score of 16-6, a huge upset.

32 Many soldiers believed (wrongly, in this author's view) that General Stuart had deliberately fudged reinforcement figures, leading to shortages of men at the front and the conscription crisis in Canada during the autumn of 1944. See Granatstein, *Broken Promises,* Chap. 6.

General Andrew McNaughton (centre-left), here visiting Canadian troops in Sicily in August 1943, was built up to demi-god status in Canada. But he lost his sway as the war went on, and his critics at home and in the United Kingdom increased. *LAC PA136200*

Lieutenant-General Ernest Sansom was NcNaughton's man, rising with his mentor to become a corps commander in Britain. *LAC PA188991*

Major-General Victor Odlum (shown here at his November 1941 farewell party in Britain) was a Great War hero and a Liberal. His appointment to command the 2nd Canadian Division was largely political, his military competence to command in a mechanized war dubious. *LAC PA188995*

Major-General C.B. Price (centre, in overcoat), a Great War veteran, prominent militiaman, and the head of a Montreal dairy, was appointed a brigade commander in the 1st Division. He then became GOC of the 3rd Canadian Division. He is shown here watching a battle drill demonstration. *LAC PA189001*

Major-General Georges Vanier (centre, in forage cap), lost a leg in the Great War and subsequently served in the army and as a diplomat. He and his wife (with flowers) were welcomed by cheering crowds at Dieppe, France, in October 1944 as they were en route to establish Canada's embassy in Paris.
LAC PA166095

Lieutenant-General Maurice Pope was a key army figure in Ottawa and Washington during the war, ending up as Prime Minister Mackenzie King's military advisor. He opposed conscription, one of the few senior officers who did. *LAC PA188985*

Major-General Hamilton Roberts was a gunner who led the 2nd Canadian Division in the abortive Dieppe raid of 1942. Roberts took the rap for the failure, though the blame properly lay much higher up the chain of command.
LAC PA153531

Lieutenant-General Harry Crerar, seen here at the wheel with General Bernard Montgomery in August 1944, was the army's best politician and survivor. He commanded the First Canadian Army's war in Northwest Europe in 1944-45 and did so successfully.
LAC PA115395

A showman, Monty was Britain's most successful general. His pep talks to the troops, including these Canadians in Sicily in July 1943, had a huge impact in sustaining the army's confidence in his leadership. *LAC PA130249*

FACING PAGE, TOP TO BOTTOM:

Major-General Guy Simonds, pictured looking over the Sicilian countryside, took command of the 1st Division for the invasion of Sicily in July 1943. He impressed Montgomery, the commander of the 8th Army, and was marked out as a comer. *LAC PA141665*

Guy Simonds (at right), with Brigadier E.G. Weeks, was the ablest commander Canada produced. Innovative, hard-driving, and ruthless, Simonds pushed his soldiers hard. His greatest victory came on the Scheldt in the autumn of 1944. *LAC PA132782*

Lieutenant-General E.L.M. Burns led the I Canadian Corps in its 1944 attacks on the Hitler and Gothic Lines in Italy. The attacks were successful, but the coldly intellectual Burns was disliked by his subordinates and finally dumped by his unhappy superiors. *LAC PA134174*

Major-General Rod Keller (centre), seen here with then Brigadier Harry Foster at his right, led the 3rd Canadian Division in the D-Day invasion. Keller was popular with the troops, much less so with his senior staff officers and brigade commanders. *LAC PA132843*

FACING PAGE, BOTTOM:

General Charles Foulkes's rise was unstoppable, or so it seemed. Few thought he did well as GOC of the 2nd Canadian Division in Normandy, but by late 1944, he was commanding the I Canadian Corps in Italy. He would become the key military bureaucrat in postwar Canada. *LAC PA132732*

Major-General Bert Hoffmeister, shown in his command tank, rose from the Militia and successfully led an infantry regiment, a brigade, and Hoffy's Mighty Maroon Machine, the 5th Canadian Armoured Division. *LAC PA204155*

Major-General Chris Vokes (at right), a PF officer, commanded the 1st Canadian Division and the 4th Canadian Armoured Division. Here at Sogel, Germany, in 1945 with Brigadier Robert Moncel, Vokes was tough-talking and popular with his troops. *LAC PA159242*

3 | THE STAFF

STAFF OFFICERS PLAY A critical role in mobilizing, training, directing, and supplying an army. They draw up the plans that their commander orders, and they supervise and control the operations. They determine the material requirements for a military operation, the time needed to prepare for it, and the orders to be passed to the troops. They calculate how to get the ammunition, petrol, food, and other supplies that soldiers and machines require to the places they must be at the time they must be there. Without the staff, no attack, no defence, and no daily maintenance and sustenance could be carried out.

In the Second World War, as in the Great War, the Canadian Army began with very few such trained and capable men. Small numbers between the wars had attended the British Army Staff Colleges at Camberley, England, and Quetta, India; even fewer senior officers had gone to the Imperial Defence College in Britain. Historian Brian Reid calculated that sixty-two Canadians had completed the British Army Staff College Course during the interwar years, but only thirty-six were available in 1939.[1] On the other hand, a substantial number of Militia officers had been through the Militia Staff Course and the Advanced Militia Staff Course, which, though they had great value, did not truly prepare staff officers for wartime operations. Producing a cadre of well-trained men who could serve as General Staff Officers, Grades 1, 2, and 3, took both time and the creation of a Canadian Junior War Staff Course in Britain and the establishment of staff courses in Canada. It took even more time to find capable officers to be Brigadiers General Staff or Chiefs of Staff at Corps and Army Headquarters.

The twenty-seven interviews that follow, grouped roughly by the commanders under whom these officers and men primarily served, give clear indications of the problems the army faced and how it dealt with them. The capable officers went from one post to another, moving up in rank and

....

1   Reid, *No Holding Back,* 22.

position as they learned on the job. They often worked for several command-ers, being poached from one brigadier by a division GOC and then poached again by a corps or army commander. W.A.B. Anderson was one such ex-ample. In fact, he was such a capable staff officer that he never got the chance to command artillery in action, much to his regret.

The youth of these men during the war is striking, as is the speed of their rise in rank and the ever-increasing responsibility they carried. W.A.B. Anderson, who was just three years out of RMC in 1939, became GSO1 at First Canadian Army HQ within five years, planning the operations of almost 200,000 soldiers. Brigadier Jack Christian was also only a few years out of RMC when he became a brigadier and Chief Engineer of the 5th Armoured Division in Italy. He was just thirty-one when he was named the Chief Engineer of the I Canadian Corps. Both men's jobs required great organiza-tional and executive ability. Brigadier Stanley Todd, by contrast, was a forty-six-year-old Great War veteran when he landed in Normandy as Commander, Royal Artillery, in the 3rd Canadian Division. He was "Uncle Stan" to some of the younger staff because he seemed so much older than they; he was also Stan "God" to many because he was such a capable gunner. Notable too – so much so that German propaganda made something out of it – was how many of the more senior non-PF staff officers (and GOCs) were lawyers or stock-brokers who had served in the Militia.

It also must be said that some staff officers could easily have been grouped in the previous chapter as fighters. Colonel Clement Dick, for example, com-manded a battalion in action in Italy, and Brigadier Frank Lace led an artillery regiment in Normandy.

Staff officers had the very best vantage point to observe the division, corps, and army commanders with whom they worked daily. Harry Crerar was seen as a capable manager or bureaucrat more than a commander, but those who served him generally liked him and thought him decent. Although individual assessments differ, those who worked with Guy Simonds generally agreed that he was an extraordinarily capable officer but far from a warm human being. Charles Foulkes was neither admired for his military skills nor liked for his personality, whereas opinions on the coldly academic E.L.M. Burns were more mixed, tilting toward the unfavourable. The most positive com-ments were offered about Generals Hoffmeister and Matthews, the two div-ision commanders who performed well in a number of roles, retained their innate humanity, and practised consensual leadership. Like Chris Vokes, who led the 1st and 4th Armoured Divisions, these two men had personalities that could inspire their soldiers, Hoffmeister most so. Indeed, he was probably the only GOC who put a personal stamp on his division, the only one whose men thought of themselves first and foremost as 5th Canadian Armoured Division soldiers. Most senior Canadian commanders, however competent, tended to be cold fish, and they remained largely unknown to those who fought under their command.

Two of the interviews in this chapter fall outside the norm. J.W. Pickersgill spent the war years working in Prime Minister Mackenzie King's office and after the war became a minister in the St. Laurent and Pearson Liberal governments. He dealt with many of the generals on a regular basis and intensely at various critical points during the conscription crises in 1942 and 1944. His comments on the qualities and deficiencies of these men were typically unvarnished Pickersgill. Lieutenant-Colonel Trumball Warren, on the other hand, was a Canadian Army infantry officer who was chosen to be an aide to General/Field Marshal Bernard Montgomery, worked for him for long periods during the war, and became quite friendly with him. His description of Monty's relations with the Canadians whom he led in England, in the Eighth Army, and in the 21st Army Group added another dimension to the story.

BRIGADIER G. EDWARD BEAMENT (1908-2005)

INTERVIEW | OLD CHELSEA, QC, 24 MAY 1991

An RMC graduate, a lawyer, and a Militia gunner, Beament served as General Staff Officer, Grade 1, in the 4th Canadian Armoured Division and then as Colonel General Staff and Brigadier General Staff from 1943 to 1945 at the First Canadian Army. After the war, he was a prominent lawyer in Ottawa.

Beament started by reflecting on serving under McNaughton in the United Kingdom.

Beament went to First Canadian Army HQ at the time of Exercise Spartan in 1943 and stayed there until July 1945.

He described the interim between Generals Andy McNaughton and Harry Crerar at the end of 1943. Charles Foulkes, the Brigadier General Staff, went to Italy; A.E. Walford was ill; and Ken Stuart, Acting Army Commander, also became ill. Beament, a colonel, was de facto in command. Montgomery was laying about and issuing orders that required decisions, and Stuart had to be asked about them. Beament went to Price Montague, sitting at the centre of Canadian Military HQ like a spider in its web, and asked to see Stuart in hospital. Montague replied, "Just tell me about it." When Beament said he couldn't, it suddenly became impossible for him to see Stuart. So he went to the hospital on his own, found a doctor who would permit it, and got the decisions from Stuart.

Beament shared Douglas LePan's positive view of McNaughton.[2] He was wonderful to work for but probably wouldn't have made a good operational commander. In 1943 Beament didn't realize that Stuart and Defence Minister Ralston, who had finally decided to get rid of Andy, were pulling the rug out from under him. McNaughton didn't focus on the exigencies of war, and he spent too much time on weapons development, things that wouldn't have an impact for two to three years. His HQ operated like a War Office in the country. Foulkes and Beament felt that it had to start operating like an HQ in the field, and though McNaughton played along on the exercises they ran, he hated war games. On one exercise during the fall of 1943, a signal came in that the I Canadian Corps (HQ and the 5th Canadian Armoured Division) was to go to the Mediterranean to fight in Italy. Andy, who had fought to keep the First Canadian Army together for the invasion of France and under his command, realized the jig was up, and his face turned white. Still, he was a delightful character who had a wonderful way with men. His staff would do anything for him. He was super-nationalistic.

The army lacked the extra engineer, artillery, and lines of communication units that it needed, and these holes had to be filled by the British. When the British units asked what shoulder flashes they should wear and what unit insignia to put on their vehicles, Andy wouldn't let them use the maple leaf, a sign of his nationalism.[3] During the post-McNaughton hiatus, the GSO1s told them to use Canadian tactical signs on their vehicles.

McNaughton was a good judge of people but not ruthless enough, Beament recalled. He had to fire his Brigadier General Staff, E.L.M. Burns, because he'd written to his girlfriend in Canada, candidly discussing military matters,

....

2 In LePan's book *Bright Glass of Memory* (Toronto: McGraw-Hill Ryerson, 1979).
3 Each corps and division had its own unique shoulder flashes and vehicle "tac signs," or tactical signs. The British units that served with the Canadians were initially ordered to keep their British Army designators.

and the censors caught him. Still, if McNaughton had been in Simonds's position in August 1944, he wouldn't have fired **George Kitching**, as Simonds did, even though Kitching was a protege. Monty had had no such qualms about dispensing with people. In Southeast Command in 1941-42, where he had charge of Canadian divisions, he used to send in notes on Canadian officers that Beament saw later: "I don't like fat brigadiers" or "I don't like gunner brigadiers commanding infantry brigades."

Victor Odlum was known as "Hoodlum," but he and George Pearkes, GOCs of the 2nd and 1st Divisions respectively, served a purpose at the onset of war. Very few Great War commanders made a real contribution in the Second World War, but in using them, McNaughton must have been showing consideration for the men he'd served with during that war. Still, McNaughton was all for keeping commanders young, and he issued an edict early on that no battalion CO could be over forty-two. That seemed very young then.

Beament said he was selected for the First Canadian Army staff by Foulkes, despite his RMC training. Foulkes was no admirer of RMC.

On Harry Crerar

When he was at Army HQ, Crerar was very different from McNaughton, who was concerned with the scientific/technical side. McNaughton's wife was nearby, his house within walking distance, and he took home files on weapons development. In the spring of 1944, Crerar was more concerned with the 3rd Division and the D-Day landings and with training. By then, HQ was ready to operate in the field. Churchill Mann arrived at the same time as Crerar – they were a team. Mann had huge numbers of ideas, of which 5 percent were good, and Beament remembered that Crerar told him early on "to keep an eye on Mann." Still, Crerar didn't want a Chief of Staff, he wanted a chief clerk.[4]

Beament sympathized with Crerar over his difficulty with Montgomery. Monty never understood that Crerar had a responsibility to Ottawa. Still, Monty was great fun when he dropped in on a mess, carrying a betting book and trying to get young officers to bet. This broke the ice. He remembered the conference at St. Paul's School in London a few months before D-Day.

....

4 The Chief of Staff's role was to relieve the commander of all detail and sufficient work so he could command, reflect, and think. Kite, *Stout Hearts*, 278-79.

Monty rattled off the list of people he was firing, including an army commander, Lieutenant-General Kenneth Anderson, who was present at the time.

Crerar as a leader had no great moments. He was a superb staff officer, however, a cautious man who never made a serious mistake. Beament first met him at Camp Petawawa in 1927, when Crerar was his battery commander. The senior subaltern was Guy Simonds. Crerar insisted that the junior officers appear at the stables early every morning, and he himself frequently turned up to check whether they had. Beer simply wasn't available in Ontario, but Beament worked out a deal with his batman (who was also Crerar's) to bring it in from Quebec. The Beament-batman relationship was good, so he was informed whenever Crerar intended to check the stables. Thus, he never got nabbed, but Simonds did. Nonetheless, Simonds was a model subaltern – handsome, trim, with piercing blue eyes.

Simonds and the Scheldt battle

The next time Beament was close to Simonds was in the Breskens Pocket during the Scheldt battle in the autumn of 1944, when Crerar was ill and in Britain.[5] Crerar hadn't been well, but trying to solve the problem of the Scheldt seemed beyond him, Beament said. His conferences were like Tactical Exercise Without Troops, indecisive and inconclusive. But when Simonds took over and when he got the facts, he went to his caravan, made an appreciation, called a conference with the air force and navy, and laid it on the line: "This is what we'll do." The staff were taken aback by the fresh wind but went away and did as they were told.

Then, at the battle for Walcheren Island, Simonds conceived the idea of having the RAF bomb the dikes, thus flooding the island, which would limit the Germans' ability to move their reserves. This idea had been considered under Crerar, and though the Chief Engineer, **Geoffrey Walsh**, was dubious, he didn't say it was impossible. Simonds met officers from RAF Bomber Command in the caddy shack on the golf course at Ghent, Belgium. They said that the mission was beyond their capacity. Simonds fixed them with his gimlet eyes and replied that he couldn't question their opinion but that

....

5　In October 1944, when Simonds was acting GOC-in-C of the First Canadian Army, the 3rd Canadian Division had to clear the area south of the Scheldt, extremely difficult because of mud, cold, and canals. The enemy in the pocket south of Breskens resisted fiercely. Stacey, *The Victory Campaign*, Chap. 16.

lives would be lost if the dikes weren't bombed. That touched something in them, they left the room, and returned to say that though they couldn't guarantee success, they'd try. This was real leadership, Beament stated.

The bombing mission succeeded, and shortly afterward, at Ostend, the Royal Navy with the Commandos aboard was to attack Walcheren. The timing was tricky, and at a certain point, matters couldn't be called off. The weather was bad, but Simonds decided to go, not unlike General Eisenhower on D-Day. His mind was made up and he acted. (Walcheren was seized and the Scheldt opened to shipping, arguably the most important Canadian achievement of the war.)

Opinions

Beament said that Monty called Chris Vokes a "good soldier – no brains."

Charles Foulkes must have been fortunate on occasion, though Beament saw him in an operational role only in the spring of 1945. Beament had a good working relationship with him, but Foulkes never impressed him as a senior commander. His guardian angel must always have been hovering nearby. His judgment of people wasn't always sound. At the 2nd Division, Foulkes wanted Lieutenant-Colonel C.R. Archibald as his General Staff Officer, Grade 1 (GSO1), even though Beament argued against it. After a week in operations, Archibald was fired. Foulkes simply didn't realize that some people thought faster than others, and at a division, the need was for quick thinking; at Army HQ, Archibald might have done well.

F.F. Worthington was a great pleasure to be with, and Beament was his GSO1 from August 1942. He was sitting in the mess when Worthy appeared, fresh from Canada. Beament informed him that he was his GSO1. That startled Worthy, who hadn't realized he couldn't put in his own man. But it worked OK. He was full of ideas, Beament said, some of which were good. His room was near Beament's in A Mess, and he'd come into it in the middle of the night, shake Beament awake, and say, "I've had the greatest idea." The next morning, he'd realize it wouldn't work. He was fifty-two in 1942, getting old for operations. Beament thought he could have fought, but he wondered if he could have withstood the stress involved in fighting an armoured division. Certainly, he was terribly broken up when he was sacked.

E.L.M. Burns was on the RMC staff when Beament was there. He liked him, but he had none of the charisma a commander needed. If you knew your stuff, there was no reason to fear him.

Rod Keller was a disaster, Beament said, and Daniel Spry was very young, only thirty-one years old. When Major-General Spry reported to the First Canadian Army in Normandy to take over the 3rd Division in August 1944, Brigadier Beament welcomed him. "Thank you very much, Sir," was his reply.

A.E. Walford, Beament said, was a great staff officer.

LIEUTENANT-GENERAL WILLIAM A.B. ANDERSON (1915-2000)

INTERVIEW | OTTAWA, 21 MAY 1991

An RMC graduate of 1936, Anderson was a PF artilleryman in the Royal Canadian Horse Artillery. Adjutant of an artillery regiment overseas, he then served in a succession of staff posts during the war: Staff Captain at the 1st Division; Personal Assistant to General Crerar at the I Canadian Corps, Canadian Military Headquarters; and General Staff Officer, Grade 1, at the First Canadian Army. He remained in the army after the war, serving at National Defence HQ, in NATO as commander of the 1st Canadian Infantry Brigade, as Commandant of RMC, and as the commander of Mobile Command.

Anderson began the interview by talking about Guy Simonds.

Simonds took command of a field regiment in 1940, after the unit, commanded by Lieutenant-Colonel Hamilton Roberts, had returned from France with only its guns (all other equipment left behind) and with its morale bruised. Those who'd been envious of Simonds had said he was a staff man and couldn't command, but he got the regiment into shape, giving it a great electric jolt. He used traditional methods (such as inter-battery competitions), but they worked.[6]

Anderson first met Simonds during his RMC third-year summer training in 1935, when he was at Camp Petawawa as a temporary 2nd Lieutenant, assigned to Captain Simonds as a gunnery instructor. Simonds was just back from the Gunnery Staff Course in the United Kingdom.[7] Anderson spent the summer carrying papers and making notes for Simonds, his "bum boy" in

....

6   Inter-battery competitions would pit one four-gun battery against the others in the regiment, testing speed and accuracy.
7   Held at Larkhill in southern England, this course trained officers to be expert technical gunnery instructors.

effect. He learned how to teach by watching Simonds. Simonds wasn't intolerant of the Militia, but he was patient and didn't frighten militiamen. He was a dandy, but so articulate. And he was good to Anderson and didn't "scare the pants off him." Anderson never had qualms about chatting with Simonds, who was pleased that Battalion Sergeant Major Anderson had chosen the artillery (Battalion Sergeant Major was the top cadet position at RMC). Anderson also said that Simonds wasn't nice to him just because his father was a general. And if they happened to meet at the Park Lane Hotel in London during the war, they'd go to a show together.

In 1938, just back from Staff College at Camberley, Simonds was posted to RMC. "Super snap," he'd been singled out, and everyone knew it. Indeed, when Anderson joined A Battery, Royal Canadian Horse Artillery, at Kingston, all the warrant officers and NCOs and even some gunners remembered Simonds from the 1920s. They sang his praises, called him "The Count," and thought he was a good horseman, a good regimental officer. They respected his ability and professionalism. By the time the war came, Anderson had great admiration for him.

Moreover, Simonds was a good technical gunner. He could teach all aspects of gunnery, though it was true that he never did handle guns in action. He didn't study gunnery, Anderson said, because he didn't need to; nor did he sit around the mess wasting time.

On PF officers

In the PF, being promoted from lieutenant to captain typically took eight years – but you could pass the exams sooner, which Anderson did after two years. The PF was very unprofessional – play soldiering and full of old officers (also some 1920s and 1930s duds). But Harry Crerar was thoroughly professional, oriented to the future, and very experienced. E.W. Sansom also had a good mind and was a real student of his profession; however, he was a bit too much of a partygoer to survive the whole course. E.L.M. Burns was serious, very bright, and dedicated.

Others were less good. Hamilton Roberts, for whom Anderson had real affection, was his battery commander. He'd married money and didn't hang around the mess. The men adored him because he could sing "Old Man River" better than Paul Robeson. He was the idol of battery parties. His battery won the inter-battery competitions, and he was no weak link. But he didn't over-exert himself, didn't get to Staff College, and didn't do Gunnery Staff Courses in the United Kingdom.

Anderson knew George Pearkes from pre-RMC days. Pearkes had called him "Billy" from the age of thirteen. As GSO1 at RMC, Pearkes had little to do with cadets and ran the Militia Staff Course, promotion exams, and Staff College entrance exams. Anderson next saw Pearkes when he was doing the practical portion of the lieutenant-to-captain exams at Petawawa, and Pearkes came out from Ottawa to watch the candidates in the field. At the end, Pearkes gave a splendid off-the-cuff pep talk on what young officers should do when the shooting started. There was nothing innovative in what he said, but he said all the right things. When Anderson next saw Pearkes, he had the 1st Division in England, and Anderson was on some job that took him to his HQ. Pearkes, who had organized a volleyball game on the lawn, called him "Billy" and dragged him into the game – a nice easy touch. He then saw little of him until 1960, when, as Defence Minister under John Diefenbaker, Pearkes named Anderson to be RMC Commandant.

The RMC old boy network

That there might be an RMC old boy net never crossed Anderson's mind, and he didn't believe in it. Simonds certainly didn't play it, nor Crerar. For every ex-cadet, such as Major-General J.V. Young, who was brought in at the top as Master General of the Ordnance, there must have been five non-RMCers. Still, though Anderson had no control over who was posted to his regiment, he was happy if he got ex-cadets. Before the war, RMC had provided the skills that had helped mobilize the Militia. For example, the Princess of Wales' Own Regiment (PWOR) in Kingston was commanded by Anderson's father-in-law, Lieutenant-Colonel R.H. Waddell, and had Ben Cunningham as its Adjutant. Cunningham was a lawyer and probably the only ex-cadet in the regiment. When the PWOR was mobilized, the Adjutant played a critical role; if the regiment was posted somewhere, he would do a reconnaissance and see who he knew, using the RMC link or his legal links. According to Anderson, this was networking and entirely proper, knowing each other and having instant mutual respect. Anderson noted that Simonds had fired Cunningham as a brigadier in Normandy in 1944. Simonds told Crerar that he intended to do this, and though Crerar might have stopped it at the cost of a war with Simonds, he didn't; after his firing, Crerar did talk to Cunningham, whom he had known in Kingston, and fixed it for him to become RMC Commandant.

Anderson doubted that Simonds would have admired Rod Keller, commander of the 3rd Canadian Division. But why did he not fire him in

Normandy? First, Simonds was on the hot seat in his biggest battle, commanding the II Canadian Corps in and around Caen. He had to satisfy General Montgomery that he could run the II Canadian Corps, and the brass got twitchy if big operations were held up. The relationship between Simonds and Montgomery was still too green for him to feel confident about firing a division GOC. Perhaps, Anderson suggested, the PF old boy net was more powerful than the RMC net – thus, it might have been easier to fire **George Kitching** or Cunningham, neither from the PF, than Keller, who was.

Tension between the Militia and the PF
The Militia-PF tension, Anderson said, was very real. There was little mutual respect in 1939, though this improved over six years of war. The PF culture was pretty strong, though some people, such as **Stanley Todd**, managed to rise *without* PF help and were well aware of it. Also, there was a gunners' network, and there was no rivalry in the artillery over regimental badges, as there was in the infantry.[8] Still, he remembered the unpleasantness of hearing people talk in the Camp Petawawa mess about "goddamn PF know-it-alls."

Rising in the wartime army
The recipe for *not* rising, Anderson maintained, was to do a poor job. People were promoted if they "completed staff action," left no loose ends, and were dependable. Remember, Anderson stated firmly, the army overseas expanded out of all recognition in just two and a half years, and hands-on control from the top was impossible. What you knew was key to being promoted, but who you knew also had a lot to do with it. Anderson cited his own case: He was Adjutant of a Militia artillery regiment in the 1st Division, where J.C. Stewart was the CRA. Anderson had good reports and his CO liked him, so when a captain was needed at Division HQ, Stewart picked him. Then he was picked for the Camberley War Staff Course (at the same time as **Ted Beament**, later Crerar's Brigadier General Staff at the First Canadian Army).

Serving at CMHQ
Anderson served at Canadian Military Headquarters (CMHQ) three times. He worked for Maurice Pope on General Andy McNaughton's main submission

....

8   Gunners were said to stick together, and all wore the same cap badge, unlike infantry-
    men, whose regimental loyalties sometimes caused difficulties.

to Ottawa on the creation of the First Canadian Army (they completely forgot to include a tank brigade!). McNaughton didn't even deal with Price Montague at CMHQ on this important question. Montague had Defence Minister J.L. Ralston's confidence that he wasn't in the PF's pocket; and if the head of CMHQ could possibly not be in McNaughton's pocket, then Montague was the man. Anderson rather liked Montague: he roamed the halls like a cricket, calling people "boy" in a cheery way. He'd poke his head into offices and chat up the staff.

On Harry Crerar

As acting Canadian Corps commander and Senior Combatant Officer (SCO), Harry Crerar had a tiny staff – one staff officer and two clerks – and Anderson was the staff officer. Crerar was conscious of the fact that Montague was junior to him, but he was also aware of the need not to bypass or short-circuit him. So if he received an "eyes only" message from Ralston or the Chief of the General Staff in Ottawa, he'd go out of his way to discuss it with Montague. Crerar was very savvy – he knew Ralston would talk a lot with Montague whenever he came to Britain, and he didn't want Montague to criticize him.

Before the war, Anderson knew Crerar only to say hello to. But in 1939-40, Crerar was around Aldershot, England, where the Canadians were based, and his daughter and her husband shared billets with Anderson and his wife. Crerar replaced Anderson's uncle (Major-General T.V. Anderson) as Chief of the General Staff, and he was a good choice. He'd served at the War Office and at RMC, and he'd set up CMHQ. Then, to everyone's great surprise, he ceased to be CGS and briefly took command of the 2nd Division and then the Canadian Corps. Anderson was his first Personal Assistant. Crerar had never worn battledress until then, and Anderson couldn't visualize him in a field command role. But he saw him each day with the wireless traffic from Ottawa, and Crerar was at ease handling this paperwork.

McNaughton, on the other hand, had an aura about him, a flamboyance without trying for it, and a great press build-up. He'd come into any group and liven it up; he was "bright as all hell." In France in 1940, where he'd have been division GOC, no one would have had any concerns about him. The brooding feelings about his ability to command in the field did not exist until 1942-43, and the British were the first to worry. The mix-ups on exercises such as Exercise Spartan put him in difficulty, as they did for Generals E.W. Sansom and F.F. Worthington. And there was the widespread feeling that all Great War veterans were has-beens.

Crerar as army commander

The First Canadian Army was not a battlefield fighting organization in North-west Europe, Anderson said. Division GOCs were apt to carry brigadiers with them while playing with battalions; so too did Bernard Montgomery, commanding the 21st Army Group, without insulting Crerar or General Miles Dempsey of the Second British Army, carry their corps along. Defeating the enemy was a Monty/corps/division job. The primary task of Crerar's First Canadian Army HQ was to co-ordinate air support for its two corps. Simonds or Charles Foulkes, the corps commanders, told Crerar what they needed, and the use of air was worked out with the RAF's 84 Tactical Air Force (whose HQ was co-located with Army HQ).[9] The second task of Army HQ was to handle logistics. The corps and divisions were supposed to be fast and flex-ible, and the necessary vast tonnages depended on trucks that HQ controlled. In effect, Crerar had a staff officer role as army GOC-in-C. He drove around and visited, showed the flag, and didn't attempt to influence the battle. Certainly, he wouldn't second-guess Simonds (who was inclined to be critical of the way Crerar ran the army). Crerar realized his lack of influence, and his Orders Groups were infrequent. If Monty wanted something, Crerar would get hold of Churchill Mann, his Chief of Staff, **Ted Beament**, and Anderson, his key staff officers, and then Anderson would send a quick sig-nal to the corps to rejiggle. At a company level, things happened fast; at division, less so; at corps slowly; at army glacially.

When a big show was on, such as the clearing of the Scheldt estuary in October and November 1944, supplies poured in, and the heat was on. Monty would call an Orders Group. At Army HQ, there'd be feverish staff activity by Mann and A.E. Walford, the Deputy Adjutant and Quartermaster General, putting the HQ plan together, and even here Crerar hung back, confident that his staff would do the job.

....

9   The job of 84 Group of the 2nd Tactical Air Force, Royal Air Force was to provide fighter and fighter-bomber support for the army. The Group flew sixteen squadrons of Spitfires, five of Mustangs, and eight of Typhoon fighter-bombers. The Typhoons, especially, were greatly feared by the enemy. The Group was made up of RAF squadrons; curiously, 83 Group, which was largely RCAF, supported the British divisions, not the Canadian ones. For an explanation, see B. Greenhous et al., *The Crucible of War, 1939-1945,* vol. 3 of *The Official History of the Royal Canadian Air Force* (Toronto: University of Toronto Press, 1994), 271-72. There is a good account of air support in Kite, *Stout Hearts,* Chap. 6.

Simonds as acting army commander

Under Simonds's command, the battle to clear the Scheldt and the attack on Walcheren were different. Simonds had a bee in his bonnet on how to bomb the dikes so as to create new beaches on which to land. He kept pleading his case, but Army HQ didn't believe in it, thinking it too clever by half. But when Crerar became ill for two months (which came as a bolt from the blue for the staff, Anderson remembered), and Simonds took over, he galvanized the staff. Mann was as nervous as a cricket – he'd never worked for someone like Simonds before. Beament was, as usual, imperturbable. Simonds, who was determined to go ahead with the bombing scheme, said that it was his job to convince the top brass to divert RAF aircraft from the attack on Germany to participate in the Walcheren operation. He managed to persuade them, and his plan worked. Unfortunately, the weather didn't co-operate, and the attack was delayed while tension built. Finally, after agonizing, Simonds sent in the assault. This was a battle directed by Army HQ, with Simonds in charge, because it required that the ground attack be co-ordinated with the Royal Navy and RAF Bomber Command. Still, things were clear, whereas before they didn't have to be. Simonds was a commander in the classic mould: he made the plan, the staff had to apply it, and his job was to see that what he wanted was done. When Crerar returned, things also returned to normal.

Operation Veritable and the battle for the Reichswald in February 1945 was the First Canadian Army's golden moment, with a huge force of Canadian, British, and American troops under control. In terms of the First Canadian Army's role, Anderson said, it was Monty's operation – he got the US troops, he made the plan, and Army HQ's job was just detailed staff work. If Simonds had been there, things would have been different: Monty might have given him more independence than he gave Crerar.

Nonetheless, Crerar was the right man for the job of General Officer Commanding-in-Chief, Anderson said. He spoke for Canada very effectively, even if he wasn't the best field commander. He had a strong sense of the proper relationship to the British Army, and his Great War experience told him how important it was for Canadians to stay together and be distinctively Canadian. And he was smoother than McNaughton, more civilized in achieving this. Every time he had a problem, one part of his mind asked, "How will this look in the history books?" As Senior Combatant Officer, he was also very conscious of his role as the de facto commander of Canada's national army.

For all his Britishness, Anderson recalled, Simonds was also a nationalist, and his attitude would have been much the same as Crerar's. He would have worked well with Monty, but he'd have had little time for politics.

BRIGADIER GEORGE PANGMAN (1910-94)
INTERVIEW | CAMBRIDGE, ON, 23 APRIL 1991

A broker in Toronto and a militiaman in the Queen's Own Rifles, Pangman went overseas with his regiment. He served in a number of staff positions, including Brigade Major of the 3rd Brigade in the Italian campaign, General Staff Officer, Grade 1 (Plans), at the First Canadian Army in Northwest Europe, and GSO1 at the 3rd Canadian Division.
Pangman started by talking about his time in the Militia and the PF.

Pangman was commissioned in the Queen's Own Rifles (QOR) in 1929 at about age nineteen. He saw no tension between PF and Militia. He respected PF abilities, and there were many PFers at provisional schools, including Charles Foulkes (who taught tactics very well) and H.L.N. Salmon (who had a keen intellect). Others were weaker. The members of the Royal Canadian Dragoons tended to be "horsey-social jumping types" and weren't very professional, he thought. Churchill Mann was an exception – he studied hard. Of the Royal Canadian Horse Artillery (RCHA) officers he met, Pangman said, some had ability (he mentioned Hamilton Roberts and H.O.N. Brownfield); M.H.S. Penhale was less good. There was a real gap in ability between the PF and the Militia.

Pangman did the Militia Staff Course and thought highly of it. There were good instructors, such as George Pearkes, who taught tactics when Pangman did the two-week full-time course held at Trinity College School. The gap in knowledge was great with the PF, and more so in the country battalions – though even here, Pangman admitted, some units were good, such as the Hastings and Prince Edward Regiment, and officers such as Howard Graham were keen.

His regiment, the QOR, was keen on RMC types and tried to get them to join. Ex-cadets didn't have to serve in the ranks as other prospective officers did. Pangman never saw any sign of the old boy network, either then or in the war, and those who got ahead did so on their own ability. Some didn't, of course, such as Harry Foster's brother Gil.

Overseas

When mobilization came, the QOR went to the 3rd Division and was mobilized in June 1940. General R.O. Alexander told its CO that it had almost been put into the 1st Division to replace the Royal 22e Régiment, which had had trouble filling its ranks.

The 1st Division had as brigadiers C.B. Price, George Pearkes, and Armand Smith. Price was a delightful man, with a Distinguished Conduct Medal and a Distinguished Service Order, but he was no commander. His Brigade Major was Charles Foulkes, and the brigade was not well trained. It left Canada ill-trained, and Pangman blamed Foulkes for this. Pearkes's Brigade Major was Chris Vokes, and Smith's was Rod Keller, a "misfit." Pearkes's 2nd Brigade was one of the best in the army, with the Princess Patricia's Canadian Light Infantry (PPCLI), the Seaforths, and the Edmontons. It was said that the PPCLI had the best NCOs, the Seaforths the best officers, and the Edmontons the best men. The 1st Brigade was also good.

Pangman was an umpire during Exercise Tiger in May 1942 and went to C.B. Price's 3rd Canadian Division HQ. Price didn't do well on Tiger (though to be fair, he had just learned his son had been killed in the RCAF). He carried on but got a rocket for his ineptitude and was soon sacked. Montgomery was supposed to have said that Price would be better running the Red Cross than a division – and incredibly, Pangman said, Price was heading the Red Cross in Algiers when next he saw him.

Pangman was very impressed with General Montgomery, a terrific fellow who tolerated no incompetence. He wished McNaughton and other senior officers had been as good at cleaning house during the first years in the United Kingdom. Monty visited when he himself was on the Directing Staff at an infantry company commanders' school. First, Pangman was impressed when Monty said he'd seen Jock Spragge, the QOR CO. That he knew a Canadian battalion CO by name was impressive. He was dazzled again when Monty asked him if he thought men could fight in full equipment, as in a demonstration they'd just seen, and then told him that their gear weighed seventy-five pounds. "How can we expect a man to fight dressed like that?" Monty demanded. Pangman wondered why the Canadian officers didn't think in those terms. Guy Simonds was the only innovative mind Canada had, the greatest soldier it ever produced. Monty did a lot to improve the fitness of the Canadians, who'd gotten soft from eating and drinking too much, especially the two divisions that went to Britain before the rest.

Andy McNaughton was a dud. He didn't know the capabilities of the men who had to do the fighting, had never commanded anything, and wasn't a soldier. He was immersed in the technical-scientific side; if he'd been a proper GOC, he would have fired battalion commanders whom he kept on. The 1st Division was pretty unprofessional, a lot of its people coming off the dole. The 3rd Division was much better, and its battalions sent men to Officer Cadet Training Units.

In the fall of 1942, Pangman came back to RMC Kingston for Staff College. Then he returned to the United Kingdom as Brigade Major of the 3rd Brigade under Penhale (who succeeded Foulkes a few weeks after Pangman was back). Penhale had been senior to Simonds in the RCHA, and Simonds had been made 2nd Division GOC. To spare Penhale the embarrassment of serving under Simonds, he was sent to the 3rd Brigade, instead of the 4th Brigade in the 2nd Division. Then Salmon died, and Simonds took over the 1st Division, so the situation the brass had tried to avoid arose again.

After Pangman's brigade did mountain training in Scotland, the report on its performance was very negative, the Commandant there saying the brigade should be replaced on operations; the West Nova Scotia Regiment and the Royal 22e Régiment (R22eR) were severely slammed. Penhale had been commanding for just a week, and Pangman had been in place for only a few months. Simonds was furious, and Penhale and Pangman had to repair matters. So they put **Pat Bogert** back in command of the West Nova Scotia Regiment and got a new second-in-command.

The R22eR had a good CO in Paul Bernatchez, but its other officers weren't good, probably because the talent pool was small. Pangman worried about what would happen if Bernatchez, who went out on patrols, got killed, so he suggested that Jean Allard, whom he'd met on the Staff College course, should be second-in-command, and this worked well. There were also problems with the Carleton and Yorks, who lost a whole platoon on patrol in Sicily, resulting in the sacking of the CO. The brigade was weak, Pangman said, because of a poor division commander before Simonds, because its previous brigade commanders (Price and Foulkes) were poor, and because Penhale was too old for the game. When Foulkes was suggested as a replacement for Penhale, Simonds refused to have him because the brigade had been in such poor shape under him.

Sicily and Italy
In Sicily, the 1st Division as a whole did well. Howard Graham and Chris

Vokes were effective as brigade commanders. The 3rd Brigade was the weakest, though it got better after changes were made. Penhale left for the United Kingdom in November 1943 and was replaced by T.G. Gibson, who was soon sacked because of a revolt of his unit COs. The COs were also chopped, one being Pangman's brother. His sister, a nurse, asked Vokes why. The reply: "It wasn't his fault, it was that bloody Gibson's fault." Vokes, Pangman said, got as far as he ought. He was a good fighting leader, like J.M. Rockingham.

Simonds did not make an impression on the soldiers, certainly not like Monty. He didn't need a learning process as division GOC, Pangman maintained. He was a keen student of military affairs, with a high intellect (though not in non-military areas). He was a professional and had the power of decision. After the war, Pangman's brother was on the Directing Staff at the National Defence College, and he said that Simonds got on well with everyone there.

Pangman thought Harry Foster would inspire men, unlike Simonds, who was no Monty. Still, Simonds was the best.

In Northwest Europe

Harry Crerar did well at the job he had to do – that is, getting on with the Poles, Brits, and so on. But he wasn't a commander: his corps did the fighting, and he had little chance to show his ability. His job was to see that Canada got proper recognition for what it did, even though there was only one Canadian corps in the First Canadian Army for most of the time in Northwest Europe. Pangman was his GSO1 (Plans) in Normandy, where Crerar went to get "the feel of battle." He had troubles with the British, especially Lieutenant-General John Crocker, whose I British Corps came under the First Canadian Army. Crocker didn't like being told what to do by a colonial, and when Crerar wrote an appreciation and directive in a Staff College way, Crocker sent it back. Crerar went off at once to see Monty, and Crocker was put in his place. Pangman would do up appreciations, and Crerar would blue-pencil them closely. He kept a card index of jokes and stories for speeches – there was nothing extemporaneous about Crerar.

Pangman said that when Foulkes joined the II Canadian Corps in Normandy, his 2nd Division took a beating and his GSO1, Archibald, was canned. The feeling was that Foulkes was at fault, and certainly the battalion COs blamed him; Foulkes survived this, but Pangman wasn't sure how. Foulkes made no further mistakes, although other division GOCs were canned. At the Scheldt, when Simonds was acting army commander, Foulkes moved up to Corps HQ as the senior division commander; even so, the Scheldt was Simonds's battle, and it was he who conceived the idea of using Buffalos, amphibious landing craft that could operate in the water and on land, and bombing to breach the dikes. His Chief Engineer said it wouldn't work, but Simonds insisted.

Shortly after this, E.L.M. Burns was dumped as GOC of the I Canadian Corps, and Foulkes went to Italy to take over; Vokes, who didn't want to serve under Foulkes, came to Northwest Europe. Burns, Pangman added, was hard done by. In Italy, Foulkes summoned all the unit COs to his HQ, which angered them all – they were busy, it was too far, and so on. He was not well liked.

Bert Hoffmeister was well liked. He was a good CO and brigade and division commander, the best division commander Canada had at the end of the war because he knew what infantry could do.

Bruce Matthews, GOC of the 2nd Division, was an old friend; Pangman had worked for his father in Toronto. Like Hoffmeister, he never got into a flap, was a capable artillery officer, and could work well with Simonds. He did well as a division commander, insisted on getting sufficient time to plan, and was no yes man.

Pangman liked Holley Keefler, who was 3rd Division GOC from late March 1945, and he became his GSO1 at the end of the war; all they did was sail, play tennis, and party. Keefler had worked for Bell prewar and Northern Electric postwar and did well. Pangman met him at Staff College, Kingston, when he came down as Director of Military Training to lecture. He used a big chart and tore off pages as he went – which annoyed General H.F.H. Hertzberg, the RMC Commandant. Keefler too was unflappable, took the advice of his brigade commanders, and planned well.

Pangman didn't know Rod Keller well but did know that he was nearly replaced before D-Day. His GSO1 and brigade commanders got together to talk about what to do with him – his drinking and the fear he was windy. In end, they did nothing.

H.F.G. Letson was Aide to the Governor-General after the war. His favourite drink was a half-and-half mix of gin and sherry. It was particularly good on a cold day, when it could be put into a coffee flask, with no one the wiser about what you were drinking. He'd got the recipe from Field Marshal Lord Alexander, the Governor-General.

A.E. Walford was a damn good administrative officer, Pangman stated, as Deputy Adjutant and Quartermaster General for Crerar. He'd been the right-hand man at Morgan's in Montreal and was well supported by his Colonel, **Beverley Matthews**. J.F.A. Lister succeeded him and was court-martialled in the Netherlands after the war.

MAJOR GILES PERODEAU (1919-2011)

TELEPHONE INTERVIEW | SIDNEY, BC, 24 MARCH 1992

He was Aide de Camp to General Crerar from August 1944 to March 1945.
His wife was the daughter of Major-General C.B. Price.
Perodeau began by talking of working as ADC to Crerar.

Perodeau was in the First Canadian Army's HQ Defence Company (armoured cars) and occasionally accompanied Harry Crerar. When an ADC departed in August 1944, Crerar asked him to come aboard – probably because he thought Perodeau was bilingual (he really wasn't, just an anglified French Canadian). His job was to travel with Crerar whereas **Finlay Morrison** was the "inside" ADC.

Perodeau liked Crerar, though he wasn't warm, was all business, very fair, shy, and not a character like Chris Vokes. Certainly, he was more patient than Guy Simonds, who wasn't happy when Perodeau misread the map and got him lost twice in one day. Crerar, on the other hand, told him simply to stop and tell him if he got lost.

Perodeau was never present at meetings with senior officers; nor did he go with Crerar to the Dieppe ceremony in September 1944 that caused the row with General Montgomery.[10] But he remembered Crerar being very upset when a staff car failed to arrive on time to get him to a meeting with Monty. He thought Crerar was a brave man and often saw bullet holes in the wings of the aircraft he used for reconnaissance. Crerar also used the aircraft to save time on trips, sending the ADC and a car (a jeep or a Buick) ahead to meet him when he landed at the airfield and drive him to his final destination.

Crerar's A Mess was not bad; only one or two senior officers picked on the ADCs. At lunch, Perodeau's role was to keep an eye on Crerar so he could

....

10   Crerar went to a Canadian commemorative ceremony at Dieppe rather than to an important meeting with Montgomery. Monty was furious. For the details, see Granatstein, *The Generals,* 112-13.

bring him his second pink gin when he raised his brow. At night, Scotch. He never saw him even slightly cut. One day at the mess, Churchill Mann (the Chief of Staff, who wanted a division but wasn't to get it) was clowning around and tossing buns at people. Crerar just said, "Here, here." **Walsh**, the Chief Engineer, wasn't friendly, but Brigadiers J.E. Genet, the Chief Signal Officer, and H.O.N. Brownfield, Brigadier, Royal Artillery, were. They ate well, on tablecloths and with silver service to put on a non-lavish show. Crerar's caravan was comfortable, his operations van well designed.

Perodeau stayed with Simonds as ADC when Crerar became ill and went to Britain to recover just before the Scheldt campaign. Simonds didn't like to fly, so he drove around (but not in the Staghound armoured car without a turret that he used as corps GOC). Perodeau didn't like Simonds, who was a cold fish, and was embarrassed at hearing him tear a strip off a brigadier. Still, there was no change in A Mess when Simonds was there, nor any sense that the pace at HQ had stepped up. Simonds, like Crerar, would go forward – to divisions or brigades. With Crerar, he once went to a battalion.

At one point, Perodeau travelled with Crerar to Monty's mess in Brussels and was terrified at meeting the Field Marshal. But Monty put him at ease, offered cigarettes, drinks, and so on. Perodeau was struck by how Monty's ADCs argued with him over lunch, just like with father at home. And he remembered General Eisenhower, the Supreme Allied Commander, coming to Crerar's HQ to stay the night and seeing Crerar salute him as he left. This was the first time he'd ever seen Crerar salute someone else, and he thought Crerar didn't like it much.

Perodeau first knew Major-General C.B. Price slightly when he went to school with his son, who was killed in the RCAF in 1942. He next met him in 1941, when he asked permission to marry his daughter. Price, in Canada to get the 3rd Division, asked him if he'd like to be his ADC, but his fiancée and future mother-in-law squelched that. In June 1942, when Perodeau got to Britain as a reinforcement officer, and Price had him to stay at his HQ, the two met again. Price took him to see an engineer exercise and promptly blew himself up on a trip-wired grenade, badly injuring his hand. In the car en route to hospital, all Price said was that the sergeant responsible was not to be punished. At the hospital, Perodeau saw that Price's ammo belt had been holed by shrapnel – he'd just missed blowing himself up. The night before, he and Price had bumped into Charles Foulkes, the GSO1, in the mess. Foulkes had been very cold, an indication that things weren't good between Foulkes and Price.

During the exercise that finally got Price fired for his failings in the field, he'd received word of his son's death in an air training crash. Possibly, his performance suffered as a result. Perodeau thought that Price was bitter at Crerar and Montgomery about being sacked, but he never complained.

FINLAY ANGUS MORRISON (1917-?)

INTERVIEW | VANCOUVER, BC, 2 MARCH 1992

> *Morrison was a junior officer in the South Saskatchewan Regiment. He was General Harry Crerar's Aide de Camp from May 1944 to 1946. He spoke on becoming ADC to Crerar.*

After apprenticing for four years as a pharmacist, Morrison studied pharmacy at the University of Saskatchewan. He did a two-year diploma course, graduating in 1942, and then joined the army. He went to Gordon Head, Shilo, and Portage for training and then to Britain in 1943 as a lieutenant with the South Saskatchewan Regiment. In April 1944, Morrison was interviewed by General Harry Crerar for the Aide de Camp (ADC) position, and he got the job. He subsequently learned that the ADC was required to have at least two years of university. The South Sasks had only two lieutenants who satisfied that criterion – and the other had just returned from a course. Thus, he got the nod.

Crerar had two ADCs, one who travelled with him and one who kept up the maps. Initially, Morrison accompanied Crerar on his trips. He took Crerar's Tactical HQ to France about D-Day+16.[11] Crerar was ordinarily at the Tactical HQ, about five miles ahead of the First Canadian Army's main HQ.

ADC duties

When Crerar arrived in France, he initially had nothing to command, at least not until the First Canadian Army became operational. The bridgehead was genuinely jammed, though Crerar also thought Monty was deliberately making him cool his heels because he mistrusted his command skills. To fill time, Crerar and the ADC travelled to brigades or divisions, bugging the

....

11   Tactical HQ included a defence platoon, operations tent, Crerar's caravan, the Personal Assistant's tent, and Morrison's own, plus two outriders and a driver.

commanders. "Where should we go tomorrow?" Crerar would ask. As ADC, Morrison picked the route, got the lunch, and handled the other details of the trip. Crerar usually drove the jeep (he almost never used a Staghound armoured car), Morrison read the map, and the driver sat in the rear. He got Crerar lost on one occasion and made him late for an inspection on another. Crerar wasn't angry, just told him that troops couldn't be left waiting: "They were five hundred men, and he was only one." In other words, it was better to arrive early and have to wait than to be late. Crerar only rarely went forward of Corps HQ, but he pushed his pilot to fly over the lines on reconnaissance, and they ran into trouble a couple of times. He was physically brave, Morrison said. Crerar had three aircraft at his disposal – a Vigilant spotter, an Auster, and an Anson for longer hops.

Morrison soon became the map-keeping ADC. If Crerar went to Montgomery's HQ for an Orders Group, he'd ask Morrison to map this for him. Morrison briefed Crerar each day at 0630.

He liked Crerar, thought he was first class to work for, considerate, understanding, not flashy. Crerar called him Finlay and wrote a nice note to his parents. They saw each other regularly after the war.

Crerar never let on to Morrison about his troubles with Monty. Morrison could see that Crerar had difficulty with Simonds, though none with anyone else. When Crerar was ill and Simonds was in charge, Morrison acted as his ADC, though Marshall Stearns, Simonds's ADC, did almost everything. Simonds was harder to please than Crerar. Incidentally, Morrison said, Crerar really was sick when he gave up command, regardless of what some people claimed.

Crerar's A Mess was for the two ADCs and the First Canadian Army's senior staff officers. They ate well, off a silver service and tablecloths, with wine at times and drinks. Crerar never drank much; nor did anyone in A Mess. It was generally a happy mess, though Brigadiers **Geoffrey Walsh** and Churchill Mann could drive the ADCs crazy.

Crerar's daily routine began at 0600, briefing while he was shaving at 0630, then the overnight telegrams and visits. The afternoons were devoted to correspondence or map study. Crerar did his own writing in longhand. He had to keep two bosses happy, Mackenzie King and Monty. And yes, he worried about the reinforcements situation.

At war's end in Canada, Morrison was still ADC. Crerar was happy with the warm reception he received in Canada, though Morrison thought that he wanted to be Governor-General.

MAJOR-GENERAL N. ELLIOT RODGER (1907-2010)

INTERVIEW | OTTAWA, 21 MAY 1991

An RMC graduate, Rodger was in the Royal Canadian Engineers, spending much time at National Defence HQ in Ottawa before the war. Overseas, he worked at Canadian Military HQ, served as Personal Assistant to General McNaughton, did the Staff College course at Camberley, and held a variety of appointments including a brief stint as a brigade commander. In 1944, he became Chief of Staff to Guy Simonds at the II Canadian Corps. After the war, he held a number of posts, including Quartermaster General and Vice Chief of the General Staff.

Rodger commenced by offering his opinion on some generals.

General **H.F.G. Letson**, the Adjutant General from 1942 to 1944, was an argumentative, dictatorial man. But he was a good mixer who got on very well in the United States when posted there as military attaché and then as head of the Canadian Joint Staff in Washington during and just after the war. Letson had married well, a beautiful divorcee whose son was John Nichol, the BC Liberal who later became a senator.[12]

E.L.M. Burns, Rodger said, was an enigmatic man whom he first met at RMC, when Burns was an instructor and Rodger a cadet. He played and sang rude ditties on the piano. Rodger then worked for him in the Survey section at National Defence HQ (NDHQ) in Ottawa, but because there was no money, he did odd jobs elsewhere. Burns was very brainy but grumpy and dour.

Maurice Pope was a great administrator, and in the Directorate of Military Operations and Intelligence (DMO&I) at NDHQ, he took Rodger on as General Staff Officer, Grade 3, from his survey work. Rodger stayed there for four years from 1932 to 1936 and worked on Defence Scheme No. 3, the plan for dispatch of an overseas expeditionary force. At that point in its development, the plan noted which command and staff positions would be required for the force, but no names were specified. He also wrote the censorship manual. Pope had tried to get the Department of External Affairs to do this, but the department felt that the manual could wait because Canada was not at war. Harry Crerar was the Director of DMO&I, but he wasn't around much. C.F. Constantine, who was Adjutant General, sent out a memo on bow ties

....

12   Rodger had accompanied me to my interview with General Letson.

and mess kits. In his response, Pope used the word "ought," saying that it would get a rise from Constantine, who wouldn't know what it meant.

Rodger also worked for Pope as GSO3 Intelligence at CMHQ in London once the war started, in effect as the go-between for the British War Office and CMHQ. He appreciated Brigadier Harry Crerar, the Senior Combatant Officer; he was a competent officer in the circumstances, certainly more so than the generals, who were all older. Junior officers had complained interwar about the old boys blocking promotion, but the elders soon disappeared once war came. Crerar was younger than this group.

After Staff College at Camberley, Rodger went to the 1st Division as Assistant Adjutant and Quartermaster General, the chief administrative officer under George Pearkes, the GOC. He had known him at NDHQ as Director of Military Training and served as his secretary when Pearkes was president of the Canadian Club or the United Services Institute in Ottawa. Some people described Pearkes as a "wonderful brigade commander," a good person, but perhaps too old when he got his high rank (he was fifty-two in 1940). At Division HQ, he was well liked. He went fox hunting to keep fit. His brigade commanders were old-timers, and if they'd been required to lead troops in battle, the result would have been a fiasco like Hong Kong. Pearkes was a fine man, Rodger maintained, but not bright.

The Deputy Adjutant and Quartermaster General of the Canadian Corps was Guy Turner, a McNaughton loyalist who clung to his coattails. McNaughton encouraged him despite his lack of brains, Rodger complained.

On General McNaughton

Rodger then became a liaison for McNaughton with Ottawa on matters outside the Canadian Corps. Guy Simonds, who had been Rodger's senior at RMC, was Brigadier General Staff and in charge of training. McNaughton spent a lot of time developing scientific projects, and Rodger kept minutes on them. But he generated loyalty. Still, McNaughton didn't devote time to training his corps, though he may have thought that Simonds could do it well. His focus was back to Ottawa and outward to research and development. On the latter, he loved seeing demonstrations. On the former, McNaughton was Canada's top soldier, and the Chief of the General Staff at NDHQ consulted him on military developments. Friction arose because the CGS effectively was junior to Andy, which was not the case for his American and British counterparts. As CGS, Crerar knew McNaughton well, and they trusted each other – they'd served together in the Great War – but there was no doubt who was junior. In effect, Rodger said, Crerar was the filling in the sandwich between Defence Minister J. Layton Ralston and Andy; Ralston and Andy could settle some things on their own, but Crerar had to mediate on others.

Rodger said the senior officer selection committee system set up by McNaughton was fair and did a good job. Even so, McNaughton wasn't a good judge of people (Guy Turner, for example). He could have stopped Victor Odlum from getting command of the 2nd Division. Worse, he backed his appointees to the end, even after they'd ceased to do their jobs. They'd become friends, not subordinates, and he didn't want to hurt them.

Dealing with the British generals was a problem, Rodger said. Before the war, McNaughton had worked on the UK Visiting Forces Act and knew what was involved in how Canadians would be treated; this meant he had a chip on the shoulder, and he resisted coming under British control. Rodger added that in 1929, when he himself was at the British Army's School of Military Engineering, he'd had to get a new commission authorizing him to command British troops; he couldn't command them with a Canadian commission.

Price Montague at CMHQ and relations with McNaughton

Price Montague was a very well-known, flamboyant, colourful polo-playing figure in Winnipeg, and when war came, like Letson, he was a prominent militiaman. He was picked to replace Crerar at CMHQ in 1940. He'd never commanded in the field, but he was outgoing and domineering. He called everyone "boy," Rodger said. Still, he was right for the job and settled most problems between McNaughton and Ottawa (McNaughton didn't talk directly to Ottawa). Ralston was acknowledged as boss, though McNaughton would fight him energetically when he wanted something or disagreed on some point. Even so, Rodger thought their relationship wasn't bad. (Rodger and Ralston were both from Amherst, Nova Scotia, and Ralston, he said, had been his "drag" to get into RMC!) Montague and Andy got on well, and Montague acted as his legal adviser. He was a nationalist, but not quite as vigorous on that front as Andy. When Ken Stuart was Chief of the General Staff, he and McNaughton also seemed to get on without bitterness, though after his firing in late 1943 McNaughton came to feel that Stuart had gone behind his back.

CMHQ's role in working with the War Office was to detail corps establishments – that is, to specify what kind and numbers of units and troops Canada would provide. The training side of CMHQ coped with the organization of reinforcement units and got training under way. In theory, CMHQ told Canada what to do on training; in effect, however, it was a post office between Corps HQ and training in Aldershot and in Canada. Inevitably, CMHQ got bloated.

Rodger lived at Corps HQ and commuted to CMHQ. In December 1943, McNaughton was fired by Defence Minister Ralston. Worried about how the troops would react to his sacking, he said to Rodger, "I hope there won't be mutiny in the army." There was none. Rodger also had to tell Mrs. McNaughton of the death of her son, Ian, in the RCAF. Even before he began to speak, she said, "It's Ian, Elliot." She sensed it.

Working for Simonds

Rodger briefly had a brigade command under F.F. Worthington, who couldn't entertain two thoughts at the same time and was no intellectual. Then Rodger went to Corps HQ as Simonds's Chief of Staff in February 1944. He never knew why Simonds chose him – he could have picked anyone he wanted. He must have seen that Rodger minded his own business and did what he was told at the 1st Division. Hugh Young, the previous incumbent, was too strong and would have tried to run the war himself.

Simonds's married life was a problem after the war, Rodger recalled, his first wife being rather retiring and shy. His second wife, Doe Sinclair, was the sister of Colonel Malim Harding and was more Simonds's style.

Simonds could be ruthless, especially in the way he sacked **George Kitching**. He didn't discuss personnel changes with Rodger or, very much, with Crerar – he just informed him. Crerar was so much the opposite – slow and deliberate – and when Simonds took over the First Canadian Army, things changed. His tactical ideas were his own, though the Walcheren dike bombings in October 1944, Rodger thought, had first been contemplated at Army HQ. Simonds was receptive to staff ideas, but he usually had them first. Rodger remembered Simonds's Orders Group prior to Operation Totalize, the night armour attack of 8 August 1944 on the road to Falaise: "But it's never been done before," some said. "That's why I'm doing it," Simonds replied. The British desert commanders, Simonds would say, "had sand in their ears."

Although Simonds addressed Rodger by his first name after the war, he was "not a man one wanted to go fishing with." During the war, Rodger called him "General" or "Sir." Still, when Rodger went to Simonds's funeral in 1974, his wife gave him Simonds's II Canadian Corps gold cufflinks, obviously something he had directed. And Simonds got Rodger put on the board of Halifax Insurance.

Simonds was very precise. In early 1944, Rodger remembered, he hand-wrote a paper on how to fight the Normandy battle. The text went to a sergeant typist to type and came back with one word missing. "Do it again," said Simonds. The sergeant made no further mistakes.

Some GOCs and opinions

Bruce Matthews, GOC of the 2nd Division, came in cold from the business world and rose on straight ability.

Dan Spry became Personal Assistant to McNaughton after Rodger. He was a real soldier who loved the infantry.

Rodger had no respect for Charles Foulkes and simply blocked out memories of his time as acting II Canadian Corps commander. After the war, when Rodger was Quartermaster General, Foulkes once dressed him down in front of everyone. Rodger thought that Crerar wanted him as Chief of the General Staff so that Simonds would have to wait for the position. The CGS needed political savvy, however, and Foulkes had this.

Crerar and Simonds recognized each other as character opposites, but there was no great tension. Certainly, Simonds saw Crerar as stodgy and cautious. One problem was that General Montgomery would bypass Crerar and go directly to Simonds (and sometimes to brigades); he certainly talked more to him than to Crerar. Montgomery and Simonds weren't friends, but there was mutual admiration.

C.S.L. Hertzberg, the Corps' Chief Engineer, was sent to India to advise on building airfields. He told Rodger that he'd "fooled the doctors" and avoided getting his smallpox vaccination. He died three or four months later of smallpox.

In the 1920s at RMC, E.J.C. Schmidlin walked around with a wrench in his pocket. His uniform looked like he was a mechanic.

LIEUTENANT-GENERAL GEOFFREY WALSH (1909-99)

INTERVIEW | OTTAWA, 24 MAY 1991

An RMC graduate and a PF officer in the Royal Canadian Engineers, Walsh became Chief Engineer of the II Canadian Corps and then of the First Canadian Army. He remained in the army after the war, served as Quartermaster General, commanded in Western Canada, and became

Chief of the General Staff in 1961. He retired in 1966 as Vice Chief of the Defence Staff.

Walsh started by talking of the future generals he knew at RMC.

Harry Crerar was his company commander at RMC and was Commandant when he was there as an Engineer officer at the end of the 1930s. Hard-nosed and very strict, he freely dealt out Confined to Barracks as punishment for cadets. Walsh didn't get into trouble with him as company commander and therefore had little to do with him. Crerar was aloof from the cadets, as he was all his life. As Commandant, he rode hell out of Walsh for four months as Engineering officer, as he did to all. He tried to break you, but once you passed his tests and he made up his mind you were OK, things improved. And when Walsh became Chief Engineer of the First Canadian Army, he didn't have to go through Crerar's mill again as he'd already proven himself. Still, Crerar was very competent.

H.H. Matthews was a nice old gent, with not a clue on engineering but who interfered nonetheless. Walsh had to fire a workman at RMC to establish his control over engineering matters.

Very different, Walsh said, was Major-General R.O. Alexander, who, though strict, had a sense of humour and was good to serve under at the start of the war. At Toronto in 1939, when there was a terrible screw-up building barracks, Alexander didn't panic.

Guy Simonds would ride people too. He was a half-battalion officer at RMC, and Walsh was a company commander at the end of the 1930s. Simonds wouldn't delegate. He was extremely shy, and after the campaign in Sicily, Walsh was the only person in the 1st Division's A Mess that he talked to – until he got to know the others. Walsh had scored with him because, when Simonds and Admiral Philip Vian of the Royal Navy flew to Africa to plan the Sicily campaign, they discussed the August-September 1941 raid on Spitsbergen and Vian told Simonds that Walsh was the only officer in the participating Canadian troops who knew what he was doing.[13] Moreover, because several ships were sunk on the way to Sicily, many officers ended up

....

13 In the summer of 1941, Canadian troops under Brigadier A.E. Potts briefly occupied Spitsbergen, a Norwegian archipelago six hundred miles from the North Pole, and disabled coal mines there. Then Major Walsh was officer commanding the 3rd Field Company, RCE. Stacey, *Six Years of War*, 301-7.

without their kit. Fortunately, Walsh's batman had loaded his kit on a different ship, so it wasn't lost. He used to loan Simonds socks!

Training in Britain and McNaughton

Training in the United Kingdom remained at the low prewar standard for some time, Walsh maintained. Absenteeism was high and stayed that way in the 1st Division until 1942. But once the Militia officers without staff training had been sacked (he named Brigadiers H.N. Ganong and A.E. Potts), things got better. As he put it, "You can't teach an old dog –." Still, the army couldn't have done better at the beginning of the war, and the old boys did a great job organizing and getting people overseas. If the Canadian troops had been called on to fight, however, the results would have been disastrous.

McNaughton was invisible, never seen, and more interested in the mechanical side of things. Even on exercises, he wasn't around and his staff ran them. He wasn't a leader for the troops.

On Salmon and Simonds

Harry Salmon was innovative and a terrific trainer. He'd screw up General Montgomery's exercises by trying something new. He took over the 1st Division from George Pearkes, also a good trainer, and got rid of all Pearkes's staff. For three months, while he worked his way down the list and decided who should be sacked, he didn't speak to Walsh. After firing nine COs, he came to inspect Walsh's engineers, liked them, and then couldn't be nicer. At the A Mess, everyone congratulated Walsh for having survived. The 1st wasn't a bad division; it was just Salmon's way of command. In fact, Walsh thought the 1st far superior to other divisions in Northwest Europe (though he admitted that some of its battalions weren't good, such as the West Nova Scotia Regiment). Also, the 3rd Brigade wasn't good when it was under M.H.S. Penhale, and some COs weren't tough enough.

George Kitching was a good General Staff Officer, Grade 1, but he didn't do well as Brigadier. When he became a GOC, Walsh could see the writing on the wall – he wasn't tough enough. The 4th Armoured Division was not in good shape – the Engineers weren't good, the Signals a mess. The previous GOC, F.F. Worthington, had no Staff College training and knew little about the other combatant arms; he relied on his staff, and his GSO1 (Lieutenant-Colonel J.E. Ganong) was ropey.

Simonds and Crerar were around, and after Sicily, men followed Simonds, Walsh said.

He once watched Simonds win a battle over the telephone. A brigadier wanted to withdraw his troops from action, and Simonds made him stay by telling him that the Germans would withdraw by dawn. They did. He had everything thought out and relied on people to follow his instructions. When Walsh was Chief Engineer (CE) of the 1st Division, he got a call from the Corps CE about land mines. Had they been cleared on a certain route? No. Simonds, the GOC, had made no mention of mines at the evening orders, and Walsh had simply followed his instructions. Walsh then told Simonds he needed twenty-four hours to organize things in future, and from then on Simonds kept him informed in advance. In other words, Simonds could learn. Nor was he really ruthless. But he wouldn't confide in anyone.

On the 3rd Division in Normandy

Rod Keller's 3rd Division was so overtrained for D-Day, so keyed up, that it had lost the knack of field operations and mobile warfare.[14] Walsh was horrified to find that a 3rd Division Royal Canadian Engineers Field Company spent eight hours to build a bridge; in the 1st Division, this task took just one hour. Keller nonetheless was a good all-rounder, and Walsh knew nothing about grumbling against him.

Crerar and Simonds as army commanders

Crerar operated differently from Simonds. He relied on his staff. In this, he had little choice, as his job was impossible, in substantial part because he had to write dispatches to Mackenzie King every night. The role of the First Canadian Army was logistics and air, Walsh said, whereas the corps fought the battle. Crerar and Simonds, in other words, were in the right places. But when Crerar was ill (of colitis, Walsh said), and Simonds became Acting GOC-in-C of the First Canadian Army, Army HQ ran things. Crerar, however, did fight the Rhine crossings from Army HQ.

The Walcheren dike bombings had been canvassed at First Canadian Army HQ. The Dutch said the bombings wouldn't work, and Walsh relayed their assessment to Simonds, who refused to accept it. Simonds discussed his plan with Walsh, the CE, who then agreed to it. Simonds's tactical ideas were his

....

14 An interesting comment. The usual criticism of the 3rd Division immediately after D-Day was that once ashore, the soldiers believed their job was finished and that others should take over. Walsh's variant seems more likely to be correct.

own; even at Camberley, his papers had impressed everyone and were for-warded to the War Office. He was always looking for the element of surprise. He expected you to use your initiative, and once you showed you could be trusted, he trusted you.

On senior officers

Harry Foster was a sound brigade and division commander who had been GSO1 to Salmon. He was solid.

Bruce Matthews was first class, young, and efficient.

As GOC of the 1st Division, Chris Vokes was an awful letdown after Simonds. During an Orders Group, Vokes stated that the sappers would build a bridge in a certain spot. There'd been no reconnaissance, no equipment emplaced, nothing. Walsh asked if he was still CE. Simonds wouldn't have done that. Walsh went to the location and could hear that the Germans were still there. He told Vokes, and Vokes never forgave him. He was rash and unthinking, as when, after his brother was killed, he said he wanted no pris-oners taken. Still, he wasn't stupid, and he did well when he served under Simonds, who knew how to handle him.

Charles Foulkes was cold, Walsh said, and you never knew where you stood with him. They were both captains together in Toronto. Crerar said he'd recommended Foulkes as Chief of the General Staff because he was a good politician. Simonds, on the other hand, was all for firing Foulkes in Normandy. When Foulkes came to Italy, Vokes asked to go to Northwest Europe as they couldn't get on.

H.F.H. Hertzberg was a great friend who was at RMC when Walsh was a cadet. He was also District Officer Commanding in Halifax when Walsh went there, and when Walsh's CO wrote a negative assessment of him, Hertzberg effectively countermanded it: "This officer is much better than this report would indicate."

C.S.L. Hertzberg was an engineer but not a real soldier, a bit of a fuddy-duddy and gadgeteer. That was why he got on with McNaughton.

Pearkes took over from H.F.H. Hertzberg at RMC and was then a good Director of Military Training. He once directed traffic when an exercise broke down in England. Pearkes noticed that Walsh had shown some initiative in getting his own vehicles through, so he made him Chief Engineer of the 1st Division. If he'd led the division into battle, he'd have done well.

MAJOR-GENERAL ROBERT P. ROTHSCHILD (1914-2000)

INTERVIEW | OTTAWA, 24 MAY 1991

An RMC graduate,[15] *Rothschild was a PF member of the Royal Canadian Horse Artillery, and he served in regimental artillery roles in wartime England. He attended the Canadian Junior War Staff Course and served in the 5th Canadian Armoured Division and the 2nd Armoured Brigade before becoming General Staff Officer, Grade 1, of the II Canadian Corps. He remained in the army after the war, serving in many posts, including Quartermaster General.*

Interviewed in hospital, Rothschild began by talking about the PF.

Rothschild thought that PFers were professional, though not quite as much as present regulars. Many had Great War experience, including many senior NCOs. The captains and down were largely postwar. Essentially, the PF role was to be a training cadre for the Militia, which was not of high quality, though better than the present-day reserves, he believed, and more enthusiastic.

The attitude to RMC people was not very good, and it took time to get integrated. Still, there was no sign of an old boy network, though it certainly helped to know senior officers. There was always an artillery protective society, but artillerymen rose because of the combination of the technical and the tactical in artillery and because the provision of fire support demanded tactical skills.

Hamilton Roberts was Rothschild's first battery commander in the Royal Canadian Horse Artillery (RCHA), and he was a gentleman who looked after his men. Certainly, he was very competent by the standards of the day and well liked. At Dieppe in August 1942, where he commanded the raiding force, he was a loyal soldier who tried his best and did as he was told. Still, he may not have had the intellectual capacity for high command. He was no E.L.M. Burns or Guy Simonds, but he was as bright as Harry Crerar.

....

15 Rothschild's nickname at RMC was "Baron." A decade earlier at the college, Simonds had been dubbed "The Count" because of his bearing.

Serving under Simonds

In 1940, Simonds took over command of the RCHA in England, and Roths-child was his Adjutant. During its hasty evacuation from Brest in June, the RCHA had managed to save only its twenty-four guns (as well as one gun picked up on the road from a British regiment). The RCHA was bruised. As CO, Simonds was first-rate. He undertook basic training and did beautifully – he'd been one of the best prewar gunnery instructors, he was an excellent gunner, and he was a fine CO in training men. He related to the gunners, even if he frightened the junior officers. Rothschild had met him at Petawawa in 1935 but didn't know him well until 1940. He was as good a CO as anyone could have, and he was also understanding. For example, he once told Rothschild to work out a training plan, but Rothschild, who had no staff training, had no idea of how to do it. Eventually, he went to Simonds and admitted this, and Simonds spent a half-day explaining what to do. Thereafter, Rothschild was expected to understand. Simonds was very demanding in a professional way. In the mess, he played the CO's role and took part, if a little stiffly.

Canadian training in Britain was generally of low standard until 1941–42, when the Canadians began to achieve fighting capacity. Still, such training as there was mainly aimed at upgrading individual skills. Remember, Rothschild said, not a single division (except possibly the 4th Canadian Armoured) was well trained when it arrived in Britain.

Andy McNaughton stayed aloof from the troops, and he was inclined to be sidetracked by technology. He loved to go up to the guns.

Rothschild went to a staff course, run by Simonds, who was excellent, simply good at anything he tackled. He could talk about anything, not just military matters. Rothschild remembered an incident in the prewar RCHA mess when the CO, Lieutenant-Colonel C.V. Stockwell, asked the battery commanders what their ambitions were. Hamilton Roberts said he wanted to be a battery commander. But Simonds said, "I'm not stopping until I'm Chief of the Imperial General Staff." (In 1946, Simonds went to the Imperial Defence College in the United Kingdom. Before he left, there were rumours that he planned to transfer to the British Army, but he squelched them at a farewell mess dinner.)

Rothschild then went to the 5th Armoured Division under Major-General E.W. Sansom, who had to deal with a strike by the Cape Breton Highlanders: being miners, the men took industrial action, though they had no real grievance. Sansom asked them what the problem was – evidently, the bread was stale, which he promised to fix. Then he changed the unit's officers.

At the II Canadian Corps

After a stint with the 2nd Armoured Brigade, Rothschild became GSO1 of the II Canadian Corps in August 1944, during the Falaise operations in Normandy. Simonds picked him for this post, and he succeeded **Robert Moncel**, just promoted to Brigadier. There was no panic when he arrived, though the II Canadian Corps had been in operations for only a few weeks, and the battles were big. Simonds had really taken hold and was whipping it into shape – in Britain, there hadn't been much corps activity. Simonds ran a tight ship, and when he sacked someone, he replaced him with a man he could count on. **Elliot Rodger**, the Chief of Staff, was good, "the staff officer par excellence," and his administrative side was great. It was a very strong team, and Simonds's Orders Groups were models of brevity, clarity, and simplicity. You always had the feeling that if everyone did what Simonds told them to do, the operations would go well. Simonds ran a happy ship and simply inspired confidence; Rothschild thought the troops felt this too. They knew he was in command, and he went around visiting units. He knew more about what was going on than anyone else.

The plans were Simonds's own, Rothschild said, and so were the innovative ideas. He picked people's brains, talked to specialists, and then produced ideas. He was approachable.

Simonds was also good at talent spotting. He had few friends, notably **George Kitching**. The only time Rothschild saw him upset was when he sacked Kitching as GOC of the 4th Armoured Division in August 1944, and possibly he felt he'd overreacted there. He didn't tolerate fools or incompetents. Even as RCHA CO, when a bad apple arrived in a group of reinforcement officers, he canned him on the spot.

Rothschild didn't know why Simonds hadn't fired Rod Keller as GOC of the 3rd Division in Normandy, though the impression was clear that Keller was the weakest of the GOCs. Perhaps it was due to the PF protective society, as Keller was popular, if a bit of a bully. Good GOCs were **Bruce Matthews** of the 2nd Division and Holley Keefler of the 3rd, though Keefler was much less good than Matthews.

Rothschild heard rumours of infantry reinforcement shortages in late 1944, but he saw very little sign of a problem. Certainly, it didn't hinder the operations of the II Canadian Corps.

On Charles Foulkes

At the end of September 1944, Simonds became acting First Canadian Army commander, and Foulkes was then made acting II Canadian Corps commander. He ran a looser ship than Simonds. He didn't have the same control over the formations, and he didn't seem to be as tactically competent, though obviously he was better politically. Why he rose was a mystery to everyone.

After the war, when Rothschild was Director of the Joint Staff at NDHQ, he reported to Foulkes as Chairman of the Chiefs of Staff (CCOS). His strengths were compromise and accommodation. He understood the political mind and how it would react. Some thought he let the army down as CCOS, but Rothschild remembered at least one meeting, during which the navy and air force tried to seize control of the military budget. Had Foulkes not intervened on behalf of the army, there would have been no army. Simonds didn't think much of Foulkes, but Rothschild never heard him criticize.

On Harry Crerar and Chris Vokes

Harry Crerar's relations with Simonds were good but not close, though Crerar wasn't close to anyone. Simonds probably thought little of him as a tactician, but a good part of the time, the II Canadian Corps was under British command. And yes, Simonds and General Montgomery talked together and bypassed Crerar. At Crerar's HQ, Churchill Mann, the Chief of Staff, was erratic, but the Brigadier General Staff, **Ted Beament** – "The Hat" – was steady as a rock.

At the 3rd Division in the Canadian Army Occupation Force, Rothschild and Vokes got on well. Vokes was widely said to be a bully who would make your life miserable if he thought he could get away with it. But he was always amiable with Rothschild.

LIEUTENANT-GENERAL S.F. CLARK (1909-98)

INTERVIEW | VICTORIA, BC, 24 FEBRUARY 1992

A PF officer from 1933 in the Royal Canadian Corps of Signals, Clark, who had two engineering degrees, was the Chief Signal Officer in the 5th Canadian Armoured Division, served at Canadian Military HQ, and then became Chief Signal Officer under General Simonds at the II Canadian Corps. He became Chief of the General Staff in 1958.

Clark began by talking of Simonds and Crerar.

A technical officer at Army HQ in Ottawa before the war, Clark then went to RMC as a professor of engineering in 1938. There he was in Guy Simonds's half-battalion and lived across the street from him in Hogan's Alley, the officers' married quarters. After the war, he attended the Imperial Defence College under Simonds as well. After retirement, Simonds would call him every Sunday – "When are we going to tie flies?"

Clark was not a great fan of Harry Crerar. He had a run-in with him over his RMC quarters, which were filthy when he moved in. He got them cleaned and bought new appliances, tossing the old ones out back, which led Crerar to complain. Clark also took over the RMC laboratories and pitched the junk in them into the lake. The college's Administrative Officer and Crerar were not amused. In 1939, when Crerar was trying to get away from RMC to go to the war, he didn't want to let Clark leave the college. Later, he tried to block Clark from going to Staff College, saying, "He's a technical officer."

Clark remembered that after Simonds came to the II Canadian Corps in early 1944, he introduced himself to his staff officers by saying, "Good morning, gentlemen. There are some of you in whom I have not much confidence. I will see you all individually the next day and tell you why." The Chief Engineer and the Deputy Director of Medical Services were sacked, and only two or three others were kept, including the Chief of Staff, **Elliot Rodger** ("the best Chief of Staff and worst driver in the army"). Clark remembered Darrel Laing, the Deputy Adjutant and Quartermaster General, saying, "I've been through and not sacked. What about you?" Clark thought that officers who were right for Simonds might not have been so for others. Simonds wanted people who could make quick decisions and stick to them. This was very Montgomery-like. Clark stayed as Chief Signal Officer, and he remembered Simonds asking him what he was doing one day. Clark replied that he was trying to get a more efficient line communications system. "Well, you'd better," said Simonds. He was very demanding and very close-lipped. For example, he wouldn't say if he liked Crerar. Certainly, Clark didn't.

Simonds's A Mess had some style. Clark bought silver plate for it, and he still had one small piece at the time of the interview. Simonds liked the silver service and got first pick at war's end. He drank more after the war than during it. They'd go duck hunting and drink afterward, but Clark never saw him drunk.

Clark visited Foulkes one day and stayed for lunch, being given two or three cases of brandy and liqueur. He got Laing, the A Mess President, to mix up cocktails, and Simonds liked them and had them every evening. Clark then got three truckloads from Foulkes. A Mess was a happy place. To divert Simonds, they'd try to get him going on non-military topics. He had read widely.

Simonds never stayed in chateaux during the war. He lived in tents or caravans, taking watering-can showers, Clark said.

As a planner, he would consult his staff, but only after producing his concept. He didn't make outrageous demands but never once asked Clark about communications. Overall, Simonds did the plan and then told his Chief of Staff "this is my plan."

Unlike Crerar, Simonds had commanded a division in Sicily and had field experience. Clark thought that Crerar disliked him because of this. He was simply envious of Simonds, and this probably prompted his letters of December 1943, in which he suggested that Simonds had snapped under the strain of battle. The letters claimed that Simonds was crazy, and Clark said they were "the worst things he'd ever seen." Certainly, Clark never saw Simonds "out of gear" or even upset. Tight, yes, but not upset. The war was a rough game, remember.

At Walcheren in October 1944, Simonds got meteorological data so he could tell where water would collect and where the high ground would be after the dikes were breached. The spots the enemy couldn't walk to would be hit with artillery.

Other senior officers

Clark thought Rod Keller was competent, though he knew about his drinking. He was with him when he was wounded in a friendly fire incident of August 1944. Keller went under a truck and was hit in the blast, but Clark, in a ditch, escaped.

He knew **Bruce Matthews** well because their caravans were set together. Moving from 1st Division Commander, Royal Artillery, to II Canadian Corps CRA was a big jump for Matthews, but he ran a good show.

Charles Foulkes was one of Crerar's boys, who wouldn't have risen without him. Despite Crerar's nitpicking, he didn't argue with him, unlike Simonds. As Clark recalled, Simonds warned Foulkes that he was to be sacked in Normandy, though Clark wasn't present. There was only one British officer in the room.

Clark thought a signals mix-up at the 4th Armoured Division led to Kitching's sacking in August 1944, along with other incidents.

H.A. Young was a signaller with little signals experience. He had passed Staff College and held staff posts.

Price Montague was a great guy who didn't interfere and who had to be pressed for decisions at CMHQ.

As a lieutenant-colonel, Clark was McNaughton's representative on the Munitions Assignment Board. At one point, Andy wanted five Bailey bridges, but Clark failed to get them. McNaughton told him to clear his schedule for the next day, and the two of them went to the War Office to see General Alan Brooke, the Chief of the Imperial General Staff.

"Morning, Brookie," said Andy. "What's this nonsense that I don't get five Baileys? I'll phone my government. Just because I have only a lieutenant-colonel on the board –."

Brooke was not impressed. Clark had never seen one general swear at another like that, though he did see McNaughton and Montgomery have a go at each other about artillery range finding.

McNaughton: "Why not do something about this?"

Monty: "It works."

McNaughton: "The hell it does."

Still, Clark admired McNaughton and hung his picture on the wall at home.

LIEUTENANT-COLONEL J. DOUGLAS CRASHLEY (1921-2003)
TELEPHONE CONVERSATION | TORONTO, 14 MAY 1991

Crashley served with the Governor-General's Horse Guards in England and Italy. He was Aide de Camp to Lieutenant-General E.L.M. Burns twice in 1944. After the war, he became a successful businessman in Toronto.

Crashley spoke of Burns.

He was ADC to E.L.M. Burns for two three-month stretches, once before the Liri Valley battle in May 1944 and once before the Gothic Line attack in August-September 1944. He said he merely kept the maps. Burns was so dour that when he went to a Royal Canadian Electrical and Mechanical Engineers workshop to congratulate the unit for its superb tank repair efforts during the Liri fight, he got distracted from his task. A soldier was wearing a felt beret instead of a "cap, mechanical," which was washable. Burns ended up lecturing the unit commander about this gaffe instead of offering his congratulations.

Crashley said that **John Bassett** knew Burns well. His father was a friend of Harry Crerar's, and Bassett came to Britain as a captain in the Black Watch (Royal Highland Regiment) – but the Black Watch wouldn't accept him as a captain, so he wangled his way to Italy as Crerar's Military Secretary. Then Burns took over, and Bassett stayed with him for eight or nine months. He tried to be a public relations adviser to Burns and to improve his image.

A stickler for meticulous detail, Burns spent much time on personal reconnaissance. He'd been an air photo interpretation expert during the 1930s, so he frequently went aloft to look at the ground before he made his plans. He even crawled up a mountain overlooking the Liri Valley to get the lay of the land. (On a forward slope of the hillside, he apparently met General Bernard Freyberg, GOC of the New Zealand Division, and the two lunched under a camouflage net.)

JOHN W.H. BASSETT (1915-98)

TELEPHONE CONVERSATION | TORONTO, 20 MAY 1991
INTERVIEW | TORONTO, 5 JUNE 1991

The son of a newspaper proprietor, Bassett was a reporter before the war. He joined the Black Watch, went overseas, and became Military Secretary to Generals Crerar and Burns as I Canadian Corps commanders in Italy. After the war, he owned newspapers and television stations.
Bassett spoke first about Burns.

Bassett worked under E.L.M. Burns for six months or so. Burns was fired largely by the British Eighth Army commander, General Oliver Leese, "one of the great assholes of all time. On any list of assholes, he'd rank third or fourth." One cold day, he visited the Governor-General's Horse Guards. "It's a bit chilly," he said to an aide. "Get me my woollies." Leese was about six foot six, and it was all the Canadians could do not to burst out laughing. He was a joke to them.

Burns's press liaison, Ian Wilson, was an alcoholic and did him no good. By contrast, Chris Vokes's public relations were good and remained so. Vokes was a great showman, but he was absolutely despised by many as a big bullshit artist.

Bassett suggested that Harry Crerar and Burns were unique among Canadian generals in having seen action during the Great War before they achieved high rank. Others, such as Vokes and Guy Simonds, were Brigadiers or Major-Generals at the start of action. Thus, having lived through the slaughter of the Great War, Burns and Crerar had some sense of what the troops experienced and were attuned to the problems of front-line soldiers. Very simply, Bassett said, they wouldn't have put up with a repeat of the 1914-18 carnage.

Burns was Canada's most underrated soldier, and Bassett knew him well even though he himself was a captain and Burns a lieutenant-general. "Tommy" (nicknamed after a pre–Great War champion boxer) was very shy and not articulate. As a result, he didn't get on well with the Brits. Standing on a jeep and addressing the troops or handing out smokes to the men was out of character and even psychologically impossible for him. He had difficult relations with the press – and absolutely no charisma. Moreover, his press officer was a drunk and not very competent, so Bassett, who'd been with the *Globe and Mail* before the war, kept an eye on this, as well as handling his Military Secretary duties (promotions, appointments, reversions, honours, and awards). If Burns had been better at dealing with people, he might have been remembered as one of the best Canadian commanders. Certainly, Bassett tried to push him here and wrote material for him. Burns would listen, but he couldn't change.

It took time for Burns to open up with Bassett, but he did. He knew Bassett was loyal and an admirer. It helped that Burns had graduated in the same RMC class as Graham Avery, Bassett's maternal uncle, who was killed in the Great War. Burns went by the book; he had few social graces, but he was thoughtful and concerned. He was horrified to find he'd been given a Distinguished Service Order (DSO) after the Gothic Line battles of August–September 1944; that decoration was intended for lieutenant-colonels, and he wanted to turn it down. But he discussed it with Bassett, who persuaded him to take the medal. (Vokes, Bassett said, would have grabbed the DSO and loved it.) As that suggests, they talked freely in private. Bassett also discovered after the war that Burns had written regularly to his, Bassett's, father to say how he was doing. Burns also toured the hospitals to visit the wounded.

Bassett said Burns was separated from his wife and noted that he had learned of Burns's girlfriend after the war.[16]

....

16 But see Mary Burns's interview on page 227.

Burns got the Military Secretary job upgraded on the war establishment to major and sent Bassett off to the Seaforth Highlanders for some battle experience with the promise he could have the job back. But Bassett decided to stay with the regiment. Burns was impressed by this decision, as he apparently told **Bert Hoffmeister** – after the war, Hoffmeister told Bassett's father how impressed Burns had been that Junior didn't take the soft job.

Bassett claimed that he was able to pay Burns back in 1958. While Burns was in command of the United Nations Emergency Force in the Sinai, he met him for dinner in Tel Aviv and remarked that Burns was still a major-general. Burns allowed as to how he'd never be promoted. "Yes, you will," Bassett said. When he got back to Canada, Bassett saw Prime Minister John Diefenbaker (who, Bassett said in passing, was a liar but believed his lies were truth) and easily persuaded him to raise Burns back to lieutenant-general. At the same time, he boasted that he got Diefenbaker to open a separate embassy in Israel, not Greece and Israel as hitherto.[17]

On senior officers

Hoffmeister was a legendary figure in the Seaforths and would drop in on his old regiment when opportunity allowed. He was a good-looking man, inspiring, very popular.

Crerar was a human, decent man whom Bassett knew all his life because Crerar was a friend of his father, the publisher of the Montreal *Gazette*. Crerar knew people in high places and got on with them. Bassett had done a story on RMC for the *Globe and Mail* at the beginning of the war when Crerar was its Commandant. Bassett was in Italy in November 1943 as Adjutant of a reinforcement battalion but was unhappy there. Around Christmastime, he saw Crerar at a mess function and asked him "to get me out of here." Two weeks later, Crerar made him Military Secretary. He was a helluva fellow, very human, social, thoughtful, dignified, and warm. Within six weeks, he was back in the United Kingdom as First Canadian Army commander. Bassett asked to go with him, and Crerar, with a smile, said, "We really don't move captains from Italy to England." Crerar looked fit and looked good in uniform.

....

17   This was incorrect. In 1958, Canada did have an embassy in Israel but without a resident ambassador. In 1958, presumably after Bassett's intervention, a resident ambassador was posted there.

Simonds, whom Bassett didn't know, was the idol of officers on the rise.

Bassett was no admirer of Vokes, whom he accused of cronyism. Vokes wanted a DSO for Lieutenant-Colonel Pres Gilbride, his Assistant Adjutant and Quartermaster General, and pushed for it. Bassett had to write the citation, and it was awarded. After the war, he said, he always ribbed Gilbride about this. Vokes also wanted to make Gilbride a brigade commander. As a lieutenant-general, Vokes could appoint battalion COs and seconds-in-command, and he could recommend brigadiers, though these had to be approved in London.

Burns was reluctant to give Gilbride a brigade, but on the principle that a GOC should have the brigadier he wanted, he agreed. However, in the United Kingdom, Crerar refused to approve Gilbride's promotion on the grounds that he had no command experience.

PFers thought the top posts were theirs by right, Bassett said. This attitude was generally accepted, but no one worried much about it in wartime. For the PF, nonetheless, the war was like dying and going to heaven.

Military Secretary to Corps GOC

As Military Secretary, Bassett saw officer assessments (the best one was **Robert Moncel's**). Bassett lived in the corps' A Mess with a lieutenant-general, three or four brigadiers, a few lieutenant-colonels, and two lieutenant ADCs. The quarters weren't grand – a caravan for the General and tents for the rest. The food, in accordance with Eighth Army policy, was issued rations only – though Bassett said that Eighth Army HQ had livestock and geese, and ate well. He once traded for a goose with some Italians, but Burns gave him hell for violating the rule on rations only, and the mess didn't eat it. Under Burns, A Mess was not unhappy but was restrained. He saw no sign of backbiting against Burns.

When George VI visited the Canadians in Italy, Bassett, as Military Secretary, had to arrange a lunch under marquee tents. He showed the plans and the list of invitees to Burns, who told him he'd omitted one name – his own. To Bassett, that showed what a decent man he was.

Bassett then served as a company commander with the Seaforths. He said troops (and he himself) looked on grandiose messages from GOCs as bullshit. To a company officer, battalion is far to the rear, brigade might as well be in London, and the GOC is someone you never wanted to see.

On reinforcements and repatriation

Bassett was never pro-conscription, but there were real reinforcement problems in Italy. He recalled that his battalion once received a Royal Canadian Army Electrical and Mechanical Engineer mechanic as an infantry reinforcement. He saw Ralston during his September 1944 visit to Italy and told him horror stories. This, he claimed, may have had an impact because Bassett Senior was a friend of Ralston's, and Ralston's law partner was related by marriage to Bassett's wife. Ralston had brought letters from Canada for Bassett.

Bassett added that his father and father-in-law got him nominated as a Progressive Conservative candidate in Sherbrooke, Quebec, in the 1945 general election – so he'd be able to get home early from overseas. (He lost to the Liberal candidate.)

HAROLD MORRISON

TELEPHONE CONVERSATION | TORONTO, 27 JUNE 1991

Morrison was an army sergeant clerk who worked for senior officers at National Defence HQ in Ottawa. He lived in Toronto after the war. E.L.M. Burns was effectively his first boss, Morrison said.

Morrison had joined the army as a private and was assigned as a clerk to the Deputy Chief of the General Staff at NDHQ.[18] E.L.M. Burns was an adviser to Harry Crerar, the Chief of the General Staff in 1940, and his office was across the hall. He and Morrison hit it off. Though Burns looked cold, cruel, and calculating, in fact he wasn't. His writing was brilliant, clear, and lucid, though he drafted and redrafted submissions for the CGS, sometimes nine or ten times, on long foolscap. Crerar, who was no fool, had an eye for people with brains, and thus he happily used Burns to draft his papers, which he signed in green ink.

Burns worked terrifically hard, long into the evening. Sometimes, however, Morrison saw him reading *Alice in Wonderland*. He recalled that Burns used the pen name Arlington B. Conway in the 1920s and 1930s articles he wrote

....

18   In 1991, when I served on a City of Toronto task force with Morrison, he mentioned his wartime service, leading to this interview.

for H.L. Mencken in the *American Mercury,* but he didn't know if he wrote during the war. Burns had a lady friend in Montreal, and his work – seeing to Ram tank production at the Montreal Locomotive Works – took him there just as often as possible. He also wrote her very frequently from Ottawa. He and Morrison would talk in the late evenings, and Burns would let his hair down. His marriage was unhappy, but he loved his daughter, **Mary Burns**. He was a strong, intelligent man, but he had a bruised personality. Perhaps his brains impeded his ability to move up in the ranks.

Morrison thought that Burns was sent back to Canada in mid-1941 because a letter that he'd written to the Montreal lady, in which he'd criticized McNaughton's fitness to command, landed on McNaughton's desk.[19] After his return, Burns was in a bleak, depressed mood. But not long afterward, he was promoted again.

On Maurice Pope and Ken Stuart

Morrison worked for Maurice Pope on the Canada-US Permanent Joint Board on Defence and remembered him coming to the office on Sunday with his poodle in tow, smoking a corncob pipe. Once, when the board met in the royal suite at Montreal's Windsor Hotel, Morrison had to destroy the secret papers at meeting's end. He tried flushing them down the toilet, which didn't work; he then lit them on fire in the bowl, but the seat and then the curtains caught fire. Extinguishers had to be used. Pope was furious and swore him to secrecy.

Ken Stuart was, he recalled, an immensely intelligent man who worked like a bugger.

COLONEL H.O. MORAN (1908-2002)

TELEPHONE CONVERSATION | OTTAWA, 19 AUGUST 1992

A Toronto lawyer, Moran went overseas in 1940 and quickly became a staff officer, rising from lieutenant to colonel during the war. He later enjoyed a distinguished career in the Department of External Affairs.

Moran initially spoke of his war service.

....

19   See Granatstein, *The Generals,* 128-29.

A corporate lawyer in Toronto in 1939, Moran enlisted in 1940 and went overseas immediately. He was at the Canadian Reinforcement Unit in Britain as a Staff Learner, then a Staff Captain. He did a course at Oxford on personnel administration, went to CMHQ for eighteen months as a major, then to the 5th Canadian Armoured Division, and back to CMHQ as a lieutenant-colonel and Director of Organization. He reverted to major to get back to the 5th Armoured Division in Italy, and in April 1944 he went to the 21st Army Group as Director of Organization under Brigadier A.W. Beament. He went to Normandy as Colonel in charge of Administration and was E.L.M. Burns's second-in-command. When Burns left after V-E Day, Moran took over his job at the 21st Army Group and retained that position until December 1945.

On E.L.M. Burns
Burns was quite different during and after the war. He was always dour, but during hostilities he was very concerned that war be a serious business. His mess was silent, and he made people uncomfortable by seeming to refuse any light conversation, not drinking, and conveying that no one else should.

An officer once remarked to him, "Lovely day, General."

"Have you been out?" asked Burns.

"No, sir."

"Oh."

What this conveyed, Moran stated, was his dislike of mindless chitchat and his need for accurate information. Another time after dinner, an officer asked if he could smoke. Noticing that another officer hadn't finished his meal, Burns replied, "Yes, but I don't think you'd want to with one still eating." His comments always seemed to be phrased as a rebuke when he was merely being considerate of one man. He didn't drink during the war – it was bad for efficiency – but did afterward. Moran saw no intellectual vanity in Burns but could understand how others might. Certainly, Burns was swift to dismiss ideas with which he disagreed. His mind worked very quickly, he was meticulous in his approach, and he was curious. But he didn't have a leader's personality. He was more intellectual, more scholarly.

On Vokes
Chris Vokes, Moran said with some irony, was "our Patton," and certainly no two men could be more different than he and Burns. You'd want him as a leader in war, even if he were a bully and macho, but not anywhere else.

On Simonds

When C.R.S. Stein, who was very popular, quiet, and interested in the troops, was sacked at the 5th Armoured Division, no one knew who would replace him. Thus, there was great surprise when Guy Simonds arrived in Italy – wearing a black beret with two badges, just like Monty – to take over the division. When he ran Tactical Exercises Without Troops, he sat in his chair as if it were a throne, saying nothing; this was his idea of an armoured training college for himself.

But Moran thought that Simonds was open to criticism and receptive to contrary ideas. As deputy to the Assistant Adjutant and Quartermaster General of the 5th Armoured, Moran attended a few morning meetings. During one of them, when Simonds discussed a move and said to Moran that it could be done, Moran explained why it couldn't, even though he'd been told never to challenge Simonds's views. There was no problem; Simonds understood and accepted the situation. He was such a decisive man that people were afraid to challenge him and feared there was no room for disagreement. But there was. Moran then had dealings with him on repatriation after V-E day, and they got on well. When Simonds paid his farewell calls at the 21st Army Group, he invited Moran to spend a few days with him at Apeldoorn in the Netherlands. He had a human side.

Moran didn't think Simonds was an intellectual and believed he was well read only on military subjects. He was a creature of war. He'd had an affair in the United Kingdom – which was understandable, as he, unlike Burns, was a good-looking man.

On Price Montague

Moran found Price Montague given to hasty judgments, though they weren't always wrong. He didn't take time to analyze, as Simonds would. For example, after the Dieppe raid, Montague made the decision to quickly notify next of kin that men had gone missing in action. In fact, this simply caused needless anguish at home because many of the "missing" weren't missing at all – they were scattered throughout the United Kingdom, having landed in small boats at various ports.

Moran wrote an assessment of the administrative side and was critical of the early notification of next of kin. Montague called him in and asked, "If you knew I'd made the decision here, would you still have said this?" When Moran said yes, Montague leaped up and said, "Get out." The next day they were on an elevator together, and Montague clapped him on the back and said Moran was right, but added, "I was under tremendous pressure." On another occasion, Montague claimed to know more useless information than any other man in the army. No one disagreed. The real problem was that he was aloof, didn't mix, and didn't see anyone but the senior officers.

On McNaughton
Moran hadn't been a wartime admirer of Andy McNaughton, but he came to like him afterward when he was at the United Nations in New York as Canadian representative. On one wartime visit to his HQ at Leatherhead to discuss reinforcements, Moran found McNaughton on his hands and knees with a model tank and was treated to a long talk on armoured developments. But when the talk turned to reinforcements, Andy called in A.E. Walford and Charles Foulkes, who ran the discussion. McNaughton's own special interests got his time and attention, not reinforcements.

LIEUTENANT-COLONEL E.T. WINSLOW (1913-96)
INTERVIEW | VANCOUVER, BC, 2 MARCH 1992

An RMC graduate and Militia artilleryman, Winslow was on the I Canadian Corps staff as General Staff Officer, Grade 2 (Artillery), from 1943 to 1945.
He began by talking of RMC.

Winslow graduated from RMC in 1934 and had some Militia service in Vancouver. He had some good connections – Ken Stuart was a family friend, and he'd known George Pearkes at RMC.

He believed in RMC and wanted ex-cadets in his unit. With an RMC graduate, you could say in ten words what otherwise took fifty because he spoke your language and had undergone the same training. Still, there was no "ring-knockers" club or favouritism.[20]

Winslow knew Rod Keller from RMC (he'd taken Mrs. Keller's sister to a June ball at the college) and greatly admired him as a damn good soldier. He looked like a soldier, carried himself well, and had a good memory.

....

20   RMC cadets bought class rings on graduation; the complaint of outsiders was that this guaranteed admission to a select club of ring-knockers.

On the PF

What did get favouritism was the PF, Winslow recalled, though perhaps this was deserved, given the quality of its training. But there were real duds and drunks – he got his CO, a PFer, fired for drunkenness. After all, the Militia wasn't very good: training amounted to just one hour of drill per week and then off to the mess. Still, some Militia officers were very good. **Bert Hoffmeister** was, and he was helped by being in the Seaforths, who were good. In addition, he was in the 1st Division, which meant he was an old hand by comparison with 2nd and 3rd Division officers.

McNaughton, Crerar, and Burns

Winslow knew Andy McNaughton through family connections and said he had a great ability at remembering names. When he was sacked in late 1943, no one seemed to care.

In Italy, Winslow attended Harry Crerar's meetings as GSO2 (Artillery) at the I Canadian Corps. He admired his meticulousness and discipline. Crerar understood artillery and used it well, and certainly he was the best corps commander that Winslow served under. He could command.

Crerar was precise and knew what he was doing, but E.L.M. Burns was no good. He was a dawdler. The only note of humour that Winslow ever heard from him came during a meeting when the Corps' Medical Officer said that penicillin was available to treat VD-infected soldiers. "Penicillin for putrid pricks," quipped Burns. He was slow and didn't show his ability. Winslow blamed Burns for not exploiting the situation when the Canadians easily broke through the Gothic Line. Instead, they waited for days, even though the Commander, Corps Royal Artillery, Brigadier E.C. Plow, begged Burns to push on. After that, a lot of officers were called in to talk about Burns's leadership competence, and he was soon gone.

Winslow thought Charles Foulkes a "social" general, but he didn't have much opportunity to do anything in Italy or Northwest Europe.

MAJOR-GENERAL H.A. "SPARKY" SPARLING (1907-95)

INTERVIEW | OAKVILLE, ON, 18 APRIL 1991

An RMC graduate, Sparling served in the Royal Canadian Horse Artillery of the PF and went to the British Army Staff College. He served at National Defence HQ, in the 2nd Division in England, in the 5th Canadian

> *Armoured Division in Italy as Commander, Royal Artillery, and in Northwest Europe as I Canadian Corps' Commander, Corps Royal Artillery. He remained in the army after the war, serving in Washington and in a variety of posts in Canada.*
> *Sparling started by talking of RMC.*

Sparling's father was in the army, and he himself and his brother went to RMC. He was clearly an RMC believer. For example, he listed the ex-cadets who were at the HQ mess at the 5th Armoured Division in 1944: the CRA, Chief Signal Officer, Chief Engineer, Supplies and Transport, Assistant Adjutant and Quartermaster General, 11th Brigade commander, and more. But he stoutly maintained that the RMC connection didn't result in favouritism. He never saw any difficulty in relations with the Militia and never knew any PFer who did. Promotion was always based on the quality of the individual. Still, RMC people did shine because of their college training.

The PF and the Militia

Sparling made the point that, as an officer in the Royal Canadian Horse Artillery (RCHA), he got to know the Militia well. After a month or so of PF training, he spent his summers instructing the Militia batteries at Camps Petawawa or Sarcee and later at Shilo. He knew all the Militia gunner officers as a result, and a good part of his winters was devoted to instructing at provisional officers' schools for promotion exams and for NCOs. The bonds between the Militia and the PF were good, and in his view, there was really very little difference in quality or training between the two – after all, the PF had very little modern equipment either. He cited the example of **Stan Todd**, the very able Militia gunner, as good as any PF officer, who was CRA of the 3rd Division and whom he knew from the mid-1920s. He added, too, that the only time the PF had as much as a brigade in the field was in 1938 at Petawawa, and even then the infantry units were understrength and there were too few vehicles.

Study in the PF

Sparling's first posting was to B Battery, RCHA, in Kingston, where he discovered that everything he had learned at RMC about artillery was virtually useless. He learned more from NCOs and from the Adjutant – who had the job of preparing officers for promotion exams. He studied almost every night for the British Army promotion exams (which were used in Canada). His routine was September-April study and provisional schools, May RCHA training, June-August Militia training, and September leave. To instruct at the provisional schools, you had to pass the Artillery Staff Course, which took a year, largely in Halifax, on theory and so on. At the same time, the army sent him and a few other officers to take courses at Dalhousie University and Nova Scotia Tech – he didn't get a degree (all he'd needed was one year after RMC) as his courses were split between the two places. He said Royal Canadian Engineers officers were sent for a year to university to get a degree, but his was the first group of artillery officers to go.

Sparling wrote the Staff College exams in 1938. There were four Canadian vacancies a year, three at Camberley and one at Quetta. Camberley and Quetta had equal status, and the first-place finisher could choose which one to attend. Sparling came first and picked Camberley because Quetta tended to focus on Indian conditions, and he figured the coming war would see Canada fighting in Europe. There were compulsory subjects on the exams but also supplementary voluntary ones where 30 percent of the marks were added to the competition scores. The Staff College course had a junior and a senior wing – the best Canadian after the first year would stay for a second year in the senior wing. His course closed down early at the beginning of the war (Sparling had been tapped to stay), but he got his psc. The Commandant, General Bernard Paget, told him he had it and added, "Now go out and earn it." In the summer of 1939, he and H.L.N. Salmon, attached to the War Office in London, were to go to the Continent together. Sparling was supposed to write a report, but Salmon said if they didn't go now, the impending war would put paid to their travel plans. And when hostilities began, no one would care about Sparling's report. They went.

Churchill Mann was on Sparling's course. On one occasion, Bernard Paget asked Mann how he would get over the barbed wire on a certain exercise. Mann, an inveterate jokester, pointed to a nearby Australian and said that he'd raise a battalion of kangaroos, put Bren gunners in their pouches, and have them hop over. Paget, not normally a funny man, broke up.

At National Defence HQ

On his return to Canada in September 1939, Sparling went to NDHQ, briefly working on the administrative side. Then he went to the Directorate of Military Training (DMT), where he worked for Colonel John K. Lawson. The plan was to bring men back from the United Kingdom for eight months to feed into the Canadian system what they'd learned there.

He was at the DMT in the fall of 1941, when the question of sending troops to Hong Kong came up. T.G. Gibson, who was the Director of Staff Duties GSO1, came to tell Sparling, the DMT GSO1, that two battalions were needed for garrison duty in a tropical post. He wouldn't say where. Lawson told Sparling to prepare a three-part list of battalions: battalions from which selection could be made at once; battalions that needed more training before selection; and battalions that shouldn't be selected. He compiled the list and took it to Lawson, but Lawson had gone home, so he signed the memo and sent it up. The selection, by Crerar, the Chief of the General Staff, was made from the second part of Sparling's list – battalions that needed more training. No one protested, though Sparling recalled that he was surprised at the choice – both battalions had done garrison duty. When the Royal Commission on Hong Kong was held in 1942, he was called and questioned by the counsel for the Opposition, Colonel George Drew. The Conservative Leader of the Opposition in Ontario, Drew was a Militia gunner whom Sparling had trained and knew well. He thought Drew, who asked him about the troops' state of training and their equipment, was trying hard not to hurt him. He also thought that the Quartermaster General, Major-General E.J.C. Schmidlin, unfairly took the rap for the problems of the Hong Kong force.[21]

Sparling knew Harry Crerar well. At RMC, Crerar had been his company officer and had asked him to join the artillery. Crerar also got RMC Commandant C.F. Constantine's permission to let the senior class come to his house for beer in the evenings. He told the students that even if he wasn't there, they could help themselves. That, Sparling said, was when he realized how thoughtful Crerar was of his subordinates. Crerar was no hail-fellow-well-met, but he was nice. In 1938, before Sparling went to Staff College, he also briefly served under Crerar in the Directorate of Military Operations and Intelligence to get some staff experience. Crerar told him to write a report on anti-aircraft defences for Canada, a subject about which he knew nothing. He swotted it up from Committee of Imperial Defence papers in the classified section of the NDHQ library and gave drafts to Crerar, who marked them up very thoroughly indeed. This taught Sparling about memo writing. He

21   For more on the Hong Kong royal commission, see J.L. Granatstein, *The Politics of Survival: The Conservative Party of Canada, 1939-1945* (Toronto: University of Toronto Press, 1967), 119-22.

thought Crerar had good sense, good political sense, and got on well. And at the DMT, he used to accompany Crerar as Chief of the General Staff on visits to training camps.

General E.C. "Squeaky" Ashton was a nice guy. As CGS, he came to Winnipeg in 1935 and called in Sparling, who was Acting CO of the RCHA battery. The RCHA's guns were mechanized, but it still had about thirty horses for officers, etc., and everyone liked this. Fearing that Ashton might want to do away with the nags, Sparling had prepared an elaborate justification for keeping them, based on how useful they were at getting around between guns and so on. Ashton said he didn't care about that. "As far as I'm concerned," he stated, "we'll keep them; and you should all play polo."

T.V. Anderson was in his last stretch as CGS when the war began, and things didn't start humming until Crerar took over.

In Italy with Hoffmeister

If he had to fight a war again, Sparling said, he'd want to do so under **Bert Hoffmeister**. He was a good tactician, good at dealing with troops and at man management, and good-humoured. A helluva good soldier. He had commanded the Seaforths, then took Vokes's brigade when Vokes got the 1st Division, and when Burns went to the I Canadian Corps, Hoffmeister got the 5th Armoured Division. Morale in the 5th was weak – it had been under Stein, then Simonds briefly, then Burns briefly, and now Hoffmeister. But Hoffy quickly established himself. The division was out of the line before attacking the Hitler Line and, having done only static defence, was learning how to move like an armoured division. It was practising an advance behind a barrage when Sparling had to locate Hoffmeister; he was told he was with the leading infantry battalion, teaching it how to lean into a barrage. When word of this got around, morale soared, and the Mighty Maroon Machine got its start. Hoffmeister could command an armoured division because he had as much experience as most Canadians at command; he'd fought through Sicily, and for most of its early life the 5th Armoured was in static positions; Italy, moreover, wasn't exactly ideal tank terrain.

After V-E Day, the 5th Armoured threw a party in northern Holland, to which Sparling went although he was no longer on the division staff (he had become CCRA). Hoffmeister, who had been tapped to command the division going to fight against Japan, got hold of him and demanded to know why he hadn't volunteered for the Pacific. He had.

"Will you go?" asked Hoffmeister.

"Of course, if they'll let me." (Sparling had been told he was to command an occupation division in Europe.)

A few minutes later, Hoffmeister came back to say, "I've been on to Army HQ; you're my CRA." Most of the Pacific Force staff were 5th Armoured, and Sparling thought the whole division would have volunteered.

E.L.M. Burns

E.L.M. Burns was 5th Armoured GOC from January to March 1944. He was a very intelligent engineer and staff officer, but he had no sense of humour, which was a real flaw. Still, Sparling liked him and had known him since RMC, where Burns taught him Statics. He never looked on him as a commander, and he recalled that Burns had foolishly gotten himself sent home from Britain in 1941, apparently because of a defeatist remark. When the 5th Armoured first went into the line, Burns asked Sparling at dinner whether he had arranged for Very flares to be used to call for artillery defensive fire. Sparling said no, as the flares were too easy for the Germans to mimic, and wireless and line communications were a safer bet. Burns said he didn't care. Very flares had worked in the Great War, and he wanted them. At breakfast the next morning, Burns asked Sparling if he'd organized the flares. Sparling, who disagreed and hadn't had a chance in any case, said no. At that, Burns lit into him in front of everyone, so Sparling threw down his napkin and walked out, returning to his caravan, basically to pack and leave. Then he was summoned to see Burns, who had his top administrative officer with him. Burns apologized, saying that he wanted someone who had been in the mess to be there "when I apologized. I was upset over something else." Sparling said he took his hat off to him for doing that.

On senior officers

Sparling was briefly a brigade major under Victor Odlum, GOC of the 2nd Division. Odlum was good for the division at the time, but under no circumstances could he have taken it into action. He was too old (sixty in 1940). He ordered his commanders and staff officers to walk five miles a day – but Sparling and his brigadier used to do their five miles playing golf!

Sparling knew Rod Keller well; his regiment had been just across the way in Kingston. He wasn't the kind of person that Sparling would willingly follow into action. He would fight like mad, but he wasn't up to it.

Sparling was an admirer of Charles Foulkes, though they got off to a bad start. Along with F.F. Worthington and a Royal 22e officer, Captain Foulkes was attached to the RCHA, and he denounced RMC in the mess. Sparling defended it. Despite this, they got on OK. In Malta, when Sparling was with a 21st Army Group mission, Foulkes was there as Brigadier General Staff to Andy McNaughton, waiting to get to Sicily. Foulkes arranged for Sparling to see McNaughton, and Andy sent him to Sicily to attach himself to the 1st Canadian Armoured Brigade and to report back to him. Then Sparling was Foulkes's CCRA in Northwest Europe and found him good to work for. If he didn't take your advice, he had good reason; he got on well in the mess. As CGS after the war, Foulkes got Sparling promoted and made Vice CGS, where he again got on well with him.

And after Guy Simonds became CGS and Foulkes Chairman of the Chiefs of Staff, Simonds avoided Foulkes like the plague, leaving Sparling to deal with him and the Cabinet Defence Committee. Simonds did what he had to, which was to go out in the field to see the Korea brigades, NATO, etc. Simonds was always clear about what he wanted done and was very professional – the best field commander in the army. He'd been very good in Sicily and as a corps commander. Sparling knew him from the PF; when he'd joined the RCHA, Simonds had been a brevet captain, and Sparling had taken over Simonds's job as artillery instructor in Kingston during the mid-1930s.

He thought Chris Vokes was crude and smutty. Vokes hated Foulkes, who got a corps command that Vokes thought was his, and after the war he refused two or three jobs in Ottawa because he didn't want to work with Foulkes. Still, Vokes was a good division commander and would have been a good corps commander. Sparling knew him intimately because Vokes's brother married a cousin of Sparling's wife, and he served under him postwar.

Sparling offered a final note on the relations between the Canadians and the British. In the I Canadian Corps in Italy, Sparling had a British Air Observation Post, a heavy battery, and a medium regiment under his control. When the corps was to go to Northwest Europe in early 1945, the COs of these units asked him if they were going too. There was a great protest when the answer was no – they were, they said, as much a part of the corps as any Canadian battery. Sparling got the decision reversed. This all showed how close the British-Canadian relationship could be.

COLONEL ROBERT RAYMONT (1908-2005)

INTERVIEW | OTTAWA, 23 MAY 1991

An officer in the Loyal Edmonton Regiment, Raymont was a staff officer
at Canadian Military HQ and served in England from 1942 to 1948.
After his UK service, he went to National Defence HQ and worked as a
key staff officer to General Foulkes, the Chairman of the Chiefs of Staff
Committee.
Raymont began by talking of his war and postwar service in England.

Raymont spent much of the war in charge of intelligence at CMHQ. After
the war, Charles Foulkes asked him to stay in the army and offered him a
variety of jobs.[22] Raymont remained in London for some time, working on
intelligence questions. He had good access to the War Office and a good
sense of its organization, and he was writing papers on Department of National Defence postwar organization too.

Working for Foulkes

By the beginning of the 1950s, Raymont said, he had become Director of the
Joint Staff at NDHQ, in effect the staff officer for Foulkes as Chairman of the
Chiefs of Staff (CCOS) Committee. Foulkes mainly dealt with international
military problems, inter-service co-operation, and relations with the United
States and Britain.

He always wanted to get things on paper, so he kept foolscap in front of
him at all times. He was meticulous, a man's man, and shy. Tactful and patient,
he exercised good judgment and didn't react quickly.

Mrs. Foulkes, who was fond of hats, was elegant and very demanding. She
looked out for her husband and tried to stop him from working too hard or
too late (though he could work like the devil). Raymont pitied Foulkes's
ADCs, who had to deal with her. The Foulkeses were private people. Their
son Philip was an engineer with Alcan who worked all over the world and
partied hard. He died of cancer soon after the death of his parents.

....

22   Raymont's collection of records, housed at the Directorate of History and Heritage,
     NDHQ, covers Foulkes's postwar career. But there is very little manuscript material
     on his military or personal life to 1945, and my discussion of Foulkes in *The Generals*
     suffered as a result.

Raymont personally knew nothing of Foulkes's war service. But **George Kitching**, who had been his Chief of Staff in Italy, said that his judgment was very good, his orders succinct and forthright.

On Simonds and Foulkes

Raymont thought Guy Simonds was also a shy man, reserved and austere. When he was commanding the Canadian Forces in the Netherlands, stories arose about the misbehaviour of certain senior officers that made Ottawa unhappy. Foulkes as Chief of the General Staff told Simonds to deal with the situation, so he arrested some officers, notably Brigadier Lister, who promptly called in their lawyers. This caused problems and did not make Simonds popular. The same was true of his postwar visit to Ottawa, when he and his aides brushed by Defence Minister Douglas Abbott at the Château Laurier Hotel, more or less trampling the civilians. "Tell General Simonds the war is over," Abbott said later. Still, Brooke Claxton, the new Defence Minister, invited Simonds to his cottage and got to know him, even like him.[23]

Foulkes clearly didn't like Simonds much, Raymont remembered. Simonds's marital problems, however, didn't interfere with Foulkes's relations with him. Their business dealings were civil, and they respected each other. But when Simonds became Chief of the General Staff, it obviously troubled him that there was another army general at the table as CCOS. Still, Simonds knew nothing of alliance planning and nothing about staff procedures in NATO. He didn't understand force goals or the budget process at home. He and Foulkes differed on how to put the military's requirements to government. Foulkes always made a realistic assessment and tried only for what he could get; he sounded out the public service mandarins first and thus paved Claxton's way at the Cabinet Defence Committee. Simonds, however, got frustrated at the time involved and more or less wanted to put ultimata to the government.

Claxton and Simonds had an agreement that Simonds would make no speeches, Raymont said. But as CGS, Simonds spoke to officers on the East Coast about the need for peacetime conscription, and this hit the press. He then spoke to the Canadian Club in Montreal on the need for two years of

23 On Claxton's relations with Simonds and Foulkes, see David Bercuson, *True Patriot: The Life of Brooke Claxton, 1898-1960* (Toronto: University of Toronto Press, 1993), Chaps. 9-12.

universal military training (conscription). Foulkes, on the other hand, knew conscription simply wasn't on politically.

Simonds, Raymont believed, expected to be CCOS after Foulkes, and when this didn't happen he – and the army – was hurt. Raymont felt sorry for Simonds, who had no political sense; he was a wartime soldier.

BRIGADIER JOHN D. (JACK) CHRISTIAN (1914-99)

INTERVIEW | THORNHILL, ON, 31 MAY 1991

Christian was an RMC graduate and a Militia officer in the Royal Canadian Artillery. He went overseas with a Royal Canadian Engineers Field Company, was posted to the 5th Armoured Division as Chief Engineer, and then served as Chief Engineer of the I Canadian Corps.

He started by talking about how he joined the Royal Canadian Engineers after RMC.

Christian graduated from RMC in 1935, having seen Brigadiers W.H.P. Elkins and H.H. Matthews as Commandants. Elkins was a pretty good fellow who let the place run on its traditions, but Matthews changed old traditions and eased up on "recruiting," the breaking-in of new cadets. He remembered Rod Keller on staff as sharp, good, snappy, and a tough disciplinarian. Christian served in the artillery in the Toronto Militia for two years, then worked in the mines in the north. He joined up in 1939, and because "they wanted an RMC grad in each field company," he went into the Royal Canadian Engineers (RCE).

Generally, Christian saw no resentment in the army toward RMC. The college's training qualified its graduates for responsibility, and he remarked a few times on the fact that he was accorded a certain respect from others because he knew drill and could halt a platoon on the proper foot. As for PF-Militia tensions, they too were minimal. The PFers were older and were spread thinly, and many had to be gotten rid of. Some were Great War types who couldn't understand or accept wireless, new weapons, and the speed of operations; others weren't healthy enough for the strain of war.

The 1st Division

The 1st Division, with which he went overseas, was a pretty loose bunch. "We didn't know a damn thing," Christian recalled. This was true of sappers

(RCE) and everyone else. The Militia was weak and ill-qualified, and Andy McNaughton, a fine fellow, worked hard and tried, but a few PFers did not an army make. One day, Christian's Field Company was inspected by the king, and the turnout was so poor that he went to his CO and got permission to drill the unit in RMC style. By the time the Canadian Corps was organized in the summer of 1940, things were better and the weak sisters had been chopped. Still, Christian said, no one expected McNaughton to take them into battle.

With the 5th Canadian Armoured Division

He went to the 5th Armoured Division when C.R.S. Stein was its GOC. An engineer, Stein was a nice, weak man. Christian went to Italy with the 5th as its Chief Engineer; he was only thirty. He thought that the I Canadian Corps was excellent – Eighth Army's commander General Oliver Leese told him so. And because it had time to get used to operations, the 5th Armoured Division was very fine. Everyone co-operated and understood each other's problems. Christian remembered seeing infantry returning from the line and saying to his sappers in the rear, "Hiya, suckers." That suggested the esprit.

GOCs of the 5th Armoured

When Guy Simonds was GOC of the 5th, Christian spoke to him about the tanks churning up mud. He wanted armoured regiment men to help fill in the ditches (the sappers lacked the manpower to do this), the idea being that it might encourage the tanks to stir up less mud. Simonds agreed, and the troopers even came to like shovelling.

Simonds was a tremendous soldier, with battle experience in Sicily. He was just what the 5th needed – he was very strict and he imposed dress discipline. In the United Kingdom, the 5th had been disciplined, but things had slipped when it saw what other units in Italy were like.

In Britain, the Tactical Exercises Without Troops had usually forgotten the RCE. In Italy, Simonds ran a sand table exercise for the division's officers, sitting on his throne like God. Christian had gained experience during a brief attachment to the New Zealand Division, so he put up his hand and pointed out a number of things, such as the requirement for fresh water and more vehicles, that needed to be addressed. Simonds agreed at once and gave sappers top priority. This was followed henceforth – when Simonds spoke, things happened. The troops had confidence in him: none liked him, but all admired him. One day after Charles Foulkes became the corps GOC, he remarked to

Christian and A.E. Wrinch, the Chief Signal Officer, that they hadn't yet received any decorations. What would they like to have? "A medal for surviving Simonds," they replied. That was a reference to the sackings Simonds had made in the 5th Armoured, but people who did their jobs well lasted.

E.L.M. Burns succeeded Simonds as GOC of the 5th. He was another engineer, a nice chap, but he had no Second World War battle experience. When he gave orders, he didn't have the same grasp of his objective as Simonds. Still, Burns got Christian another RCE company to work with, which made a great difference, and he was willing to countermand orders when they couldn't be carried out.

Bert Hoffmeister was the next GOC of the 5th. By that point, Christian and Wrinch were the senior people in A Mess, and they gave Hoffmeister a hard time by jacking around, all of which he took in good spirits. The only major problem with him, which they had to talk to him about, was his habit of going off to the front-line battalions. That left the division staff to try to fight his battle. Hoffmeister became a first-class GOC; he took advice, and his Orders Groups were preceded by discussion. On one occasion in the Netherlands at Arnhem, he actually began a snap Orders Group by asking Christian to give his orders first, and then he himself followed, knowing that the RCE equipment would determine the attack. You could work in a team with him. He had lots of guts and was a good leader. And in his A Mess, he was a participant. Christian and the Commander, Royal Artillery, Brigadier J.S. Ross, went on leave to Cairo with him.

In Italy, fresh water was critical, given the mud and flooding. In the 5th Division, Christian took great care with the water supply, and flank units used to get the 5th's water because it was so much better. He even had white picket fences to set up around his water points so the freshness was emphasized. And he used his RCE Field Park unit for cemeteries too, after seeing bodies by the side of the road. The unit would dig a cemetery, collect and bury the dead, and erect crosses over them, all of which he thought good for morale.

At one river crossing, Christian remembered, he didn't like the selected bridging point, but the infantry and armour wanted it. So, entirely on his own hook, he built a second bridge upstream; the first bridge washed away, and his bridge saved the day. Still, Hoffmeister gave him hell, even while thanking him ("Thanks for doing it, but don't ever do it again"). Hoffmeister hadn't known the bridge was there; the enemy might have used it to outflank him, etc., etc. You did a better job for Hoffmeister than for Simonds because he was easier to talk to, easier to convince, and easier to concede to. You couldn't ordinarily do so with Simonds, who knew so much more than everyone else.

On Foulkes

Christian went on to be the I Canadian Corps Chief Engineer under Charles Foulkes in Northwest Europe. Foulkes was easy to get on with, but there was little fighting under him. Perhaps this was fortunate, as Christian had the sense that corps plans weren't quite up to 5th Division standards. Foulkes was a bit like an insurance man, not his type. He rose, Christian said, because he was qualified, he was in the right place at the right time, and he did nothing wrong. He could also act sensibly: a British division's attack at Arnhem was called off after one of Christian's reconnaissance officers reported adversely on the river crossing point. An officer named Sloan told Christian and then Foulkes that this "was no place for Mrs. Sloan's little boy."

COLONEL ERNEST A. CÔTÉ (1913-2015)
INTERVIEW | OTTAWA, 19 JULY 1991

An Alberta francophone, Côté went overseas with the Royal 22e Régiment and then went to McNaughton's Canadian Corps HQ as a staff officer. He served in a number of staff posts until he became Assistant Adjutant and Quartermaster General of the 3rd Canadian Division. He returned to Canada in late 1944 and served at National Defence HQ. After the war, he became a diplomat and a deputy minister in Ottawa.
Côté began with his early wartime career.

He was not in the Militia in 1939 but had been in the Canadian Officers Training Corps (which he described as a farce). But in September 1939, while he was articling in Edmonton as a lawyer, he was commissioned in the Royal 22e Régiment (R22eR) and went to Britain with it in December. He became Adjutant in February 1940 as one of the few bilingual officers. In the spring of 1940, Côté showed French General Maurice Gamelin around the R22eR, and he impressed someone from the Canadian staff; as a result, he was sent to VII Corps HQ in July, Andy McNaughton's Canadian-British corps. He was still a lieutenant, and he worked on war establishments. He remembered Lieutenant-Colonel Guy Simonds coming to draw up the plans for the

Canadian Junior War Staff Course: sitting in a room with just a table and chair, he created the whole thing in two weeks. That was impressive.

Côté said he worked for Guy Turner, the Brigadier General Staff, who worked hard and was difficult to get close to but seemed very human. Turner got him an assistant when he found that he couldn't keep up with the work despite working six-and-a-half days a week. He saw little of McNaughton but thought him intelligent, capable, and a good organizer, with a feel for the men. But he doubted that McNaughton would have been successful in the field: he was a universal man and not military enough. For example, he complained to Defence Minister Ralston about a truck design, not something the GOC should worry about.

In September 1940, Côté went to Staff College with the highly capable **Ted Beament** and after this to the 8th Brigade as Brigade Major (though he was still a captain), first under Brigadier J.P. Archambault and then K.G. Blackader. Then he went to the 1st Division's administrative side under George Pearkes in May 1941. Côté was the only French Canadian in the HQ and had been the only one at Corps HQ. This was just an error of omission, not evidence of ill will. He was useful, however, because he could advise Pearkes about problems that arose in the R22eR after the CO, Lieutenant-Colonel Percy Flynn, left. Côté couldn't remember for sure how he'd voted on the conscription plebiscite of April 1942 but expected that he must have chosen "non" – the reason being Great War history.[24] He added that there were very few French-speaking officers outside the infantry battalions and the 5th Medium Regiment. There was a sense of being at home in French Canadian regiments – for example, his first job as Messing Officer of the R22eR in December 1939 was to lay on the Christmas feast, something especially important to Québécois. And the sense of familiarity probably kept French Canadians from going to Staff College too. There were, of course, some "speak white" (anti–French Canadian) sentiments at division and corps until 1944.

Pearkes was sympathetic and empathetic, but Côté couldn't tell whether he would have been good in action. Certainly, he wasn't in Simonds's class for brains. Côté stayed at the 1st Division until August 1942 and then went

....

24 In April 1942, the King government asked Canadians to release it from its pledges not to implement conscription for overseas service. French Canadians and ethnic Canadians, especially Germans and Ukrainians, massively voted no; English Canadians heavily voted yes.

to be Deputy Adjutant General at the I Canadian Corps under A.E. Walford, a man for whom he had great respect as an intelligent, capable organizer. Harry Crerar was GOC of the corps, and he knew him only as a father figure. Solid and methodical, he inspired confidence, as did McNaughton and Simonds, the latter also inspiring fear. Côté was with the I Canadian Corps for Dieppe, which, he said, was expected to be a success.

Côté then went to the 3rd Division as Assistant Adjutant and Quartermaster General. The GOC was Basil Price, and **W.J. Megill** was the General Staff Officer, Grade 1. Price was a nice guy who wouldn't hurt a flea, but at least the division was run honestly. In the 2nd Division, by contrast, there was administrative corruption – if they lost ten jeeps, they'd ask for fifteen replacements, which meant they wrote stuff off instead of trying to recover it. This was ultimately corrosive, and it led to the 2nd Division having to be pulled out of the line in Normandy, with manpower and equipment shortages. His 3rd Division, on the other hand, was honest, a fact that his predecessor hammered into his mind.

D-Day

Côté digressed to say that for D-Day, he'd found a couple of extra barges and loaded them with additional gear, including an extra uniform for Rod Keller, who always wanted to look good. But he refused to take crosses for graves – the corps had told the division to carry a quota. He also made his Roman Catholic and Protestant padres learn enough of the other's ritual so they could give last rites to all. And, moreover, he insisted that paymasters be Assistant Adjutants in action. As a result, they would know the casualty figures, the only way of preventing fraud.

Rod Keller, GOC, 3rd Division

Côté said that he, GOC Rod Keller, GSO1 **Don Mingay**, Commander, Royal Artillery **Stanley Todd**, and the three brigade commanders were summoned to London in January 1944 to do D-Day planning. He remembered the horrible show that month, when Monty took over command of the invasion, firing senior commanders in front of a crowded room.

There had been amphibious exercises before this, but in December 1943, the 3rd Division had been moved out of barracks and into tents, and Keller was furious: "Bugger me, to have water exercises and to have troops die in tents" in a damp winter. So Côté found five or six thousand houses in Southampton to billet the troops.

Keller, a good figurehead, was highly regarded by his troops. He had physical presence, was punctilious about his appearance, and would take on a challenge. The story was that he'd lost a lung swimming in icy Lake Ontario when he was at RMC. He drank too much, liked the ladies, who were important to him, and was easily frightened and jumpy. He wasn't very intelligent. Plans were made, not by him but by Don Mingay, Stanley Todd, and P.W. Strickland on Mingay's staff. His jumpiness wasn't widely known outside of Division HQ. Keller wanted a well-trained division, and indeed it was, though possibly so well trained for the landing that it forgot how to operate on land.[25] Still, Keller was doing his job.

On senior officers

Côté remembered Guy Simonds's Operation Totalize in August 1944 as a brilliant classic that showed that the German army wasn't the only one that could be inventive.

Dan Spry was intelligent and able as GOC of the 3rd Division. Monty came every few weeks to teach him his job. Whereas Keller had been a rough bear, Spry was a gentle gentleman. Even so, he exercised a firmer hand on the administrative side than Keller. Keller was a temporary gentleman.

Harry Foster had the 7th Brigade in the 3rd Division. He was a typical RMC product, with good presence almost of Keller's type, good discipline, and stature. He did well as a brigadier, and Côté heard nothing but compliments about him.

Back to Canada

In November 1944 by lottery, Côté returned to Canada and worked at Army HQ in Ottawa for Walford, the Adjutant General.[26] Army HQ was a classic rear-area HQ, working on the big picture. His job was minding the Medical and Dental Corps, which did good things for the health and oral hygiene of French Canadians. He said Walford and other civilians – Walford was a Militia officer but was a senior business figure before the war – brought know-how and stability to the staff.

....

25 Geoffrey Walsh also expressed this idea (see page 147).
26 In late 1944, the army instituted a home leave scheme for soldiers who had served overseas for five years and had good records. Côté was one of these.

Côté ended by talking about his time at the National Defence College (NDC) as a civilian officer in the Department of External Affairs under Simonds as Commandant in 1949. Simonds was very civil, very good, and he took an active role. The British greatly respected him. Côté thought the NDC was a good transition for Simonds from the command role to Chief of the General Staff – he saw the "biggies" and had a chance to deal with them.

LIEUTENANT-COLONEL DONALD MINGAY (1915-2004)
INTERVIEW | CREEMORE, ON, 6 JUNE 1991

Mingay was a junior officer in the Essex Scottish, attended Staff College at RMC, and then served in a number of staff posts before becoming General Staff Officer, Grade 1, to Rod Keller in the 3rd Canadian Division. He worked in business – including Creemore Springs Brewery – after the war. Colonel Mingay opened with his Militia service.

Mingay joined the Essex Scottish in 1934 as a second lieutenant because his friends were in, and his future father-in-law had founded the unit. He attended two or three Royal Schools of Instruction run by the PF at Wolseley Barracks, London, where he met Dan Spry, then a young lieutenant. His unit, Mingay said, was enthusiastic and reasonably large. It went to Cedar Springs on Lake Erie each summer for training. He had no recollection of resentment against the PF in his unit or of any real antipathy to RMC graduates. He did say that there was a sense early in the war that PFers and RMC grads got the good jobs, but this changed: the Militia officers simply proved more competent – he pointed to **Bruce Matthews**, **Stan Todd**, and K.G. Blackader – and Canada was fortunate this was so.

Mingay enlisted on 3 September 1939 and went overseas ahead of the 2nd Division. He did the Staff College course in Canada in 1941, where he had **Bert Hoffmeister** and Jean Allard as classmates. Then he went to I Canadian Corps HQ as GSO3 (Operations), to the 4th Brigade as Brigade Major, to the Essex Scottish as second-in-command, and to the 3rd Division as GSO1 in the fall of 1943.

On senior officers
As 2nd Division GOC, Victor Odlum couldn't really cope, Mingay recalled. Like all the Canadian senior officers at that time, he was still fighting in terms

of the Great War, but his GSO1 was good. There was a lot of parade square training and no serious field training. After the fall of France when directional signs were removed from English roads, Mingay and Peter Wright worked out a way of navigating the countryside by directing troops from pub to pub.

Mingay never saw Andy McNaughton and had no perception of him.

He worked under Guy Simonds when he was Brigadier General Staff and Mingay was GSO3 (Operations) in the I Canadian Corps. Simonds was unquestionably the ablest senior officer in the army, a man who knew what was up, who thought ahead. He was very unhappy about the Dieppe raid, largely because Canadians had had no input into the plan. Simonds thought things through and was highly intelligent, compared to Rod Keller, who had nothing to think with. He was very demanding to work for and stayed so. After the war, when Simonds was drafting a book, he wanted to talk to Mingay. He rang him up on a Sunday and ordered him to report on Monday at 1000, when Mingay was supposed to go to Vancouver on business. "Can't you change this?" Simonds had asked. Everyone had confidence in his decisions and planning.

Mingay was at Corps HQ during the Dieppe raid and felt great sympathy for Hamilton Roberts, the GOC of the 2nd Division. The Essex Scottish had been savaged in the raid, and Mingay said it blamed Mountbatten, not Roberts, for the disaster. Still, Roberts was just a nice PFer who showed no outstanding characteristics or attributes at anything. Mingay added that the lessons of Dieppe made little impact on training. At the 4th Brigade, they did route marches and toughened up, however. M.H.S. Penhale was Brigadier for part of this period and drank very heavily. One of his friends was a Scotch manufacturer, and Penhale got a case a month. He never came to dinner with fewer than six Scotches in him!

Rod Keller as GOC, 3rd Division

The previous GSO1 in the 3rd Division before Mingay was Willis Moogk, a PFer who later became an antique dealer. He seemed to have little interest in training, and the division was not very well trained, even though it had already been designated for D-Day. When Mingay reported to General Keller as GSO1, he was greeted thus: "Well, Mingay, I don't know you, I didn't ask for you, and I will give you a week to prove yourself." That frightened him, but he quickly discovered through Keller's batman that Keller required three gins to get out of bed. Mingay was sober and Keller wasn't, so he knew he'd survive. Keller was a hard drinker, but he never went out of control. Still, he was an unfortunate who should never have been in command of a division. Mingay had been with the division for only a few days when the brigadiers took him aside to fill him in on Keller. And Keller, he said, appeared to have little interest in anything other than his girlfriend in London. Thus, Keller enjoyed the time on the planning staff in London, though if he played any role in the planning of D-Day, Mingay was unaware of it.

Mingay thought his superiors knew of Keller's difficulties, but he couldn't figure out why no one acted. On the other hand, the division staff were good, and they covered up for him. Moreover, the soldiers thought Keller was a god – they called him Killer – and when he passed through troops on D-Day, they cheered and applauded him. He put on a great act as a tough guy. Also, the brigadiers in the division were top-flight, and they carried the can for Keller. Harry Foster, for example, used to come to Mingay's caravan every night while Keller was asleep, to inform him of his brigade's actions and plans. Keller stayed in his dug-in caravan and was effectively yellow. Before the attack on Carpiquet airport, Mingay went on a reconnaissance with Briga-diers **Todd** and Blackader, but Keller didn't come. That was typical: he didn't participate. The only time you'd be sure to find Keller was at meals. It didn't seem to bother him in his A Mess that he wasn't doing his job. He was drink-ing heavily in France too.

As GSO1, Mingay had to report to Keller regularly, but it didn't seem to matter. And when Brigadier Ben Cunningham had to be fired, Mingay had to be the one to tell him. Keller wouldn't do it.[27] Finally, Guy Simonds came to HQ – Keller always managed to be elsewhere when Simonds was around – and let slip to Mingay, Todd, and another brigadier that there would be a change in command. A few days later, Keller was wounded in the bombing raid south of Caen, the best thing that could have happened to him, Mingay said. He thought Simonds must have talked to the brigadiers.

Things changed when Dan Spry became GOC of the 3rd Division. He wanted to know what was happening, and he was always visiting the units. Under Keller, Mingay had called and run the daily staff meeting without Keller, but this changed too. Spry did it all. He could go a bit wild with drink, though, and once picked up Mingay and threw him through the doors of an

....

27   Cf. the W.A.B. Anderson interview on page 126.

armoire. Still, he wasn't a big drinker. Drink, Mingay said, was the curse of PFers, except for Simonds and Crerar.

BRIGADIER P.A. STANLEY TODD (1898-1996)
INTERVIEW | ANCASTER, ON, 8 MAY 1991

Todd was an RMC graduate, a Great War veteran, and a Militia artilleryman. He became Commander, Royal Artillery, of the 3rd Division, and then Commander, Corps Royal Artillery, of the II Canadian Corps. In his nineties and very sharp, Todd spoke of the Militia.

After taking a war-shortened one-year course, Todd graduated from RMC in 1916. He then joined the British Royal Artillery, served in the United Kingdom and the Middle East, and was invalided out after being paralyzed by diphtheria. It took him about seven years to recover fully. He then joined the artillery Militia in Ottawa, where he worked for an insurance company and was a lieutenant-colonel in 1939. He went overseas as a battery commander, got a field regiment, and then became CRA, 3rd Division, and CCRA, II Canadian Corps.

The prewar Militia, Todd said, was very tiny. His artillery unit in Ottawa had just enough men for four gun crews, but there was a lot of education going on in the training of officers and NCOs. The Militia Staff Course involved an eight-month commitment of evenings and a month off work in the summer for full-time classes. He met many of the wartime senior commanders at Camp Petawawa. In other words, Permanent Force and Militia people got to know each other.

On Harry Crerar
Todd knew Harry Crerar in Ottawa and was then on a first-name basis with him. He found him well trained, slow, and serious – so serious that Todd doubted whether he ever laughed. Crerar did a military appreciation on everything he had to think about, took his time, and came up with the right answers. In no way was he glamorous. When Todd was a brigadier, he attended a dinner with Crerar at II Canadian Corps HQ – it was serious too. He was an excellent officer, 100 percent sound, and very real, but one problem was that it took too long for people to get to know him.

Certainly, Crerar clashed with Montgomery, who greatly favoured Guy Simonds. When Monty had been at Camberley Staff College, Simonds was a student there.[28] Crerar got Monty's back up, just as Andy McNaughton did when he tried to get into Sicily to visit the 1st Canadian Division. Sicily was Monty's show. When Crerar finally got into action in Italy, Simonds was already there and favoured. What this meant, Todd said, was that Monty bypassed the First Canadian Army to give orders directly to Simonds. He recalled phone calls from Monty to Simonds that consisted of "Yes, Sir, right away" on Simonds's part, followed by stalling and obfuscation when Crerar tried to find out what was up.

The root of the problem between Simonds and Crerar was that both were artillery. From the height of his six foot two, Simonds looked down on Crerar as a stuffy old man, whereas Crerar saw Simonds as an upstart to be put in his place. Crerar's stability led him to take a dim view of Simonds, Todd claimed.

Montgomery

Monty "won the war," and Todd was frightened of him because he did things officers didn't do. But he could inspire soldiers. He'd call them around his jeep and tell them he'd beaten the Germans before, they were best soldiers in the world, and together they'd beat them again. The troops loved this, but the officers said "bullshit." After the war, **Trumball Warren**, Monty's Canadian Aide de Camp, was Todd's neighbour in Hamilton, and Todd got to dine with Monty several times. He wasn't so bad, though very opinionated. Still, his treatment of Crerar wasn't ethical.

The Dieppe raid

Todd was in the 2nd Division at the time of Dieppe. He generally took Brian Villa's view of the genesis of the raid, adding that Crerar and McNaughton wanted action for fear the troops were going stale.[29] They weren't, he said. The Dieppe plan was unsound, which McNaughton and Crerar must have

. . . .

28 This was not correct. Montgomery was not at the Staff College when Simonds was a student.

29 In his book *Unauthorized Action: Mountbatten and the Dieppe Raid* (Toronto: Oxford University Press, 1989), Villa argued that Admiral Lord Louis Mountbatten of Combined Operations HQ undertook the raid without full authorization.

known. As commander of the 4th Field Regiment, supporting the 4th Brigade, he pleaded with Mountbatten's Combined Operations HQ to let his guns provide covering fire while the men got ashore, but he was told the attacking infantry would capture enemy guns and use them against the Germans. The GOC, Major-General Hamilton Roberts, was put in an impossible spot. Wanting to reject the plan, Roberts discussed it with Royal Navy Admiral Guy Grantham, who was also against it. But Roberts couldn't contradict McNaughton and Crerar, who were, after all, also artillery and his superiors. In the end, he was sacked because, as operational commander, he could have called off the raid; therefore, he was at fault. It was, Todd said, a "frightening thing" to command thirty thousand men in action; wearing a general's red tabs was pleasant in peacetime but not in battle.

McNaughton

Todd knew McNaughton socially in Ottawa and had Andy's sons in his Militia unit. He also briefly served on his staff as Brigadier, Royal Artillery (BRA). McNaughton was a good man in the wrong place. For a start, training was elementary under him. As a result, Todd himself was obliged to teach every man in his regiment how to drive and how to lay guns, as well as various other essential skills. He clearly felt that the army was learning only some of its roles. McNaughton had been a good officer in the Great War, but Todd doubted he'd ever spent much time on tactics. As proof, he cited Exercise Spartan, held in 1943 before the army was ready for it. McNaughton's two corps became hopelessly tangled in traffic jams, and Andy himself stood at a crossroads, trying to direct traffic. There was no question of his brains or dedication, but he typically did things himself rather than sending his staff. His weaknesses weren't perceived at that time, however, and he was considered a great man from whom great things were expected. Todd was BRA when McNaughton was sacked in 1943. He remembered that the six brigadiers at First Canadian Army HQ sat in A Mess while Defence Minister Ralston was upstairs in a bedroom, doing the deed.[30] He had no doubt that Crerar made a better army commander than McNaughton.

....

30 See Granatstein, *The Generals*, 74-79. Ralston described this interview with McNaughton as "the most painful I have had since I took over the Department. I was deeply sorry for him." Quoted in Bill Rawling, "The Generalship of Andrew McNaughton: A Study in Failure," in Horn and Harris, *Warrior Chiefs*, 86.

Guy Simonds

Simonds, of course, would have been better yet as army commander. Todd knew him before the war from Petawawa and disliked him intensely as a person – he was snooty and snobbish. And his behaviour didn't improve when war came. Todd recalled him walking down Sparks Street in Ottawa, with his nose in the air as a major. Todd's dislike was so strong that when he and **Bruce Matthews** were made brigadier on the same day, he took 3rd Division CRA and Matthews the 1st Division, just so he wouldn't have to work with Simonds. But he couldn't avoid him in late 1944, when Simonds summoned him to I Canadian Corps HQ and announced that Matthews was promoted to major-general and Todd was the new CCRA.

Simonds was cold and aloof. As a young officer, he'd spent all his time studying and reading, and Todd doubted that he was interested in or knew very much about artillery. But he did know strategy and tactics, and he had a good understanding of politics and national psychology. At Christmas 1944, for example, Simonds stayed in the mess for a long evening, something almost unprecedented, and spoke at length on the future course of the war and on the great powers. Obviously, Todd was impressed.

Todd grew to admire Simonds enormously as a commander. He and British Lieutenant-General Brian Horrocks were the best. He could be ruthless in getting where he wanted to go; if something held him up, he'd sack people until he'd put someone in place who could achieve what he wanted. The tactical ideas he produced were almost certainly his own, the product of long nights of thinking in his caravan. He went to sleep at about one in the morning and was up at about six to go off in his armoured car. When a big attack was on, he would go to the start line to make sure that things went well, and he was not beyond pushing and pulling the infantry to get it moving. But this caused problems for Todd, as Simonds wanted his CCRA to be with him. As a result, he wasn't at HQ, where all his communications were, and as the artillery had the best information from Forward Observation Officers with the lead units, he was therefore hampered in his work.

Simonds almost never questioned Todd's artillery plans. He'd derive his appreciation and make his plan, and then ask Todd to tell him how the artillery could help achieve it. Todd recalled a late March 1945 attack on Emmerich, where the Rhine makes a sharp turn west. Simonds had to attack on a certain day, and Todd was to soften up the hill that lay at the heart of the enemy position. Todd worked out a system of dividing the hill into 100-yard squares and then put one gun on each square to fire four shells per hour at irregular intervals. Simonds questioned this and ordered a Victor target – firing every gun in the corps – despite Todd's protests. After the Victor target was used for a day, Todd's system went back on. The attack went in without opposition, the Germans putting up white flags.[31] They'd been unable to get either food or sleep due to the continuous shelling. Simonds then apologized to Todd and after that never altered his plans.

At the end of the war, Simonds contemplated not returning home. He'd sacked a lot of prominent men, who would now try to do him in. Todd thought he was a lonely man, a social climber who had enjoyed hobnobbing with the greats in the United Kingdom. This latter aspect was, Todd said, why he divorced his first and very shy wife.

D-Day and Keller

Todd spent seventeen months preparing for D-Day. He had to retrain his gunners on self-propelled armoured 105-mm Priests (these were scrapped after the invasion when the artillery went back to towed 25-pounders, and Simonds used the Priests for his armoured personnel carriers in Operation Totalize in August 1944). He also had to design the run-in to the beach and learn how to fire from the sea. This, he said, was hard because guns need aiming sticks, survey, and so on to be accurate. But he had time to address these challenges, unlike the British 3rd Division, which had only one month to prepare and was sending drafts to the Middle East up to a few weeks before D-Day. He added that the British Army, having lost so much materiel during the 1940 evacuation at Dunkirk, was at a real disadvantage compared to the Canadians, who had four years without casualties. That was why they were better.

Todd said that Rod Keller was a bluff, hearty man, a bully, someone who would always say he didn't care what X or Y thought. He had a difficult marriage, and he had a girlfriend in London who was married to a Royal Marine officer. On occasion, Todd had to ensure that the officer, who was apparently serving under the Canadians, was assigned to weekend duty so Keller had a free hand. Todd was also blunt about Keller's lack of courage. "Keller," he said flatly, "was yeller."

---

31   In fact, the 3rd Division's attack on Emmerich featured "vicious fighting" and cost 172 Canadian casualties. See Stacey, *The Victory Campaign*, 541-43.

He was foolish, too. During the D-Day planning, the 3rd Division's planners were in row houses in London near Victoria Station under tightest security. Everyone was supposed to stay indoors for twenty-four hours, but Keller managed to get out of the buildings and into a hotel, and he ordered Todd to accompany him. Within moments of reaching the hotel, he was out on the street in civvies.

Then, on the Isle of Wight, Keller and Todd lived with a Royal Navy admiral who was to carry them into Juno Beach. After a short period, the Admiral's No. 2 came to see Todd privately to say that Keller worried them. Todd replied that he could say nothing without being disloyal and suggested that the Royal Navy should go through channels if it was unhappy. Then the three infantry brigadiers (K.G. Blackader, Harry Foster, and Ben Cunningham) came to see him with their complaints, mainly that Keller was never around and that his GSO1, Lieutenant-Colonel **J.D. Mingay**, was running things. Again, Todd gave them the loyalty argument, and he used the word "mutiny." In fact, the complaints about Keller were accurate. Mingay was a brilliant staff officer who did run things; whenever he had a problem, he and "Uncle Stanley" Todd worked it out. (By that time, Todd was in his mid-forties and was thus older than almost everyone else.) In effect, Mingay and Todd ran the division, Keller signing everything put in front of him.

Once ashore in France, Todd went on, Keller's cowardice showed. His caravan was dug in and he stayed in it. When he was wounded in the US Army Air Force bombing during Operation Totalize in August 1944, he whimpered and moaned from his two small wounds. Apparently, everyone was greatly relieved when he was taken away.

Todd couldn't explain why Keller hadn't been fired. Years later, he had a long conversation with Simonds, who said that when Brigadier Cunningham was sacked, he had wanted to overturn it, first because he was an RMC classmate and second because he had no confidence in Keller's judgment. But Simonds had no real answer as to why he didn't fire Keller.

Dan Spry as GOC

Dan Spry succeeded Keller. He was very young indeed, but he was an excellent GOC. Todd couldn't judge his tactical skills, but he was a great change from Keller and wasn't frightened. Still, at the Scheldt, on one occasion, Spry wanted to surrender, but Todd talked him into hanging in for another day, and the tide turned. He wasn't himself that day, was tired out. But the next spring, when the 3rd Division put in a brigade attack, Simonds was at the start line and Spry wasn't. The attack was a mess, and when Simonds went back to Spry's HQ, he discovered that Spry and his CRA were asleep after an all-night poker game. Simonds sacked him on the spot and the CRA, Brigadier E.R. Suttie, too. The real mistake here, Todd said, was Spry's choice of GSO1, Lieutenant-Colonel N.L.C. Mather, a rich man from Montreal who had no brains and who couldn't handle his job of planning for the division. He attributed Spry's problem to being too inexperienced to see that Mather was a bad choice. He was just a kid.

Other senior officers

Todd found Harry Foster hard to know; indeed, he didn't know him at all until he turned up at 3rd Division HQ. His bags were in the hall, and he said he couldn't find Keller. "So what's new?" Todd said. He was a tough man and one of the strongest officers. His brigade was very good, and he took orders from Division HQ with a grain of salt. His brigade was the only one to reach its D-Day objectives.[32]

Todd knew Charles Foulkes but not well, mainly from his time as Brigadier Royal Artillery in late 1943. Charlie was amusing and a great talker. He had a knack for looking out for himself, so when Andy McNaughton was out and Crerar was in, bringing with him his own Chief of Staff (Churchill Mann), Foulkes managed to get the 2nd Division. He acted like a field marshal even when he was a brigadier, and as Brigadier General Staff he pushed major-generals around. He wasn't shy, Todd said.

During one action, Simonds ordered Chris Vokes, GOC of the 4th Armoured Division, to push the attack hard. Said Vokes, "I'll not just ram one finger up their bums, I'll use two and then I'll twist." Vokes had fingers like sausages, so this was a threat indeed.

A.E. Walford, who was the auditor of Todd's company in Montreal, had an artillery battery in that city during the 1930s. He was a good talker who could put proposals in a knowledgeable, capable way. But he was never a combatant officer in the war, and he stayed on the quartermaster side.

Ken Stuart was a nice guy, but the fighting divisions had no contact with him except through the army commander. There was a major division between combatant and staff in Todd's view.

....

32   That was not correct. Only one armoured troop reached its objective on 6 June 1944.

George Pearkes was a character who led by being a good fellow. The 1st Division was very undisciplined, but because it was the only one in the United Kingdom that had full equipment after Dunkirk, it thought "its shit didn't stink."

"Bugger" Odlum was a joke, Todd claimed, a Great War brigadier who was twenty years out of date and who still thought in terms of trench warfare. All he could do was go for spit and polish, and he was big on shiny trucks. Once, the trucks of Todd's unit splashed him with mud. Still, you had to give credit to the old boys who gave up their businesses to take the army overseas and to provide the eighteen months or so that gave the time for everyone else to learn their jobs. If the Canadian troops had gone into battle at that point, the numbers of casualties would have been excessively high.

On experience

Todd had eighteen months with a battery and twelve months with a regiment. He knew his job very well after that, and this made it easy to be CRA and CCRA. There really wasn't anything he didn't know about the work of artillery regiments.

There was no RMC old boy network, Todd claimed. He had found good and bad ex-cadets.

In closing, Todd stated that there was no soldier like the Canadian for initiative. He was amenable to discipline if properly led and if he could be persuaded that discipline would help save his life in action. What you had to do was instill pride and get him away from his civilian attitudes.

COLONEL W. CLEMENT DICK (1912-97)

INTERVIEW | TORONTO, 7 MAY 1991

A member of the Queen's Own Rifles and the Argyll and Sutherland Highlanders in the Militia, Dick joined the Royal Hamilton Light Infantry on mobilization. He served at Dieppe and with the British in North Africa, then went to Sicily with the 1st Division. He became Brigade Major to Bert Hoffmeister in the 1st Division and his General Staff Officer, Grade 1, in the 5th Canadian Armoured Division in Italy and Northwest Europe.
The interview began with Dick talking of the Militia and the PF.

A rifleman in the Queen's Own Rifles (QOR) during the early 1930s, Dick was asked to become an officer. In the QOR, you had to buy your own uniform – the cost was $600-plus, which, as an ad salesman for Maclean Hunter, he couldn't afford. So he was invited to join the Argyll and Sutherland Highlanders in Hamilton, which provided the uniform. He then joined the Royal Hamilton Light Infantry (RHLI) when it was mobilized and went overseas with the unit.

Dick had not been impressed with the prewar PF – the PFers who were attached to his regiment were nine-to-five types who did little. During the war, it was the Militia that was doing the fighting, and when some militiamen began to progress faster than the PFers, there was some hard feeling, though not tension. After the war, however, the PFers made up yards with promotions. He never saw any sign of an RMC old boy net.

Training in Britain

Dick had no sense that any training problems existed in the United Kingdom. As a lieutenant in the RHLI, he worked hard, marched a lot, and took courses. He couldn't tell whether his battalion commander was or was not capable. He landed with his regiment at Dieppe and was one of its three officers to get back. He then went to the British Eighth Army in North Africa, served through to Tunisia, and returned to the United Kingdom to join the 1st Division in Scotland as it prepared for the invasion of Sicily. He said that, unlike the 3rd Division,[33] which was in top form prior to Dieppe, the 1st was a bit bored and tired, though it was fit. He was Staff Captain under Lieutenant-Colonel Pres Gilbride, the Assistant Adjutant and Quartermaster General, who was superb. Then out of the blue, he was sent to the 2nd Brigade as Brigade Major. **Bert Hoffmeister** didn't greet this RHLI outsider warmly, and he got a cold shoulder that lasted until he saw the Brigadier and said he could do more for him back at Division HQ. After that, things went well.

With Hoffmeister's Mighty Maroon Machine

After the battle for Ortona at Christmas 1943, Dick was sent to Staff College at Haifa for three months. Hoffmeister wrote to him there and asked if he'd

---

33   Although Dick mentioned the 3rd Division, he probably meant the 2nd, of which the RHLI was part.

come to the 5th Armoured Division, which he did. Dick then took command of a light anti-aircraft regiment that had been converted to infantry (the Lanark and Renfrew Scottish),[34] a post that he held for three months until Hoffmeister came to see him and told him he was now his GSO1.

Dick was a great admirer of Hoffmeister, who was very close to his unit commanders, so much so that he did his own liaison by going to see them. This was unusual. He was up front so much that it caused problems for his staff – it was "a bloody nuisance." Hoffmeister personally knew what was going on, and he wouldn't ask others to go where he wouldn't go himself. The soldiers knew this. Dick thought Hoffmeister managed to get on with his superiors and knew he had little love for Simonds. He recalled one incident where Hoffmeister's division and a New Zealand division were to attack over appallingly muddy terrain. Hoffmeister and the Kiwi GOC saw E.L.M. Burns, who was I Canadian Corps commander, said it couldn't be done, and got him to delay. (Dick thought the New Zealand GOC said he might have to refer to his government, and this, not Hoffmeister's words, was probably why Burns backed down.) Hoffmeister was the kind of man who called a spade a spade. He didn't curse, however, and was a light drinker. He got the maximum out of everyone in the division, and Dick thought the 5th was as good as any division in Northwest Europe. He added that in the 1st Division, you couldn't get a staff job without battle experience. You were dealing with men's lives, after all. Hoffmeister, he said, was really bothered by the possibility of casualties, and that was why he went forward so much.

On senior officers

Chris Vokes, GOC of the 1st Division, was just "a great big kid." Pres Gilbride ran the show, so much so that **George Kitching**, who was GSO1, had little to do. Why Kitching let him horn in, Dick didn't know. Vokes was friendly and everyone got on well with him, but he drank a lot each night, even if he wasn't drunk. Gilbride used to keep him on track. When they were in Italy, Gilbride once told Dick to see the mayor of a nearby town and ask him to provide "ladies" for a dinner party that Vokes was holding. Dick refused.

....

34 In Italy, the Luftwaffe had become an almost negligible presence, so an anti-aircraft unit seemed superfluous; hence, its conversion to an infantry battalion, a decision that was not received eagerly by the gunners.

Vokes moved among the troops and was great for getting around and seeing people.

Dick couldn't understand why Kitching rose so fast. He was a crony of Simonds, but even so, Dick was astonished when he got a division.

Simonds was very good in the field but difficult. After the war, Dick was Commandant of the Canadian Army Staff College in Kingston when Simonds was at the National Defence College there; there was some tension between them. Dick added that he never forgave Simonds for the way he left his wife and family after the war: he just ditched them.

Burns was OK, quiet, and never had much to say. Charles Foulkes, who came to Italy from Northwest Europe, thought the latter was the big show and that Italy was minor league.

Crerar was "Uncle Harry." Dick couldn't judge him as army commander, but he was a nice man who went around to the divisions after V-E Day and talked to the men.

Dick worked with **H.F.G. Letson** in Washington after the war. One day when he went to pick him up, Letson's wife came out with his artificial leg and asked Dick to help him put it on. He was a great guy, good to work for.

Northwest Europe versus Italy

There were major differences between the Italy and Northwest Europe campaigns. The pace was slower in Italy, and the Desert Air Force was on call and prompt there. In the north, you had to wait for air support, very different from Italy. As proof, Dick cited the April 1945 fight at Otterlo in the Netherlands, where the 5th Division had tried for a couple of days to get air support and was nearly overrun by Germans.

Dick never saw any sign of real reinforcement shortages and heard nothing to suggest that infantry reinforcements were untrained.

Staying in the army postwar

Intending to leave the forces, Dick was paying a courtesy call on Foulkes to say goodbye, when Crerar came in and told Foulkes to offer him a job to keep him in the army. Dick and Crerar had talked for an hour or so in Holland after the war ended. Foulkes offered him military attaché in Moscow (he said no) and then military attaché in the United States (he said yes).

BRIGADIER-GENERAL R.T. BENNETT (1918-95)

INTERVIEW | OTTAWA, 22 MAY 1991

> *Bennett graduated from RMC in the late 1930s and served with the*
> *Royal Canadian Ordnance Corps at Canadian Military HQ and with the*
> *5th Canadian Armoured Division in Italy and Northwest Europe, rising*
> *to lieutenant-colonel by the end of the war. He remained in the army*
> *afterward.*
>
> *Bennett began by speaking of RMC, Guy Simonds, and other senior*
> *officers.*

At RMC, the breadth of instruction was very good, though the emphasis tended to be on rote learning rather than on how to be an officer. Guy Simonds and Ken Stuart were probably the best of those who showed you how to be an officer. (Bennett recalled M.V. "Baldy" MacQueen telling him that an officer had three things to do: look after his horse; look after his men; look after himself if time permitted.) He remembered Simonds organizing a radio so the cadets could listen to one of Hitler's addresses at Nuremburg. Simonds had got to know historian and military commentator Liddell Hart when he was at Staff College at Camberley. Simonds was an utterly impersonal, strange man, who was dedicated to his mission. Nothing would distract along the way.

As Commandant at RMC, Brigadier H.H. Matthews was a remote, small figure with white hair. It was said that his wife had died in a Permanent Married Quarters fire. When he went off to be Adjutant General, the cadets said woefully, "Oh boy, this is what the army needs."

Harry Crerar was Commandant for a year. When lightning killed Bennett's brother, Crerar took the time to talk to him. He also changed things at RMC, including having cadets to dinner.

What RMC did was give a feeling of self-confidence, Bennett believed. You developed initiative and learned to respond and how to get along. It was all for one and one for all. The seniors then were entirely responsible for dormitory life, which had a very negative impact on their juniors. In effect, the system exposed the horses' asses. In the service, wherever you were posted, there were RMC classmates nearby. You could pick up where you'd left off at once.

At CMHQ with M.V. MacQueen

In 1939, Bennett went to CMHQ in the United Kingdom under "Baldy" MacQueen, who gave everyone a hard time until they measured up. He was from Nova Scotia and had graduated from RMC in 1914. He served overseas and returned a major. He was a typical Canadian Scot; he looked dour, but he had a good hidden sense of humour that lit up his face. His marriage was childless. He had a steel-trap mind, Bennett stated, and was one of Canada's most intelligent officers. After the war, he was Master General of the Ordnance for four years, then president of Canadian Arsenals. He had a lot of enemies, didn't suck up, and was independent.

Tension between the PF and Militia

There were tensions between militiamen and PFers early in the war, and there was some antagonism against RMC people too. But the poor ones were eventually weeded out. The problem was that the PF had too few officers to man the army at the beginning, which meant that Great War vets had to be put in. They did a good job of basic training, but if Canadian troops had fought under them, it would have been a disaster.

On senior officers

Bennett started up the overseas vehicle depot in England and discovered that Canadian-designed trucks had three hundred individual bolts that had to be removed to get at the engine. They also had undersized cabs. He complained, his complaint reached General Andy McNaughton, and McNaughton's ADC called to say that Andy was coming down. McNaughton test-drove a truck and told Bennett he was right: "This is a lot of bloody nonsense." Still, Bennett thought Andy was a lousy commander, a man who was still a troop commander. He "could dissect any problem," but he had to do it himself.

Victor "Hoodlum" Odlum was avuncular, but his methods were Great War. The troops liked him.

Hamilton Roberts had no brains, Bennett stated bluntly. When he took over the 2nd Division, he shuffled his feet and looked at the floor, telling the officers that he'd forgotten what he was going to say.

Bennett was a young lieutenant-colonel when he joined the 5th Armoured Division. **Hoffmeister**, he said, was a soldier's soldier without pretensions. There was a job to do, and he grew in the job. He commanded from the front and was more human than Simonds. When Lieutenant-Colonel Fred Vokes was killed at the Gothic Line, for example, Hoffmeister himself told Chris Vokes, his brother.

Harry Salmon was not unlike Simonds and would have risen had he not been killed in an air crash in 1943.

Charles Foulkes was a brilliant horse's ass, but out only for himself. He tried to shut down RMC. He was no gentleman, Bennett said.

F.F. Worthington was a character, and very few characters go anywhere. He was delightful, pragmatic, and hard-nosed. He took the 2nd Tank Brigade overseas and designed a shoulder flash that featured a ram – with its genitals on full display. Oddly, this embarrassed the soldiers, who picked out the offending parts. When Worthy heard of this, he ordered them sewn back in. The troops loved him, and he could do anything they could do, including driving and maintaining tanks, but he rose above his ability.

C.R.S. "Bud" Stein had been Director of Cadets at RMC. He wasn't a successful wartime GOC, because he was too nice. A GOC, Bennett claimed, needed to be a bit of a shit.

BRIGADIER FRANK LACE (1911-2005)

INTERVIEW | TORONTO, 17 MAY 1991

Lace attended RMC and joined the Militia artillery regiment in Toronto. He served as Brigade Major, Royal Artillery, in the 1st Division, as commander of field regiments in the 3rd Division and the 4th Armoured Division, as General Staff Officer, Grade 1, Royal Artillery, in the First Canadian Army, and as Commander, Royal Artillery, of the 2nd Division. Lace started the interview by talking of the Militia and the PF.

After leaving RMC, Lace served in the Militia in the same artillery unit as **Bruce Matthews**; they went to Britain on the same ship but never served together until 1944 in the 2nd Division.

Lace saw no tension between the Militia and the PF. He himself had trained at Camp Petawawa with PF units in the summer after RMC, and he saw many PFers at subsequent camps. RMC graduates tended to gravitate to the artillery because of the college training in survey and engineering. Where they had an advantage was in their officers, who later rose: Harry Crerar was Lace's RMC company commander, Rod Keller the PT and infantry instructor, and George Pearkes the GSO1. They knew your name, and though there was no secret language, they were assured that if you'd gone to RMC, you knew something of discipline, loyalty, and soldiering. RMC made the good better – and the worse worse. There were RMC failures, and some officers (such as gunner Brigadier R.J. Leach, an ex-cadet) liked the Militia types, who, after all, came from a larger talent pool than the small PF.

In England

Lace served with Pearkes in the 1st Division. In England, a local Master of Fox Hounds at Crawley used Pearkes to get hunting started again. Pearkes encouraged his officers to participate in the chase by giving them two afternoons a week off for this. Pearkes himself got in at the kill and was awarded the fox's pads. He was a delightful fellow, with an unusual sense of humour, who once even wrote a play using the fox hunt as a metaphor for the infantry division. His funny crooked smile didn't radiate warmth. Still, Lace thought he was capable of commanding in action.

When Lace was CO of the 15th Field Regiment in the 4th Armoured Division, he worked with Major-General F.F. Worthington. Worthy was a great fellow, and they became close. He would fly around in a small Lysander aircraft to see the units. And when Lace was sent to the First Canadian Army, Worthy staged a farewell dinner for him – which Lace missed because he was at a lecture in Brighton.

Lace thought the Canadian training in the United Kingdom was fantastic; by 1944, the 3rd Division was the best in Britain. Certainly, Canadian artillery was as good as any, including the German; it could quickly put shells anywhere it wished.

As GSO1 to H.O.N. Brownfield, the Brigadier Royal Artillery at the First Canadian Army, Lace often saw Andy McNaughton. He was a nut on gunnery, a good technical gunner. Crerar took over soon after he arrived. He was dour, apparently humourless, a solid gunner.

Guy Simonds, by contrast, was an excellent commander but not really a gunner, because he never commanded guns in action. Lace had known him a bit before the war, where he was always the brilliant captain with the great future. He exerted enormous pressure on his unit commanders and pushed them hard. Although Lace praised Simonds, he claimed that he sacked people to enhance his own prestige and satisfaction.

In Northwest Europe

Lace joined the 3rd Division at Calais in September 1944. Keller, whom he'd known at RMC, was gone by then. At RMC, the cadets had to call on Sundays to pay their respects and leave their cards; Keller's quarters was a popular stop because his wife was "colourful." Keller was dashing, but he lacked the smarts to be a good GOC. Dan Spry took over from him. Lace had met him when he was a cadet and Spry did the Militia Staff Course held at Kingston; then Spry went to the PF. He was very capable.

Bruce Matthews was next, a dedicated Militia soldier, one of Canada's best GOCs. He wasn't a great technical gunner, but he had the knack of getting good people to do the job. He got along with everyone, gave his commands clearly and firmly, and to everyone's surprise, even dealt well with Brigadier **W.J. Megill**, a PFer who resented serving under a Militia GOC. For Lace, the key was that, though Matthews was artillery, he didn't try to interfere with his CRA. Matthews created a wonderful atmosphere in which to work. Perhaps his only flaw was not being tough enough in dealing with failures, but fortunately, his GSO1, **Peter Bennett**, was.

Lace thought the gunner network was pretty strong, but the secret to rising was the contacts made through duty. He served briefly on a COs selection committee and was impressed with one question about potential COs: "Does he court popularity?" He worried about the articulate officers who rose through glibness, citing **George Kitching** as an example.

The Second World War belonged to artillerymen, Lace said.[35] Perforce, the artillery learned about all arms co-operation. Thus, even though Bruce Matthews had never commanded an infantry unit or a brigade, he made a good division commander. Matthews himself never believed it was an issue that he'd never commanded infantry – he'd worked closely with the three brigadiers and knew them and their problems. He had a wonderful rapport with his brigade commanders, and Lace never heard of any serious tensions, though Megill was a difficult, idiosyncratic man.

BRIGADIER BEVERLEY MATTHEWS (1905-97)

INTERVIEW | TORONTO, 16 OCTOBER 1991

A Toronto lawyer, Matthews went overseas with the 48th Highlanders after brief service with the Queen's Own Rifles. He soon became a staff officer

....

35 This was surely true: McNaughton, Crerar, Simonds, Matthews, and Keefler were all gunners.

*and served at the VII Corps, First Canadian Army, as Assistant Adjutant
and Quartermaster General with the 5th Canadian Armoured Division,
and with the I Canadian Corps. After the war, Matthews was a powerful
senior partner at the law firm McCarthy & McCarthy.*

Matthews began by talking of training in Canada and overseas.

Matthews had been in the Militia with the Queen's Own Rifles but left.
He joined up in 1939 with the 48th Highlanders and went overseas as a reinforcement officer in 1940. He was unimpressed with training in Canada
(he trained at the Canadian National Exhibition grounds in Toronto with his
regiment).

Overseas, Matthews thought the 1st Division worked hard at training but
conceded that under Lieutenant-Colonel W.B. Hendrie, his regiment wasn't
exactly well trained. Hendrie was a gentleman but not a soldier. General
Montgomery, Matthews believed, had it in for Hendrie, surprised him by
coming via an unexpected route for an inspection, and rattled him. He was
sacked. Even into 1941, there was a party atmosphere among many regimental
officers.

Matthews saw little of the PF, but some PFers were good and some weren't.
They had the basics. On the other hand, they took care of each other, helped
each other achieve promotion, and got first crack at Staff College. Nor was
he impressed with RMC graduates. "They didn't stand out at all," he said, and
were just the same as Militia officers.

On senior officers

Charles Foulkes had no special ability, though he was pretty good at looking
after his own career.

Matthews served at VII Corps HQ for a time in 1940 and saw something
of Andrew McNaughton, whom he described as able, intelligent, and interested in the training. McNaughton's son invited him to dinner at the general's
house. They spent a pleasant evening talking politics (Matthews had been a
prewar Tory). He concluded that it was Mrs. McNaughton who had ambitions
for Andy and wanted him to go into politics. She knew what she wanted.
There was no resentment in the army toward McNaughton, and it was a
surprise when he was canned. Word of the mess in Exercise Spartan, however,
had gotten around.

George Pearkes was a typical old-time soldier, too old to be an effective
commander and more huff and puff and show.

Basil Price ran a Montreal milk company and still thought and acted like a civilian, even in uniform.

Matthews served at CMHQ a couple of times and thought Price Montague ran a good HQ. He was highly sensitive to political situations, worked very hard, and lived in HQ much of the time – to save money, said critics, but really to keep an eye on things. He was very quick, saw trouble coming, and sought advice. There was no nonsense from him about rank.

Harry Crerar was an intelligent gentleman, and Matthews had respect for him. At one point, Crerar asked his advice, Matthews offered it, and Crerar refused it. Then later, Crerar sought him out to say that Matthews had been right and he himself wrong. Crerar was really a senior civil servant, not a fighting general.

Matthews left Staff College at Camberley to go as Assistant Adjutant and Quartermaster General to the 5th Armoured Division under Bud Stein. Stein had no confidence in himself, and he sat in his office with the intercom turned on so he could hear what Matthews was doing and saying. He was sacked and Guy Simonds named to take over when the 5th got to Italy. Matthews and the GSO1, Lieutenant-Colonel W.C. Murphy, handled the move and were greeted on ship by Simonds, who informed them of his expectations. They were to run their areas, and he would assume that everything was going properly. But if it didn't, they'd be in trouble. Matthews liked this approach because it provided an opportunity to shine. In Italy, Simonds put them through strenuous training and kept the pressure on. He got around and the troops saw him and respected him. He also aped Monty. His HQ was a happy one, and though he was all business, he'd have a drink in the mess without indulging in shoptalk. Matthews thought he was intelligent but could recall no sign that Simonds was informed about literature or music. He was a single-minded soldier whose goal was to succeed.

E.L.M. Burns wasn't as aggressive as Simonds and was more academic. His prewar specialty was mapping. Steady and sympathetic to people, he ran a happy HQ at the I Canadian Corps. But he wasn't a fighting soldier, which might have been why the British weren't impressed with him. As a commander, he sought consensus rather than giving orders. One day, Burns came to see Matthews at the 5th Armoured Division and said he'd like him to come to Corps HQ. Matthews replied that he'd prefer not, as he was his own boss at Division HQ, which wouldn't be the case at the corps. A few days later, Burns came back, tried again, and got the same reply. Then Matthews said, "Sir, I'm in the army, and if I'm ordered to go I will and will do my best." Burns then ordered him and he went. That illustrated Burns's style.

He knew **Bruce Matthews** well and thought he was intelligent, in love with the army and with the artillery.

Chris Vokes made a fetish of being rough and tough. Once when a German prisoner was giving him lip, Vokes, who'd boxed at RMC, knocked him out.

Dan Spry was the top Boy Scout, his postwar job, from the beginning.

The stories about Hamilton Roberts from Dieppe were not good. Matthews's friend Lieutenant-Colonel Peter Wright claimed that Roberts was always below decks on the command ship, having a drink, and did little to command. Matthews added that when he himself was at Camberley, the Directing Staff thought Churchill Mann had messed up the Dieppe plan by having it depend on surprise and lacking in flexibility.

Baldy (or Curly!) MacQueen was unreasonable and difficult, Matthews remembered, but a great officer, one who ruthlessly sacked incompetents. He thought he was running the army, but he did a good job.

On conscription, Matthews felt the army consensus was that men were in short supply and there was no indication that reinforcements would ever come. There was no sense of being cut off from home, just that they – the men overseas – weren't getting the support they deserved. Matthews thought there was little political influence in the army, though strings were sometimes pulled to get people sent home or to prevent disciplinary action.

BRIGADIER WILLIAM ZIEGLER (1911-99)

INTERVIEW | EDMONTON, 23 OCTOBER 1991

Ziegler was a Militia artilleryman who rose to be Commander, Royal Artillery, of the 1st Division. He left the army in 1950 and went into business, working in senior positions at the Canadian National Railway and for Inland Cement.

Ziegler started by talking of his Militia and wartime career.

Unable to get into RMC, Ziegler joined the Militia in 1926 as a boy soldier and was commissioned in 1931. He was a captain by the summer of 1938, when he was attached to the PF as an instructor. There, he mastered technical gunnery and was proficient, well positioned to rise, when the war started.

He went overseas in early 1940 with the 8th Field Regiment, was sent back to Canada to be Brigade Major (Artillery) in the 3rd Division, and then attended Camberley. (At Camberley, he was told he should try to get better marks than the 10 Canadians there and not worry about the 190 other students; he was second of the 10, Dan Spry beating him out.) He next became General Staff Officer, Grade 1 (Artillery), at the First Canadian Army, CO of the 13th Field Regiment, and a colonel at CMHQ. In February 1944, he became Commander, Royal Artillery, of the 1st Division in Italy, with which he stayed to the end of the war. In 1946, he went to work for the Allied Control Commission and was governor of a province in northern Germany for five years.

On the PF and RMC

Ziegler was not overly impressed by the quality of the PF. There were princes (H.O.N. Brownfield), terrific soldiers (Chris Vokes), and others who had to be sacked, although he admitted that, as the president of a corporation after the war, he had to sack people too. The army was a cross-section of people. **Bert Hoffmeister** would have been a leader even if there hadn't been a war. Guy Simonds was a man of such quality as to be unusual in any army – even when Ziegler first met him at a Royal School in 1931-32, he knew he wasn't to be trifled with. So was Montgomery (though a little SOB). The PF's problem was slow promotion: at the end of the war, Ziegler was offered a regular army commission as a brigadier, but he refused it because he thought he could look forward to one promotion only; so he got out.

As for RMC graduates in the army, they too were good, bad, and indifferent, but they made better officers than most.

With the artillery in England

When he went overseas, his regiment was billeted with the Toronto artillery regiment (with **Bruce Matthews**). There was initially no mixing between the officers, and the westerners thought the Toronto officers were snobs. But after a large party, where everyone got hammered, there was no further problem. He thought the quality of training was about the same in both regiments.

Ziegler added that, before Dunkirk, his regiment had no guns, so he devised mock-ups out of timbers, and the troops practised with those.

He had high respect for Andy McNaughton. On one occasion, when Ziegler's regiment was at Larkhill, England, he was attempting to use a new artillery board for plotting. As he leaned over the board, trying to figure it out, he heard a voice from behind: "What's the trouble?"

"I don't know," he replied, "but if I ever get ahold of the SOB who designed this board –."

Of course, the voice belonged to McNaughton, and so did the board, but he just laughed. McNaughton's problem was that he couldn't deal with the British. He was OK as a trainer, though perhaps he'd been weak in preparing senior officers. After all, he was green, like all the Canadians. And yes, though he was good technically, he was less strong in higher command skills. He wasn't a presence, and he saw the troops infrequently.

Basil Price, who commanded the 3rd Division, was a grand old fellow, lovable, a person you'd like as a grandfather. It was hard for him to bawl out anyone. (These remarks weren't intended as compliments.) Price was an "old dugout," and it wasn't until the fighting began that such men disappeared. There had been no option but to keep the Great War officers until 1942 or so; they weren't to blame for this – the fault was Canada's, for stripping its military after 1919. If McNaughton, Price, and Victor Odlum had led the army into action, the result would have been chaos, though the sprinkling of good staff officers under them might have helped the situation. If they'd been smart, they'd have left the fighting to their GSO1s. They did their best, but they were no good.

In Italy

When Ziegler got to the 1st Division in Italy as CRA, he thought the artillery was stuck in the mud – literally. He knew that Bruce Matthews, his predecessor, was a favourite of both Simonds and Vokes, but inevitably the artillery was suffering through a hard post-Ortona winter, dug into gun pits and a bit slack on discipline. Ziegler hauled COs over the coals, ordered the guns cleaned, and restored morale.

Vokes was initially pretty unhappy with him, thinking his new broom was a criticism of Matthews. Vokes had met Ziegler only briefly before and hadn't wanted Matthews to leave, but if Matthews had to go, Vokes had wanted Jack Ross, a PF CO in his division, to get the job. Instead, as H.O.N. Brownfield made the appointment (and as Ziegler clearly was a Brownfield favourite), he got the nod – and, worse, came from the United Kingdom. Moreover, because Ziegler wore glasses, Vokes felt he simply couldn't be a real soldier. He was in the doghouse for a miserable period of weeks that lasted until the Hitler Line attacks in May 1944. Ziegler had had a month to train his regiments, and he drove them hard. His artillery fire plan was massive, double that at El Alamein, and he'd worked it out during a seventy-two-hour stretch. Vokes then wanted it changed in mid-battle and gruffly said he supposed it couldn't be done. But with just a three-hour pause, Ziegler managed to switch direction. Vokes then called him into his dugout and insisted he have a full tumbler of whisky. ("Goddammit. Ziegler, don't you understand English, a real drink.") After complying, Ziegler passed out and later realized that Vokes knew he was dead on his feet with fatigue. From that moment on, he worshipped Vokes. Vokes changed his attitude too, calling him "the best goddam CRA in the Canadian Army" from then on.

Ziegler thought it was natural for Vokes to favour the PF. He wasn't such a tough guy under his veneer. He was a real human being. He wasn't gun-shy, and he always went forward, taking Ziegler along in the jeep. They often had to hide in ditches together under fire. He was a good planner, left Ziegler alone to do his work, and left his Chief Engineer alone too (which, for Vokes, as an Engineers officer, must have been hard). He could decentralize command, and though he was no brilliant tactician, he was certainly adequate. Moreover, the troops worshipped him. One morning, when he and Ziegler were out in the jeep, they came upon some distressed Hasty Pees (Hastings and Prince Edward Regiment), who were looking at their dead comrades. Vokes stopped the jeep. "Don't bloody look at them," he said. "Get out your spades and bury the stiffs." They did. The soldiers had been ready to vomit, but Vokes got them moving and raised their morale. He could also crack jokes with troops, unlike Simonds. In the A Mess, Ziegler always addressed him as "Sir," and Vokes called him "Ziegler" or, once in a while, "Bill."

When Vokes left to become head of the Canadian Army Occupation Force in Germany, he told Ziegler, who was staying on with the Allied Control Commission in Lower Saxony, that he could have his alcohol. Ziegler expected to receive a case or two; instead, a three-ton truckload arrived!

Ziegler liked E.L.M. Burns and rejected the criticisms of him. Yes, he was taciturn, studious, and slow, and he didn't have much personality, but he was also sincere. Although Vokes didn't like Burns, he and **Hoffmeister** apparently told Ken Stuart that he was OK despite Eighth Army commander Oliver Leese's criticisms. After the war, Ziegler once bumped into Burns at the Château Laurier and was invited for a drink. Then Burns had to leave, so Ziegler paid the bill. Burns, having gone home, returned, embarrassed because he'd stuck Ziegler with the bill. Still, he didn't have much personality.

Ziegler had little regard for Charles Foulkes and no respect for him. On the other hand, Ziegler's heart bled for Vokes when Foulkes got the I Canadian Corps and he didn't. Vokes was livid as a result. There was no way he could have served under Foulkes, so he and Harry Foster switched divisions. If Ziegler could have done so, he'd have left with Vokes. Ziegler had known Foulkes since 1941, when, as a lieutenant-colonel, he'd been on ship with Ziegler. Even then, Foulkes was unapproachable. Ziegler wondered how able he'd actually been. A corps commander in Italy had to leave most things to his division GOCs, and at his first major fight at the Lamone River, the corps took a setback. Foulkes was angry and sacked Brigadier **J.A. Calder**, making him the scapegoat. That cemented feeling against Foulkes in the corps, and Ziegler never heard a good word from anyone about him. Foulkes also drank too much, once turning up drunk to open a recreation club. He thought Harry Crerar had a lot to do with Foulkes's rise.

Foster took over the 1st from Vokes, and the division suffered under him. Not that he was evil – he just wasn't Vokes. Nothing he did stuck in Ziegler's memory. They got on well, there were no problems, and he handled his battles well, but it wasn't the same.

Ziegler thought Hoffmeister was the most brilliant division GOC to emerge from the Militia – as good as any PFer, a natural leader, a helluva soldier, skilful, bold, and well thought of by his CRAs. He knew the infantry's capacities and knew how it could operate with other arms. Circumstances had put Hoffmeister into the position where he could show his ability: if the Seaforths hadn't been in the 1st Division and if the division hadn't gone to Sicily, Hoffmeister might have remained untried.

On senior officers

Ziegler was at Camberley with Dan Spry, where the four-month course was incredibly difficult, much more so than university. The homework was killing and artillery officers had special assignments. Spry had impressed Simonds and Vokes, and was pretty good in Italy.

Bruce Matthews's fire plans in Sicily and Italy were pretty simple, with regiments tied directly to brigades. When Ziegler took over as CRA, the division artillery was firing in division battles. (This wasn't criticism, just a statement.)

Ziegler met Hamilton Roberts through Brownfield, Roberts's RMC classmate. He described Roberts as the scapegoat for Dieppe.

When the 1st Division went to Northwest Europe in 1945, its artillery came under Holley Keefler's 3rd Division at one point. Ziegler had known Keefler as a lieutenant-colonel when they were both artillery COs together. Brigadier Ziegler went to his caravan, knocked, and said, "Hello, Holley." "Ziegler, you're talking to a major-general," replied Keefler. "Have you forgotten how to salute?"

After that, their relationship was strictly formal.

Artillerymen rose in the Second World War, Ziegler maintained, because artillery was a science. It was difficult to master. In 1945, virtually every senior officer was artillery; in 1991, only one major-general in the Canadian Forces was artillery.

RT. HON. J.W. PICKERSGILL (1905-97)

INTERVIEW | OTTAWA, 21 MAY 1991

Nominally an officer in the Department of External Affairs, Pickersgill worked for Prime Ministers Mackenzie King and Louis St. Laurent in the Prime Minister's Office and then as Clerk of the Privy Council. He later served as a Cabinet minister under St. Laurent and Lester Pearson.

Pickersgill began by talking in his usual acerbic fashion of the senior officers he had observed.

Maurice Pope was the best educated and informed of the generals and had the most inquiring mind. He saw both sides of the street. He was a well-connected Taschereau, not a *nationaliste,* but he knew there were French Canadians in Canada and this coloured everything he did. He had a good sense of humour. When he was in the Prime Minister's Office, Mackenzie King scarcely talked to him, but Pope wrote memos, and these had an impact on Pickersgill and Arnold Heeney, the wartime Clerk of the Privy Council. Pope could hold his own and was an illuminating fellow. Probably because of this, he wasn't entirely trusted by the military, or perhaps this was because he was half French Canadian. There were no redneck attitudes toward French Canadians in the military, but there was no understanding of them either.

George Pearkes was a policeman (he had served in the North-West Mounted Police before the Great War), a man with too little brains to act politically on conscription. He had some humour, however.

No one disliked Georges Vanier, Pickersgill recalled, though some felt he was too much of a saint. He was brave but not bright. Pauline, his wife, was much sharper.

Pickersgill stated that he wouldn't have given Major-General Léo Laflèche a job as a messenger. He wasn't dishonest, and as deputy minister in the Department of National Defence during the late 1930s, he did his duty as he saw it, in trying to get the Bren gun contract through.[36] But he had no political capacity and was a zero when he was in Cabinet. King put him in, and Pickersgill didn't oppose this because he was trying to stop the Outremont Liberal MP Tommy Vien (who was a crook) from getting in. Laflèche won a seat in Outremont in a 1942 by-election, made necessary when Vien became a senator.

Andy McNaughton was an extraordinary creature who could change his mind just like that, Pickersgill said, snapping his fingers. He had no notion that one thing had to be reconciled with another. He had been successful in creating the First Canadian Army, but he was a tinkerer. Pickersgill had to rewrite McNaughton's speeches when he was in Cabinet.

Harry Crerar was a plodding fellow, with a good second-rate mind (like Mike Pearson's, Pickersgill said tartly). Still, he had more ability than most, did his homework, and had a conventional mind.

Ken Stuart was primarily a timeserver but not stupid; he tried to fit in.

J.C. Murchie, the Chief of the General Staff at the end of the war, was a dullard whom Mackenzie King did not know well, because the Cabinet War Committee didn't count for much by the time Murchie became CGS.

A.E. Walford, the Adjutant General, on the other hand, was a first-rate fellow. In November 1944 during the conscription crisis, Pickersgill worked through all the reinforcement numbers with him, and he tried to present the picture honestly.

Guy Simonds was genuinely the best commander, with a good mind and some political sense, partly because his family had come out of the British tradition of Gladstonian liberalism.

....

36 A huge prewar scandal, the Bren gun affair affected defence procurement for some time. Defence Minister Ian Mackenzie and Laflèche recommended the John Inglis Company in Toronto to build the machine guns, and a royal commission resulted. No personal corruption was uncovered. See David Mackenzie, "The Bren Gun Scandal and the Maclean Publishing Company's Investigation of Canadian Defence Contracts, 1938-1940," *Journal of Canadian Studies* 26 (Fall 1991): 141-52.

Charles Foulkes was a real politician who got as much as he could get by taking the political temperature and not going beyond what the politicians would tolerate.

Harry Letson was never really a soldier and always underrated. He knew the score, Pickersgill stated.

Ian Mackenzie, the Defence Minister at the outbreak of war, literally never went to National Defence HQ (NDHQ), doing his business from his House of Commons office.

Military-political questions

It was essential for the army to participate in the mid-1943 invasion of Sicily to preserve its morale. Defence Minister Ralston, a politician, could see this; McNaughton overseas could not.

By contrast, Hong Kong was an entirely political decision. Imagine in 1942 what George Drew, Conservative leader in Ontario, would have said if Canada had declined it! After all, brighter people than those in NDHQ had miscalculated what the Japanese would do. Even Pickersgill himself hadn't thought that sending the troops to Hong Kong was a mistake.

Mackenzie King was greatly embarrassed by his inability to remember army and air ranks, and he had a profound sense of inferiority to the military. He hated reviewing troops, and the fact that he was always late led to difficulties, such as his being booed by troops in 1941 in England.

The military in the Second World War didn't capture the politicians, Pickersgill said. Defence Minister Ralston didn't try to create a situation where conscription would be necessary, though he clearly believed it a better system. And Pickersgill didn't believe the military tried to conspire to get conscription, except for Pearkes. But when the situation arose, there was no doubt where the generals stood.

LIEUTENANT-COLONEL TRUMBALL WARREN (1915-2001)

INTERVIEW | PUSLINCH, ON, 27 MAY 1991

An officer in the 48th Highlanders, Warren was the Canadian Aide de Camp (ADC) to General Bernard Montgomery in England, then again in Italy, and finally Personal Assistant to Montgomery in Northwest Europe. Warren spoke of working for Monty.

Warren made it clear that he was a Montgomery fan who had served the general first and foremost, if necessary ahead of Canadian interests. He went to Monty in 1940-41 from the 48th Highlanders, where he was a captain; he was selected out of a pool put up by various battalions. The brigade commander, Rod Keller ("a tough guy and a helluva boozer"), spoke to him before he went, and so did Andy McNaughton, who said, "You're not representing your regiment: you're representing Canada, and if you fail, you'll be paraded before me." (McNaughton, Warren said, was a god to the Canadians, but he was invisible – he never visited troops.) Monty made the point that he wanted to hear the truth, so on one occasion after he'd sacked brigade and battalion COs, Warren told him that he was getting a bad reputation with the Canadians. Montgomery replied that the generals had been in the wrong spots. Warren believed he found it very hard to get rid of Canadian officers, as opposed to the ease with which he replaced British officers.

In Sicily and Italy

In Sicily, on his second tour as ADC in 1943, Warren kept Monty in touch with the 1st Canadian Division. He rode around on a motorbike and would see the GOC, Guy Simonds, or the brigadiers and report more quickly to Monty than if he'd gone through regular channels. He mentioned a spat that arose in Sicily between Simonds and Brigadier Howard Graham: the 1st Division was not very fit after its sea voyage to the island, and sun and wine caused problems.[37] During one of Warren's trips to the 1st, Pres Gilbride, the Assistant Adjutant and Quartermaster General, and **George Kitching**, the General Staff Officer, Grade 1, took him aside and told him that Simonds had put Graham under arrest. Simonds had bawled him out in front of others, apparently because his out-of-shape brigade hadn't kept up with the advance, and Graham had replied that it was his brigade, and he would command it. Warren relayed this to Monty, who saw Simonds next morning, Warren having been dispatched to see Graham and to tell him that Monty was on his side. Monty would dress him down, but he should just swallow it. Monty also chewed out Simonds and told him to give Graham his job back. Two days later, Warren saw Graham to check whether everything was OK, and it was.

....

37　Warren's version of the disagreement differs slightly from Graham's, which is given in Howard Graham, *Citizen and Soldier: The Memoirs of Lieutenant-General Howard Graham* (Toronto: McClelland and Stewart, 1983).

On the McNaughton incident in Sicily,[38] Warren conceded that Monty had no sense of dominion autonomy.

After Sicily, Warren went to the 1st Division as GSO2 and stayed there into 1944. During the Ortona fighting in December 1943, Monty called him in one day and showed him the map, with the 1st Division units rather scattered and suffering high casualties. What, Monty demanded, was Vokes doing? Warren replied that because he was now in the 1st Division, he had to be loyal to Vokes and couldn't criticize him. Monty apologized. Monty liked Vokes but didn't think he was up to corps command: "He'll never get one as long as I'm around. He's not good enough for that."

Personal Assistant to Monty

When Monty went back to the United Kingdom prior to D-Day, he made Warren his Personal Assistant. A few days before the invasion, General Ken Stuart instructed Warren to keep a diary and to send copies to CMHQ. Warren told Monty, who spoke to Stuart and got the order reversed.

Harry Crerar made mistakes early on. First, he arrived in France too soon, and his HQ site was actually still in German hands. Then he wrote a memo on how to fight the battle, which offended General J.T. Crocker of the I British Corps and led Monty to ask him to withdraw it; Crerar had never fought a battle, after all. And, of course, he missed Monty's Orders Group before Arnhem because he attended the commemorative Dieppe parade instead.

It was clear to Warren that Monty did not admire the Canadian generals. In a handwritten letter of 1 January 1969, Monty had said to Warren, "If ever a man was unfit to command an army in the field it was Andy [McNaughton], and I said so to Alanbrooke in no uncertain voice." After the Sicily incident, Monty added, McNaughton "never spoke to me again. The same is true of Harry Crerar. What I suffered from that man! Canada produced only one general fit to hold high command in war, and that was Guy Simonds." Warren suggested that Monty had sent Crerar on sick leave so that Simonds could command at the Scheldt.[39]

Monty was worried about Canadian reinforcements in 1944, Warren said, and Simonds and Crerar wouldn't tell him the truth of the situation. Monty

....

38   Montgomery refused for some time to let McNaughton visit the Canadian troops fighting in Sicily. See Granatstein, *The Generals,* 76-77.
39   In fact, Crerar was ill with anemia and dysentery.

sent Warren to CMHQ to find out what was up, but Ken Stuart and Price Montague just stonewalled him, so he tried Vincent Massey, the Canadian High Commissioner in London. Massey, who knew Warren's family, told him how serious things were.

Monty thought highly of the Canadians' fighting ability and liked them for being real roughhouses; on defence, however, he preferred (British) Guards, who would hold on to the last man, whereas Canadians might duck. He once tore into the Canadians in Warren's presence, and Warren asked, "Have they not done everything you asked?" Monty's reply: "Leave the mess."

On Canadian senior officers

Crerar's system was that when you joined his HQ, he had you to dinner in A Mess. At supper, Warren sat next to A.E. Walford, who asked him about the Canadian public's response to the Dieppe raid. Warren, who'd been in Kingston for Staff College during Dieppe, replied that the casualty reporting system was a mess. Walford asked him to put that in writing and said he'd been in charge of the reporting system.

When George Pearkes started to smile, Warren recalled, you were in trouble.

Hoffmeister was on the Staff College course with Warren. He was a terrific guy who somehow clicked and could do no wrong.

Keller got on well with Monty but later lost his nerve and was on the verge of being removed when he was wounded in August 1944.

4 | THE FAMILIES

THE TWENTY-SEVEN INTERVIEWS in this chapter were done with family members – spouses, daughters, sons, and, in one case, a nephew – of twenty senior officers. Some of their relatives were key players during the Second World War – Generals Crerar, Burns, Stuart, Spry, Montague, Pope, Walford, and Vokes. Others – Generals Hertzberg, Page, Price, Potts, Turner, Young, and Worthington – were among the Great War generation who found themselves relegated to subsidiary roles as the war went on and younger officers took the helm.

Family members tended to view their generals through rose-coloured glasses, naturally enough, but sometimes their comments brought relations with other PF officers into sharp relief. Consider Marguerite Stuart Shortreed's remarks on the relationship between General Andrew McNaughton and her father, Kenneth Stuart. Stuart's mother, she said, was the "grandmother" in the McNaughton household before the war, alternating Christmases with the Stuart and McNaughton homes. When she died during the early years of the war – and before the breach occasioned by Stuart's role in the firing of McNaughton as General Officer Commanding-in-Chief of the First Canadian Army in late 1943 – she had pictures of her son and McNaughton on her breast. Ken Stuart's son added that he believed that members of his RMC class blamed his father for the reinforcement shortages that beset the First Canadian Army in the autumn of 1944. Comments such as these simply cannot be made up, and they suggest both how closely knit the interwar PF officer corps was and how intensely wartime military politics influenced the lives of those at the top.

These interviews also tell us something of the way in which officers in the tiny PF lived between the world wars. They may also say something about family life during the interwar and wartime years, at least for military families. The PF seemed to have had a large number of private-school-educated and upper-middle-class officers, and their wives came from similar origins. Very few if any wives worked, it seems, most raising their children alone while their husbands were away on interminable courses or at annual summer camps. The lifestyle was relatively spartan for most, the pay not very high for officers, but in the 1920s and 1930s there was enough money for many majors or captains and their families to have maids and sometimes a cook, and the army provided recreational facilities for the children and adults. At the same time, the officers' mess was the centre of social life and parties, a life usually with far too much drinking. Study, training the Militia, frequent postings, the need to get the children settled in new schools every few years, and friendships played a very large role in the PF family. Most families who lived in the Permanent Married Quarters provided by the army typically had few friends who were not in the military. Their existence was cloistered, separate, and quite distinct from the civil society around them. Interviews in the earlier chapters of this volume with PF officers reinforced these impressions.

Some of the officers' spouses went overseas at the beginning of the war, were made to return home in 1940, and tried – sometimes successfully – to return to Britain. As Mary Plow said tartly, "The British ladies ... were puzzled that so many Canadian wives wanted to be near their husbands when they all wanted to get away from theirs to snag a Yank." Standards then *were* different.

But what was common to all the senior officers' families was loneliness and worry. Their men were away on courses, training exercises, or fighting the war while their parents became ill, their children grew, and family decisions devolved onto others. In an age when men made most of the decisions (or thought they did), officers' families frequently had to decide things by themselves. Worry – fear – was always present during wartime. In England, even though the battlefields were distant, the German bombing and live-fire training accidents killed many. Once the Canadians went into action, first at Dieppe, then in Sicily, Italy, and the rest of the Continent, casualties soared. Generals too might be killed or wounded, and their family members shared the same fears that the relatives of more than a million Canadians experienced during the Second World War.

A few of the interviews require a brief word of explanation. First, the interviews are grouped by family. I interviewed Mrs. Evelyn Lett so that I might gain access to Brigadier Lett's papers. The Sutherland-Brown brothers were my route into the feud between Brigadier-General "Buster" Sutherland-Brown and the Chief of the General Staff, Andy McNaughton, in the 1930s. The interviews with General Crerar's son and daughter were particularly useful for their contrasting recollections. Peter Crerar wrote a hagiographic memoir of his father's wartime life that retold many of the bowdlerized stories he had told me; Crerar's daughter, Margaret Palmer, was much more candid. Similarly, the interviews with General Maurice Pope's three children, though differing in some details, said much of Pope's personality. These three interviews, added to the two with General Ken Stuart's children, were critical in shaping Chapter 8 of *The Generals*. The two Hertzberg brothers, H.F.H. and C.S.L., as charter members of the "old brigade," were not major figures in *The Generals*, but the interviews with the three Hertzberg children added to the PF story, illuminating the disappointment suffered by those who did not get the chance to command troops in the Second World War. Helen Perodeau, Major-General C.B. Price's daughter, offered her recollection of the disappointment her father suffered when removed from command of the 2nd Division. Mr. Justice Joseph Potts's account of his father's loss of command in Britain, in contrast, illustrates how rationalizations could be and were developed.

MRS. MARGARET PALMER (1916-95)

INTERVIEW | OAKVILLE, ON, 9 APRIL 1991

Mrs. Palmer was the daughter of General Harry Crerar. She went to England with her mother in November 1939, where she married a young officer, H. Zouch Palmer, in January 1940 (the first Canadian war wedding in Britain). She returned to Canada soon after.

The interview began with Mrs. Palmer speaking of life as the daughter of a PF officer.

Mrs. Palmer remembered the interwar years in the PF as a frustrating time for "Daddy," in substantial part because he saw war coming. The family often discussed this at home. They felt suffocated by the PF, which also bothered them. But they led a good life in a house full of servants. On one British posting, for example, they had a batman/groom, a cook, and a parlourmaid; in Ottawa, they always had at least a cook-general who lived in a basement room and through whose window, Margaret remembered, she would crawl into the house when she came home late. There was some money in the family – small sums from the Crerar side and her mother had some money too. There was much entertaining, afternoon teas, leaving calling cards, and so on. This all ended with the war, which marked a real dividing line. Her mother, she said, had a strong personality and didn't "suck up" like other army wives. She also had artistic interests – a trained singer, she painted and loved music and art.

On RMC

Mrs. Palmer didn't know why her father attended RMC, but it was important to him, and she remembered how very pleased he was to be made Commandant in 1938. Her brother Peter, however, wasn't the type to attend RMC, though he did go to Upper Canada College, where their father had also gone. There was, she said, no love lost between father and son. Her father didn't play RMC favouritism games, though if you knew how people operated you had an insight into them.

Friends

Her father's friends were not all ex-cadets, and he thought it important to be well rounded and to know people from all walks of life. Neither he nor her mother was terribly committed to the closed army society. Their best friends were Ike Perley-Robertson, an Ottawa lawyer, Gordon MacLaren, a lawyer, and Mike Pearson from External Affairs, who regularly came to their cottage in Muskoka. But there were also army friends – Andy McNaughton, a wonderfully unconventional man who took kids on camping trips in the woods, the Vaniers, Ken Stuart, E.L.M. Burns, and General Richard Dewing of the British Army, with whom they shot. UK friends were important, people the family had met on their three prewar postings. In all cases, Mrs. Crerar liked the wives, and the couples were close. The only enemy was Guy Simonds – it was funny the way Canadians were either Simonds or Crerar men. After Crerar replaced McNaughton in command of the First Canadian Army in 1943-44, there was some deterioration in their friendship. Bernard Montgomery was no friend, and her father would grumble about him with his male friends.

Emotions and politics

Crerar was an emotional man, full of strong feelings that he tried to control. Some people claimed that he had no sense of humour, but in fact he had a keen sense of the ridiculous, and she had to hold him in his seat at Marx Brothers films. He was serious about his work, had a sense of responsibility, and drove himself hard. A highly professional soldier, he didn't like dabblers and wouldn't tolerate sloppiness, and though he felt casualties keenly, he wouldn't let his judgment be swayed by them. Control was his watchword. One of his brothers had been killed during the Great War.

Her father had a good political sense, and Margaret thought he supported conscription for the sake of efficiency. But as a practical man, he had a political awareness of Quebec. Certainly, he had great regard for the Van Doos, for Vanier and Captain Paul Triquet, the R22eR officer who had won the VC in Italy in December 1943. She didn't know his politics but thought he probably voted Liberal for the party's policies, not for Mackenzie King. The family talked politics at home, but it was made clear to her at a young age that everything said in the house was private. She thought her father was very Canadian, but he was also an imperialist, something natural after his postings in Britain.

Crerar was a disciplinarian, a stern and authoritarian personality in his own house. He put her on a clothing allowance when she was eighteen, and she had to keep accounts and present them monthly. (She thought he did the same with his wife.) She admitted in confidence that she was terrified of him, as he could be devastating. But she also enjoyed his company – on walks, cross-country skiing, fishing, and sailing. He was sometimes hard on her mother, who was a great beauty – "stunning" – though their marriage was close, as much as army marriages can be, with their forced separations. Margaret's parents thought alike on some things, but Mrs. Crerar was more forgiving about people.

Crerar loved sailing – Margaret crewed for him – and he played golf, which he found frustrating. He rode. He was relatively fit and worked at it. They walked on holidays, and even after the war he had terrific energy and could wear out Margaret and her husband, Zouch Palmer, an RMC ex-cadet whom she'd known from Ottawa as a child.

She and her mother went to the United Kingdom in November 1939, more or less sneaking aboard the liner, which was virtually empty, with Mrs. McNaughton and one other officer's wife. Margaret planned to get married in Britain. They returned home in 1940, and after Crerar's posting as Chief of the General Staff had ended, and he returned overseas, her mother spent the rest of the war trying to get back to Britain, without success. She and her mother lived in Ottawa in separate apartments.

At the end of the war, she and her mother met Crerar at Halifax, and there was a ceremonial procession home. He looked older – she'd not seen him for three years – though he was fit. But he soon developed a sense of bitterness that his accomplishments weren't as recognized in Canada as he believed they deserved to be, but were more so in Britain and the Netherlands. This,

Margaret thought, got him drinking. He'd always enjoyed a drink, but it got out of hand, and at one point he was arrested for drunk driving, which humiliated him. He was offered the post of Ambassador to the Netherlands, but her mother, who'd had enough of official entertaining, flatly refused.[1] So he stayed in Ottawa. They lived on Acacia Drive in a house they'd bought when he was CGS, and he took a few company directorships and developed hobbies such as photography. Margaret thought he had trouble adjusting to the postwar world, but he and her mother filled their time and travelled, and he read, especially on international affairs.

PETER CRERAR (1919-2003)

INTERVIEW | TORONTO, 14 APRIL 1991

The son of General Harry Crerar, Peter said he was close to his father during the war when he served with the Royal Canadian Dragoons in Italy. He had enlisted as a trooper, rose to captain, and briefly served as an aide to his father in Northwest Europe after recovering from malaria.

He started by talking about his father, Montgomery, and Eisenhower.

General Crerar was no fan of Montgomery, who wanted a commander who commanded everything just as he did. Monty disliked him from the beginning, but the key was the incident of September 1944, when Crerar attended the 2nd Canadian Division's commemorative ceremony at Dieppe rather than going to a meeting with Monty.

"Where have you been?" Monty asked him.

Crerar replied that he'd "sent signals" to explain why he had to be at Dieppe.

"I don't think we're going to get along, Crerar."

"If you're not happy," Crerar replied, "I'll advise my Prime Minister of my actions."

Then Monty backed down: "I'm sorry, Harry." Peter said that his father was a quiet Scots Canadian but one who would fight.[2]

....

1 Crerar was named a special ambassador for the coronation of Queen Juliana in the Netherlands in 1948.

2 Peter Crerar's *My Father, the General* (N.p.: privately printed, 2001) put into print, rather inaccurately, many of the tales recounted here. For much more accurate accounts of Crerar's career, see Granatstein, *The Generals*, and Dickson, *A Thoroughly Canadian General*.

On the other hand, he got on well with General Eisenhower, probably because Canada was a neighbour of the United States, but also because, unlike Monty, he wasn't after Eisenhower's job. Besides, who would want to talk to Montgomery? When Prime Minister Louis St. Laurent invited President Eisenhower to Ottawa, one dinner party included just the Crerars, the St. Laurents, and the Defence Minister and his wife.

On Simonds

Peter believed that Monty and Guy Simonds connived so that Simonds would be given Crerar's job when he became ill in September 1944. He had gone to his friend Lady Illingworth's place in Yorkshire to recover from circulation problems and swollen ankles – Peter said his father worried about his health – when Churchill Mann, his Chief of Staff, called from his First Canadian Army HQ, told him that a plot was afoot, and suggested that he return soonest. He did. Simonds would have cut throats to get ahead, whereas Crerar was just a nice conscientious man who loved his troops. How Crerar survived all this – Mackenzie King at home, Monty and Simonds overseas – Peter didn't know. He had good co-operation from his generals – except for Simonds. The troops looked on Crerar as a kindly father, but on Chris Vokes as "blood and guts."

Crerar as commander

When he established brigades, Crerar had tried to put together units from across the country. "They don't know each other," he said, feeling that Canadians should.

He was determined to take risks: Before the Hochwald attack in early 1945, he made repeated air reconnaissances and came under fire. "I don't feel so bad sending troops in there after I've been up and shot at ahead of them," he said. And in the last days especially, he was very concerned to keep casualties down.

He could be hard. He sacked Dan Spry as a division commander after going to his HQ, where he found bottles everywhere and Spry himself in a flap.[3] He was concerned for the front line-troops. He and Spry were friends after the war.

....

3   In fact, Spry was fired by Simonds, not Crerar.

He got on well with the Brits, especially Field Marshal Alan Brooke. As he put it, once "the Brits get over their colonial status thing, they are the best of friends, but it takes a long time for them to accept you."

He let his commanders handle the German surrender. He didn't want to shake hands with the Germans. But in an Empire Club speech after the war, he urged Canadians to become friends with Germany and Japan.

After the war

When the December 1941 debacle at Hong Kong was the subject of a royal commission, Crerar took a beating from Ontario Conservative leader George Drew, who was the Opposition's counsel at the commission, but this didn't bother him.[4] During a boat trip to attend the coronation of Queen Elizabeth in 1953, Drew, by then leader of the federal Progressive Conservatives, insisted on sitting with him, and they became friends. Probably, Drew liked his post-war conscription speeches. Crerar, however, complained that he didn't want to spend all his shipboard time with Drew, as he himself was no Tory.

After the war, Crerar was quite happy. He loved his Rockcliffe home, which was paid for (it's now the Bangladesh embassy), and he enjoyed not being posted all over the place. St. Laurent offered him the Governor-Generalship, but neither he nor his wife wanted that.[5] He did enjoy being made ADC General to the queen, and he was a staunch monarchist. At one point, he wrote to St. Laurent, asking to be made a senator, but **Jack Pickersgill** blocked this somehow. He was, Peter said, head of the Citizenship Council, represented Canada at Queen Juliana's coronation in the Netherlands, and was put in charge of receiving Hungarian refugees in 1956. By the end of his life, Canadians had largely forgotten him. This rankled, although his funeral turned into a state funeral, thanks, Peter said, to public demand.[6]

Crerar was an old-line officer who kept his politics completely private. Peter didn't know how he voted but thought he voted on issues.

....

4 Crerar was in Britain when the royal commission took place in Ottawa, and he had responded to queries in writing only.

5 Not so. Apparently, the post of Lieutenant-Governor of Ontario was offered but declined.

6 Peter Crerar's comments on his father's latter years are not entirely substantiated in Dickson's biography or his sister's recollections. The "state funeral" was a military funeral, for example, and there are no references to Crerar receiving Hungarian refugees. But he was head of the Canadian Citizenship Council.

Crerar didn't drink much after the war. Although he was hauled in by the Quebec police when he drove into a hydrant after attending a country club function, he watched his liquor – a martini at noon with the BBC News and a couple of Scotch and sodas in the evening.

His postwar military contacts were few – not much with Charles Foulkes, who was Chief of the General Staff and Chairman of the Chiefs of Staff Committee. Foulkes wasn't RMC, and Crerar had little in common with him. There was little contact with Simonds. He really liked Howard Graham, J.M. Rockingham, **Bruce Matthews**, Holley Keefler, and **Robert Moncel**.

He loved RMC and would have wanted Peter to go there had the war not shut it down. After the war, he wanted Peter to stay in the army. But Crerar told RMC people after the war that the Militia officers had done very well.

GROUP CAPTAIN VICTOR C.H. STUART (1918-2007)

INTERVIEW | LONDON, ON, 31 JANUARY 1991

*He was the son of Lieutenant-General Kenneth Stuart, a key figure in the
1944 conscription crisis, and served overseas with the RCAF, mainly in
the Far East. He remained in the air force after the war.
He began by speaking of his father, the PF, and RMC.*

General Stuart was born in Three Rivers, Quebec. His father was a clergyman, and there was no great wealth at all, though Ken was sent to Bishop's College School in Sherbrooke, Quebec, from 1904 to 1908. When his father died, his mother lived with the Stuarts because she couldn't support herself on the small church pension that widows received.

Victor never asked why his father went to RMC, but he clearly loved it, "lived" for it, and believed in the place, and Victor went there too. Many members of the Stuart family had been soldiers. Ken's friends were from his RMC class, especially General J.V. Young and Colin Gibson, who served as a minister in the wartime Liberal government.

When Victor was at RMC, his father was on staff there and later was briefly its Commandant. He was friendly with Reg Sawyer, an ex-cadet and chemistry professor, and the two of them redid the curriculum. Victor had been made class senior, the top cadet position, but the Battery Sergeant Major removed him from this post after the summer, for obvious reasons. Victor walked a careful path and avoided talking about his family at RMC. His father also played the game properly and did nothing to affect Victor's postings in the RCAF during the war. Victor didn't think his RMC career either helped or hurt him. Attending the college didn't guarantee that you'd rise, but there was allegiance to classmates, mutual assistance, and a willingness to help in hard times.

His parents met in Halifax after Ken graduated from RMC. Victor thought they'd married in Britain during the Great War. She was a Bauld from Halifax, and the family had been wealthy (gold) and famous for working with blacks in Dartmouth. But the money must have been lost – certainly, Mrs. Stuart had no private means.

In the interwar years, the Stuarts lived near the edge financially, trying to meet the required PF officers' social standard on low pay. But the life had its compensations, with garrison badminton and tennis clubs that were inexpensive, and important social contacts in town. They enjoyed the moves, even Mrs. Stuart. They socialized with other officers during this period, and the kids were in and out of the McNaughtons' house at Work Point Barracks in Esquimalt and in Ottawa, and with Buster Sutherland-Brown's kids. (**Malcolm Sutherland-Brown** and Colin Gibson's son were RMC classmates of Victor's.) They were friendly with Charles Foulkes during the interwar period too.

Andy McNaughton was District Officer Commanding at Esquimalt when Ken was District Engineering Officer and lived in married quarters. Andy was a "boffin" even then: he designed a swimming pool at Work Point that was emptied by the tide, was always in the workshop, and did metalwork. The Stuarts and the kids visited frequently there and in Ottawa too, where the McNaughtons lived on Chapel Street. Before the war, there were no problems between them; the difficulty arose after McNaughton had to be removed from command of the First Canadian Army in late 1943.

Victor thought that his father had something to do with promoting E.L.M. Burns and Guy Simonds, who was on the RMC staff as a captain when he was there during the 1930s. The "progressive movers" were needed, and the dullards were frozen into holding positions as brigadiers. Ken obviously wanted the best people to command troops. Did he himself want a field command? Victor thought so but wasn't sure, in part because he saw his father very infrequently during the war – he himself was in the RCAF and mainly in India and the Cocos Islands. He did see him once in Britain and was unaware of his health problems but thought they might have kept him out of command posts. His father looked a good deal older than his age, fifty-four, when he died in 1945.

Victor was very annoyed that his father was blamed for the conscription crisis of 1944. He operated under great pressures, political and military. A dedicated soldier, he was supportive of the army and the war. Why should he be blamed? Was he given bad advice? Was he in league with Defence Minister Ralston (with whom he was very close)? There was no way he would deliberately fudge figures on the availability of infantry reinforcements in the summer and autumn of 1944 (as **Denis Whitaker** claimed in one of his books). He took the rap for the politicians and the army, but he knew he had to – that was the kind of man he was. Victor thought that ministers (and possibly generals) may have met at his house during the conscription crisis – his sister, he said, would know more.

After McNaughton was made Defence Minister in November 1944, Stuart knew his time was limited, and his resignation letter and McNaughton's demand for his retirement crossed in the mail. This was McNaughton's vengeance. He had become a bitter man. Incidentally, McNaughton was also at Bishop's College School, from 1900 to 1905, so they crossed paths there too.

Stuart understood French Canadians. He was from Three Rivers, after all, though he wasn't really bilingual. Victor thought Stuart's mother was bilingual. She was a large woman and a good cook. They had also been stationed at Quebec City for five years when Ken was District Engineering Officer, and they had enjoyed it. They liked the Vaniers.

The Stuart family stayed out of the postwar fights over conscription. There was nothing to be gained by joining in. But Victor worried that some RMC ex-cadets might harbour negative feelings against his father, and this bothered him.

General Stuart liked Harry Crerar, who was senior to him. Victor thought he had money. Crerar's daughter Margaret married H.Z. Palmer, who was in Victor's RMC class.

MARGUERITE STUART SHORTREED (192?-200?)

INTERVIEW | TORONTO, 26 FEBRUARY 1991

Mrs. Shortreed was the daughter of Lieutenant-General Kenneth Stuart, Chief of the General Staff, and then Chief of Staff at Canadian Military HQ. She began by talking about her father.

Ken Stuart had a deep interest in the Militia, and he worked with it every summer. He always seemed to return with a broken collarbone from riding accidents on exercises.

To her, he was gentle, kind, mild-mannered, and indeed almost frail, though he was a good athlete and tennis player. From his mid-thirties, he had a tendency to phlebitis and had had a clot removed while he was at Staff College in Camberley. His death certificate of 1945 noted that he died of leukemia, but she didn't think it was accurate. Certainly, he'd been very ill with double pneumonia when he was in Britain. Her brother **Victor**, who was serving in Burma in 1945, read about his death in the newspaper as the family didn't know where he was to notify him. And she said that she and her mother weren't allowed to go to the graveside during the funeral. They watched in a limousine while the military parade went by.

She thought of her father as an intellectual – he read all the time and wrote at night at home. He was non-political – "in the army you never had any politics" – and he kept silent about who got his vote. He disliked the press because it never got anything right. He'd be misquoted and would remark to his wife, "I didn't say that."

Stuart was bilingual, like his mother. He used to laugh and say he spoke patois. They had close friends in Quebec City from a posting there.

He was a true monarchist and imperialist. He had been brought up that way, and so were his kids. When Victor's son was born, Stuart was having breakfast with George VI, told the king, and had the monarch propose a toast to the new grandchild.

The conscription crisis

The conscription question in 1944 finished Stuart and broke his heart. He and Defence Minister Ralston were trained to advise the government, and they said that troops were needed. Stuart detested Mackenzie King. Mrs. Shortreed had a photo of her father standing on the ramparts at Quebec City with Mackenzie King – Stuart had wanted to push him off. He called the Prime Minister "a wretched little man." During the conscription crisis, "half the Cabinet" was sneaking into their house by the backyard, past the garbage cans, for secret meetings because no one would expect to find the ministers there. Stuart admired Ralston, a great man, and worshipped him. She recalled her mother's grief when Ralston died.

The Stuarts and McNaughtons

On the morning after Andy McNaughton became Minister of National Defence, Stuart left the house "looking like a million dollars," saying he was going to resign before he was fired. He knew that McNaughton blamed him for his sacking as army commander in late 1943, but Stuart couldn't have done this, because he had no such power. This was a sad situation, because the Stuart kids had grown up with the McNaughton children on postings in Victoria and Ottawa. She recalled horsing around on a raft with McNaughton's son, who pretended to drown her. And General Stuart's mother was almost literally the grandmother in the McNaughton house, where there were no grandparents. As a widow, she lived with her husband's family for eighteen years between the wars and travelled with them everywhere, except on a UK posting, and she alternated Christmases with them and the McNaughtons. She loved Andy. When she died soon after the outbreak of war, she was found in her nursing home with photos of her son and McNaughton on her chest (!).

She'd had a hard life. Her husband died while Ken was at RMC. Another son was killed in the Great War, and Ken spent four days on the battlefield, looking for his remains – but there were none. And her two daughters died young of disease. But she doted on Ken and loved his wife and their children. Ken had married his wife in Britain during the Great War, while she worked as a volunteer in a Folkestone hospital. This was a love match, Marguerite said, though she thought her mother had a hard time during the 1939-45 war, being constantly separated from her husband. They were about to go to Britain when the buzz bombs started, and he wouldn't permit her to come.

The Stuarts and McNaughtons led different social lives. The Stuarts, who were very social, liked Sunday night parties, and they enjoyed drinking, going to clubs, playing sports, and riding. Stuart could also stand on his head and drink at the same time, something he taught other officers to do in the mess. The family always had a girl to help in the house and a batman. But there was little cash, and she was sure her father worried over this. For example, when he became RMC Commandant in 1939, he had to get Ottawa to furnish the residence. The family simply didn't have the furniture or money to do it. They were close to the Pearkes family, and George was her godfather.

The McNaughtons were different. They had money. Andy was a very handsome man, very good to Marguerite, always with a pat on the head. He was more of a scientist than a soldier. One bone of contention early on was when her father rejected a McNaughton son for RMC because he didn't have the grades. There was also a certain frisson long after the war when one of Stuart's granddaughters fell in love with McNaughton's grandson, but despite her mother's horror at the thought of a Stuart-McNaughton match, it fell apart naturally.

On Mrs. Crerar
The Stuarts were friendly with the Crerars but not close. The Crerars had money on both sides of the family. Mrs. Crerar was gorgeous, and during the war, she and Marguerite worked for the Red Cross in Ottawa and occasionally marched together in parades. One soldier told them that they marched better than the Canadian Women's Army Corps. He hadn't known who Mrs. Crerar was, of course.

On RMC
Ken Stuart loved RMC but believed it should be a degree-granting institution. This got him into fights with professors when he was General Staff Officer, Grade 1, there. He was very popular with cadets and was made an honorary member of the class of 1936. She remembered him being hauled out of bed and driven through Kingston in his pyjamas, which would have happened only if he'd been loved. She also recalled Cadet Jake Moore, later the chairman of Brascan, regularly coming to her father's house at RMC and saying he didn't want to be a soldier. But when the war started, "he literally marched to Ottawa and demanded a place."

DR. MARY BURNS (1933-)
INTERVIEW | MANOTICK, ON, 22 MAY 1991

Dr. Burns, an archaeologist, is the daughter of Lieutenant-General E.L.M. Burns.
   She began the interview with her father's background.

The family was Irish, she said. Burns's father was a Militia colonel and a Canadian Pacific Railway investigator. His mother was a Wills from the St. Thomas, Ontario, area. Before the Great War, the family lived in Montreal, and Burns remembered riding a sleigh down Côte des Neiges. They were reasonably well off and had their own stables. But the marriage broke up, and the father eventually died a drunk.

Burns went to RMC and didn't fit in. He was dark and swarthy, like a Celt. He apparently smuggled a cow into a senior's room.

Marriage and Quetta

Burns's wife was a Phelan, lace curtain Irish, from the Ottawa area. She wanted to be a nurse but first got sent to the syphilis ward. She met Burns at Kingston when he was instructing at RMC.

They went to the Quetta Staff College together in 1929 and had a houseful of Indian things.[7] Their place was a museum. They loved India, and Mrs. Burns liked the army. Mary was born in 1933 in a gruelling caesarean birth that left her mother in difficulty for years. She was a nervous type. The marriage was good until just before the war, but the war compounded their problems. She kept the home going, took in boarders, and gave Burns the $5,000 she had saved when he came back to Canada. She died after small strokes in 1975; with the aid of a housekeeper, Burns had looked after her as well as he could.

Burns was a Protestant and his wife a Roman Catholic. This caused no difficulty, though the wife was religious "in an Irish way." He had some religion and kept a Bible by his bed in the Middle East. He wanted to be cremated, Mary said – he'd watched bodies rot in the Great War trenches.

Burns's personality and attitudes

Burns was no smiler – when his wife was dying, she told a friend that you weren't allowed to smile at their house. Planting a garden was a military drill with him. But he was very kind, and Mary fished and sailed with him. He was artistic; he painted and was serious but could laugh; and he had a good turn of phrase. He taught Mary to follow her own path, to rely on herself. The mother handled discipline, but both could communicate.

He was a Canadian patriot, but also an empire and monarchy man. He had no inferiority complex about the British, and he didn't tolerate stupidity but sometimes put his foot in it. He didn't want to be a disaffected general. Her mother told Mary not to ask him about the war, and he volunteered little.

....

7 Burns was said to have scored the highest marks of all Staff College candidates in the empire.

His friends were F.F. Worthington, E.W. Sansom, Andy McNaughton, and John Lawson, who was killed at Hong Kong commanding the Canadian force in December 1941, as well as military, civil service, United Nations, and hobby friends. He entertained a lot and always kept up a large correspondence.

When he was in the Department of Veterans Affairs as assistant deputy minister right after the war, he dressed up in seedy clothes to see how the department treated vets. Unhappy with the results, he raised hell. "I looked after the boys during the war, and I should look after them postwar too," she quoted her father.

Sidelines
Burns wrote a lot under the pseudonym of Arlington B. Conway (ABC), including some pieces with Madge MacBeth, an Ottawa writer of note between the wars.[8] He had plenty of opinions and wrote wrathful letters to the press.

He was a great photographer, a fisherman, and a squash player. He liked antiques and did woodworking.

He encouraged Mary's theatre interests and made costumes for her in Ottawa's Children's Theatre – a crocodile head and a mechanical beanstalk.

Politics
She thought her father voted Liberal, but he never said. Her godparents were C.G. "Chubby" Power, the Liberal MP from Quebec City who was a Cabinet minister under Mackenzie King, and his wife, old family friends.

JOSEPH POPE (1921-2010)

INTERVIEWS | TORONTO, 15 AND 29 MARCH 1991

The eldest son of Lieutenant-General Maurice Pope, Joseph became a very successful broker and investor in Toronto.

....

8   Burns contributed to H.L. Mencken's *American Mercury* as its military writer. His work with Madge MacBeth included a novel, *The Great Fright: Onesiphore, Our Neighbour* (New York and Montreal: Louis Carrier, 1929). His most important military writing appeared in the *Canadian Defence Quarterly* and in his two postwar books: *General Mud;* and *Manpower in the Canadian Army* (Toronto: Clarke Irwin, 1956). For more on Burns's writing career, see Granatstein, *The Generals,* 121-26.

The interview opened with discussion of General Pope as a family man in the PF.

Maurice Pope had trained as an engineer at McGill University and worked for the Canadian Pacific Railway. He enlisted in the Canadian Engineers in 1915 and joined the PF the next year. He met his wife in November 1918 after telling his adjutant to find him a comfortable chateau with a marriageable daughter. The result seemed ordained. He got engaged, returned to Canada, and had himself sent back to Poperinghe, Belgium, on a war graves posting for two years. He married and the first child, Joe, was born in Belgium.

Joe was an army brat, moving every two years from 1921 to 1939, the longest stay being under three years in Quebec City. He remembered his mother, the daughter of a Belgian count, arranging the furniture in their quarters, antiques purchased in Europe at a time when antiques were priced like second-hand furniture. He believed she bore all this happily, and Maurice used to tell his kids how lucky they were. Joe crossed the Atlantic thirteen times before he was fifteen.

There were no private means. Mrs. Pope had just two $10,000 inheritances, and the Popes largely lived on salary – about $275 a month, which wasn't bad in that era. They could certainly afford servants – in Quebec City they had three, in Esquimalt two, in Wimbledon, England, during the early 1930s three. They lived comfortably; in Quebec City they had quarters at Rues Saint Louis and d'Auteuil beside the Garrison Club that were quite grand. They had no car: Pope told his kids that they couldn't afford one if they wanted to have servants. He also looked after his own kit; Joe had no memory of a batman ever being around. In the United Kingdom, Joe and his brother Harry were sent to a private school, and during the 1930s the family lived in a service flat, where three guineas a week paid for furnished quarters, all meals, and servants. Pope was not authoritarian at home, though he disciplined his kids until they were in their teens. To Joe, Pope was a good, moral, religious man.

Both parents were fluently bilingual (Mrs. Pope spoke an accented English), and the house ran with single sentences skipping back and forth between French and English. They had a good social life. In Ottawa, that included frequent visits to Government House, and Mrs. Pope played bridge avidly in the afternoons. They attended and held formal dinner parties and drank moderately, but unlike most, they preferred wine to spirits. Pope had left Ottawa in 1906, and during the 1930s they didn't initially have civilian friends there. But they did know Mike Pearson well, and George Pearkes, a close friend, lived across the street. Mrs. Pope was a devout Roman Catholic, a happy woman who shopped every day, as in Europe.

Léo Laflèche, the Deputy Minister of National Defence in the 1930s, lived around the corner. His grasp of the interface between the political and military realms was not impressive. Joe remembered that Pope once said he "had to pack his briefcase and go round the corner to explain it all again."

Maurice Pope's father was Sir Joseph, a key official in Sir John A. Macdonald's government and the first Under-Secretary of State for External Affairs from 1909 to 1925. Pope himself had been raised in this governmental atmosphere and tried very hard to ensure that his children understood the link between politics and public service. He was also acutely conscious of the authority of the political over the military. Though ordinarily a Tory, he was a great admirer of Mackenzie King and voted for him, not least because of his acute awareness of French-English difficulties and conscription, and the way in which he brought Canada into the war in 1939. As Pope put it, voting for King was "voting for the ticket of Sir John A." Pope's father, Sir Joseph, had briefly worked for King at the end of his career (1921-25), and King certainly knew who Maurice Pope was. That was probably why he made him his military adviser toward the end of the war.

Pope was also very British-oriented and monarchical, though less so than Sir Joseph. The household was taught that the United States was not quite sound or civilized, though when Pope went to Washington in 1942 he came to admire the people he dealt with, notably General George Marshall.

The staff officer

Pope was a staff officer from about 1917 on. He had no aspirations for field command, and Joe wondered how he would have done on the parade square. Even so, he was fit. He walked to work and home for lunch each day, played tennis, and rode at Militia camps.

Pope was also more intellectual than most officers. He was the only one of Sir Joseph's sons who had a university education, though one went to RMC and was no fool. He had been well trained by osmosis from his father. Joe saw no sign of RMC envy in Pope. His brother had attended the college and turned into a drunkard, and sometimes Pope had worried about his son, Harry, who was in the last RMC graduating class of the Second World War, though he turned out well.

Pope liked J.C. Murchie and Ken Stuart, his immediate superiors during the 1930s, though Stuart wasn't a social friend. He liked Harry Crerar and understood why the British wanted him to be First Canadian Army commander in preference to Andy McNaughton. Andy would interrupt an exercise to work out an engineering problem. Pope was very close to E.L.M. Burns and didn't think Georges Vanier was very bright.

Joe claimed that his father was ambitious and that he felt bitter about the slowness of his promotion beyond the rank of major – almost twenty years. And he expressed some regret that by going to Washington, he had lost the chance to be Chief of the General Staff, something he had wanted. He was reserved regarding such things, not one to show emotion. Mrs. Pope, however, with two sons in the army during the war, did worry a lot.

MAJOR W.H. POPE (1923-2000)

INTERVIEW | UXBRIDGE, ON, 3 APRIL 1991

The second son of Lieutenant-General Maurice Pope, Harry Pope graduated from RMC in 1942. A prisoner of war and escapee in Italy, he was awarded a Military Cross for service in the Korean War.
He began by talking about his own military career.

His career was wondrous and chequered.[9] He was basically bilingual – though initially raised in English, the kids ordinarily spoke French to their mother, and when Maurice Pope was stationed in Quebec City, they attended *école*. He had seen the anti-French bias at RMC. He served briefly with the Voltigeurs de Québec, the Royal Montreal Regiment, and at length with the Royal 22e Régiment (R22eR). He said he attempted to use his father's pull just once, when he called General Price Montague at CMHQ in hopes of jumping the queue and getting sent from Britain to the R22eR in Italy. Montague agreed, but when plans changed, Harry tried to alter the arrangement, and Montague slapped him into line.

....

9 Harry Pope's memoirs are *Leading from the Front* (Waterloo: Laurier Centre for Military Strategic and Disarmament Studies, 2002).

Maurice Pope and family

Harry described his father as a very reserved, even prudish, man. He never saw him kiss his mother on the lips, for example. And when she got pregnant with his brother Joe soon after they married, one of Harry's grandmothers remarked, "So Maurice at last came down from his pedestal." Pope never told his kids about sex – that was almost inconceivable. He once complained about being introduced to the mistress of an acquaintance – "As if I would want to meet her." But when Harry, who had been divorced, married a divorced Anglican, Pope was very kind indeed. And on his death bed, he told Harry to take a gold centennial coin from his dresser at home and give it to his grandchild, who was then in utero with eight months to go.

General Pope had no use for RMC as such, but he wanted Harry to go into the army through the front door. He saw RMC as a club, one he wasn't part of, and felt excluded from the esprit that cadets shared. When Harry was General Burns's Aide de Camp in Italy, nine of the fifteen members of A Mess at I Canadian Corps HQ were ex-cadets. Even so, the only thing the RMC experience did was offer good training. After you'd gone through its "recruiting" (rough first-year hazing), you could cope with anything.

Joe, the first son, had no interest in the military and was still working in the bank in 1941. But when his father said he didn't want a conscript in the family, Joe enlisted.

Harry admired his father – hardworking, intelligent, and devoted to duty. He was also career-oriented and not one to rock the boat. His pension was very important to him. He was reasonably fit (with a bit of a potbelly) and liked fishing and hunting but was clearly a staff man. He was authoritarian at home, didn't discuss things or offer moral advice – except telling the boys that if they got a servant girl in trouble, they didn't have to marry her, as one Pope uncle had done. He was a gentleman and was always polite to servants. He got cranky as he aged, including with his wife, and Mrs. Pope once told Harry, "Don't be a nuisance to your wife." Pope didn't drink much, but puffed a pipe or a cigarette.

Pope was devoted to his career and had few friends – E.L.M. "Tommy" Burns was one. He had no private means. His wife's inheritance came in 1929, and she put it into the stock market at the wrong time and then withdrew it in 1933, again the wrong time. She had about $25,000 in 1960, which Joe, a broker, invested. When she died, her estate was worth about $1 million, counting her house.

Pope was very interested in politics, and he admired Mackenzie King, who kept Canada together. One day in 1945, when Harry got back from the war, his father took him to the Rideau Club, and they sat with Paul Martin, Brooke Claxton, and Louis St. Laurent. At that point, Andy McNaughton was the Defence Minister, even though he'd been defeated in two elections. When Harry asked how McNaughton could possibly still be a Cabinet member, Pope gasped – he was the soul of discretion. But Martin simply said, "Wait." And sure enough, McNaughton was soon gone. Years later, during the Korean War, Harry was a soldier in the R22eR, training for Korea. Chasing hard after some lady, he attended a weekend Trotskyite conference in Seattle and ended up on the FBI's black books. Harry said he apologized to his father.

When Harry left the army in 1959 because he disagreed with Diefenbaker's defence policy, his father was very upset. "Why don't you see a psychiatrist?" he asked. And when his resignation reached the desk of Defence Minister George Pearkes (an old friend of Maurice's), Pearkes said, "Good God, but what about his pension? Should I talk to Maurice?" When Harry later ran for the NDP against Progressive Conservative Defence Minister Douglas Harkness, his father gave him money to help finance his campaign.

Pope was favourable to the Militia, seeing it as an essential mobilization base. Harry knew nothing of his role in drafting the Defence of Canada Regulations before the war.[10] But his view of General Pope's attitude to Japanese Canadians (the regulations authorized their forced removal from the BC coast during the war) was harsh. His father knew the West Coast and had served there. And in the early 1970s, when he was interviewed on TV about the evacuation, there were tears in his eyes. There may have been an element of guilt there.

Pope was also very near to being a French Canadian. His mother was French Canadian and he himself was bilingual. English Canadians in the army saw him as French Canadian, Harry said, but to francophones, he was an Anglo.

Harry thought he'd died of prostate cancer. He'd refused to be checked out – prostate was an old man's disease.

....

10 The draconian Defence of Canada Regulations were prepared in Ottawa before the outbreak of war and implemented under authority of the War Measures Act on 3 September 1939, one week before Canada's declaration of war. See Granatstein, *The Generals*, 211-12.

On Burns

Held as a prisoner of war in Italy, Harry escaped, spent seven weeks as a guerrilla, and finally made his way back to the Allied lines. In friendship for Harry's family, E.L.M. Burns, then GOC of I Canadian Corps, called him in and asked him to be his ADC. Harry refused, but as an escapee, he couldn't be used in the line. It was too risky: if he were recaptured, he might well have been executed. The same was true for Captain Paul Triquet, who got the VC and also couldn't be in the line afterward. So Harry became Burns's ADC anyhow. Harry thought this was because Burns liked Mrs. Pope. He once tried to get himself sent behind German lines with a radio to be an artillery spotter, but Burns wouldn't allow it – how could he explain that to Mrs. Pope? As it was, Harry lasted only fifty days as ADC before being sent back to the R22eR. That job kept him out of the Hitler Line battles in May 1944, which were very hard.

Burns was decent and hardworking, but he couldn't get his two division commanders to push as hard as they needed to. Essentially, he was a staff officer and couldn't dominate others. He would give minor officers hell but couldn't do so to his GOCs. Probably he lacked the battle experience that gave confidence in his own ability. He had little personality. Harry said that once the Canadians had been in battle, promotions could come only from those who had experienced combat – Burns came in at the top and this sat uneasily with his subordinates.

Chris Vokes, Harry thought, was OK though crude (Maurice called him a "good solid cook"). After Canadian troops had come out of cover to meet surrendering Germans, only to be killed by other Germans on their flanks, Vokes gave instructions that Canadians would know how to deal with German prisoners – kill them. Nor did he believe that Military Crosses should go to lieutenants – showing bravery was just part of the job.

MRS. SIMONNE POPE FLETCHER (1928-2003)

INTERVIEW | OTTAWA, 23 MAY 1991

Mrs. Fletcher was General Maurice Pope's daughter.
She began the interview by describing Pope at home.

Her father was very strict, and she was terrified of him while adoring him. You had to watch your "p's and q's," and not talk at the table unless spoken to. Still, Pope was easier on her than on her brothers. His views were very strong and clear, though he mellowed later. It was important to be correct and to do the right thing. During the war, he showed no emotion about his sons in the army, although Mrs. Pope would.

The marriage had its strains, and Pope could be very difficult. He lost his temper and wouldn't tolerate being interrupted. Once Mrs. Pope went to Europe and thought about not returning. Still, the marriage was good, even if he wasn't easy to live with. Probably, he had to let off steam at home, as he had to be a diplomat at work.

Pope could throw a good party and knew how to get the right mix of people. He and his wife were both very good cooks, and their table was always good. But they drank little, didn't smoke, and were frugal; even when Pope was an ambassador postwar, his wife did the shopping. They had good taste and worked the antique shops in Europe. After retirement, money was tight, and the pension seemed small until indexing began.

They enjoyed Washington during the war, when Pope was head of the Canadian Joint Staff there. They lived in an apartment just off 16th Street and had a batman who cooked and served. Pope liked Americans and got on well with them. In Berlin after the war, where he headed the Canadian Military Mission, he used his US connections to get good rations.

He liked Europeans too and understood them. He saw lots of the French and did better with them than with either UK or US officers. He read *Le Monde* every day, she recalled. He was fluent in French, though he had a bit of an Anglo accent.

Pope was friendly with Generals J.C. Murchie and Ken Stuart, but he thought Andy McNaughton a fool. He liked Mike Pearson and admired Mackenzie King – everything rose and shone on Mackenzie King.

TONY FOSTER (1932-2012)

INTERVIEW | HALIFAX, NS, 2 OCTOBER 1991

The son of Major-General Harry Foster, Tony was also the author of Meeting of Generals, *a dual biography of his father and SS General*

> *Kurt Meyer; General Foster presided over Meyer's military trial just after*
> *the war.*[11]
>   *The brief interview, done while he was letting me borrow some of his*
> *and his father's papers, focused on personalities.*

On Charles Foulkes and others

Tony remarked on his father's dislike of Charles Foulkes. When Foulkes was
I Canadian Corps commander in Italy, he owned a large collection of por-
nography and had a soldier who kept it for him. Apparently with the intention
of showing Foulkes that they were aware of his collection, Foster as GOC of
the 1st Division and his General Staff Officer, Grade 1, Lieutenant-Colonel
W.S. Murdoch, acquired some porn and sent it to him. The idea was that this
would keep him off the 1st Division's back. It seemed to work: before that
point, Foulkes would poke around, looking for things to criticize, but afterward, he did not. Foulkes was the only senior officer of whom General Foster
spoke ill – he thought he was a fraud, an incompetent, and a nasty man.

Tony recalled a conversation with his father about fear. Tony had said that,
as a pilot, he thought he knew what he was doing in the air and wasn't afraid.
General Foster ventured that he himself lacked the intelligence to have been
afraid in battle; he was "too stupid." People who had enough imagination
to think about what might happen to them sometimes went to pieces, but he
didn't have that problem.

Tony mentioned the stories about Rod Keller after D-Day – that "Keller
was yeller." He hadn't mentioned them in his book, because he was a friend
of Keller's son. He was unsure of his father's reaction to Keller, but he said
the 3rd Division brigadiers had tried to get rid of Keller before D-Day.

After Tony's mother died during the war, his father visited him and his
brother at school in British Columbia. He said the good air made him feel
like turning somersaults.

"Why don't you?" Tony asked.

"OK," replied the General.

So he did, doing a succession of flips down the school driveway.

And after the war, Tony recalled his father saying that he'd figured out
a way of saving $365 a year – by buying a brand of rye that cost $1 less a
bottle.

....

11   Tony Foster, *Meeting of Generals* (Toronto: Methuen, 1986).

PETER HERTZBERG (1921-2009)

INTERVIEW | TORONTO, 19 DECEMBER 1991

He was the son of Major-General C.S.L. Hertzberg, nephew of Major-General H.F.H. Hertzberg, an RMC graduate of 1940, and an officer in the Royal Canadian Engineers, most notably with the 5th Canadian Armoured Division in Italy and Northwest Europe.
He opened by talking about the Hertzberg brothers, C.S.L. and H.F.H.

The brothers were very close, riding over to see each other during the Great War whenever they could and staying in close touch after hostilities ended. The children of C.S.L. visited H.F.H. in Kingston and in Nova Scotia during the summers, for example. H.F.H. was RMC Commandant in Peter's last year, and this was when they became close. It "broke H.F.H.'s heart when he didn't get overseas in 1939," presumably because he was on the wrong side politically, or so Peter thought. C.S.L., however, was no Mackenzie King fan and was a Tory. Fifty-two at the outbreak of war, he was a crony of Andy McNaughton and thought very highly of him, as did his brother. Very active in the Militia, C.S.L. was head of the Royal Canadian Engineers Association and had high stature as a consulting engineer. His firm was the leading one of its kind in Ontario, and it advised on the Bank of Commerce Building in Toronto. C.S.L. was also friendly with C.D. Howe. Lack of money during the Depression may have played a part in Peter's going to RMC rather than university.

C.S.L. Hertzberg in the war

Though he'd been severely wounded in February 1917 by a rifle grenade, C.S.L. was fit and athletic in 1939, playing tennis, cricket, and aquaplaning. The 1st Division officers were his contemporaries at NDHQ – it was something of a club. C.S.L. overseas had good rapport with younger Royal Canadian Engineers officers and spotted the comers – **Jack Christian**, for one. His friends were the McNaughton A Mess crowd – R.M. Luton, Burgon Bickersteth, an academic adviser, and Guy Turner. In Britain, Peter saw his father a lot during the war – where he really got to know him – but he never talked about his contemporaries. The story that he'd refused a smallpox vaccination before going to India in October 1943, where he died of smallpox in January, angered Peter, who refused to believe it. His father wasn't afraid of medication, and vaccinations sometimes didn't work.

Peter's mother was sickly, and he implied she was a Christian Scientist and that there were problems between his parents. There was no sign that she tried to join her husband overseas, and they didn't see each other from the time C.S.L. left for overseas in 1939 and his death in 1944.

Peter added that Howard Kennedy, who became a major-general in the Second World War and later the head of the National Capital Commission in Ottawa, was a close friend of his father. Kennedy had been badly shot up in the Great War; he saw C.S.L. regularly during the interwar years and was close to him in England. He was godfather to Peter's younger brother.

C.S.L. was called Bud in the family, Charlie by friends outside. Unlike H.F.H., he wasn't ordinarily referred to by his initials.

On the generals
Peter ended the war as General Staff Officer, Grade 3, in **Bert Hoffmeister's** 5th Armoured Division. At Otterlo in the Netherlands in mid-April 1945, when the Germans broke through, he recalled General Hoffmeister emerging from his caravan in very colourful pajamas. He was a believer in the Mighty Maroon Machine and said the division had a real rapport. It had a football team and ran a bus company in Holland after V-E Day.

He described Chris Vokes as "an asshole and a criminal" for the Lamone River attack in December 1944, where his cousin, H.F.H.'s son Peder of the Royal Canadian Regiment, was killed.[12] On 4 December, just before the assault, which went in after midnight, Peter had a drink with him. He told Peter he'd not see him again as they were being sent into a hopeless attack.

THEA HERTZBERG GRAY (1927-2015)

INTERVIEW | TORONTO, 12 FEBRUARY 1992

The daughter of General H.F.H. Hertzberg, she lived in Vernon, British Columbia.
Mrs. Gray described her father's early years.

....

12   Vokes had passed command of the 1st Division to Harry Foster on 30 November 1944, so he was not responsible for the Royal Canadian Regiment during the Lamone River debacle. Perhaps Peter confused Vokes with corps commander Charles Foulkes. The similar pronunciation of the two surnames, Vokes and Foulkes, constantly gave rise to mix-ups.

H.F.H.'s father was a Canadian Pacific Railway engineer but not terribly well off, though the kids went to Upper Canada College or St. Andrew's. But when H.F.H. wanted to go to RMC, there wasn't the money. Thus, Mrs. Gray said, he was very moved when, as RMC Commandant, he was made an honorary member of the last Second World War class.

He joined the Militia before the Great War; she didn't know why he didn't join the PF then, though he did in 1915 from overseas. As she put it, the war saved him from a civilian life he disliked. He was more a soldier than a businessman. His brother, C.S.L., was a gentler soul than he was, but they were very devoted to each other. C.S.L. was more clever, less of a military mind, more academic, and more intellectual. H.F.H. wasn't blustery, however, and she thought he was a soldier with soul, who read poetry and loved the Old Testament. Certainly, he didn't talk about his war experiences or refight battles with salt cellars.

At RMC

H.F.H. really loved his two tours at RMC. When Thea went to Peter Hertzberg's fiftieth graduation anniversary in 1990, she was feted as H.F.H.'s daughter and told by one cadet in his class "we loved him." His speech on closing RMC in 1942 was still remembered. General **W.A.B. Anderson** told her that "we loved your mother," too.

And certainly Mrs. H.F.H. was a great lady who kept her husband human. Hertzberg's own mother had been very bigoted and was strongly anti-Catholic, but Mrs. H.F.H. was different and liberal. At RMC early in the Second World War, the wife of the Medical Officer was German and had two brothers in the Luftwaffe; she was badly treated until Mrs. H.F.H. had a party and made much of her. A Jewish wife was similarly treated. They also had three British child refugees living with them during the war, and she used a small inheritance from an uncle to pay for this. There was more money when the uncle's wife died. Mrs. H.F.H. loved the army and loved being a general's wife, but she wasn't stuffy. The family was strapped for cash, largely because they had to entertain at postings in Halifax, Kingston, and Toronto. They lived an upper-class life on a middle-class salary. Still, the H.F.H. kids all went to private schools – though when the daughters married, H.F.H. had to borrow the cash. This was when he was in retirement.

As a child at RMC, Thea hung around with an officers' kids gang – all of whom knew the cadet gossip and would go to check out scruffy incoming recruits and say they'd never be any good.

Hertzberg's posting to RMC as Commandant in 1940 was a demotion: he was sacked as Quartermaster General in April 1940, she claimed, because he refused to recommend a Militia officer to be District Officer Commanding in Halifax. This was a wartime post, and it needed a PFer in charge. When H.F.H. persisted, Mackenzie King said to him, "General, I refuse to be swayed by your famous rhetoric." He always cherished that remark. The family suspected that the sacking was Finance Minister Ralston's doing – he was no favourite, nor was King. But there was real shock when Defence Minister Norman Rogers was killed in an air crash in June 1940. As the above suggests, H.F.H. was a wonderful orator.

Military friends

H.F.H.'s military friends were Generals F.F. Worthington, Harry Crerar, and Andy McNaughton. Of Andy, he said, "Put him in a cage and feed in questions from one side, and he'd pass out answers from the other," a favourable, if odd, comment on his brains. She noted that H.F.H. was also a friend of Air Marshal Gus Edwards of the RCAF.[13]

In the Second World War

Thea had never heard the story that H.F.H. might have become GOC of the 2nd Division. But she knew it almost killed him when he wasn't given an overseas command. He thought of himself as a commander, not as a staff officer. But he was good at staff work – very meticulous and precise. For example, when he was Quartermaster General, he did the transport planning for the 1939 royal tour of Canada, and he made a point of ensuring that the seat heights were correct.

He went overseas on a tour in 1943. She thought this was the PF's way of compensating him for not getting a command, but it was good because he saw his son Peder and his brother for the last time.

Peder, who was in the Royal Canadian Regiment, died on 5 December 1944 during the Lamone River attack. The family blamed Vokes for this meaningless affair, and H.F.H. showed his contempt by refusing to shake Vokes's hand. Thea described Peder as a "scapegrace," AWOL on occasion, screwing around, but good-looking and charming. H.F.H. favoured his

....

13   Edwards, a nationalist, favoured "Canadianizing" the RCAF overseas. See Greenhous et al., *The Crucible of War, 1939-1945.*

daughters (perhaps because his sister had died at age eight) – but on the anniversary of Peder's death, he'd reread all his letters in a private ceremony.

In the late 1950s, when H.F.H. was physically very shaky, he presided at the Royal Canadian Engineers' officer cadet graduation parade at Camp Chilliwack, British Columbia. He gave out the C.S.L. Hertzberg sword. He'd gone to the event expecting that the cadets would be dreadful in their drill, but he loved the parade. And he said, "This is my last parade. I thank you for making it such a good one."

MRS. DAGMAR HERTZBERG NATION (1924-2012)
INTERVIEW | VICTORIA, BC, 27 FEBRUARY 1992

She was the daughter of General H.F.H. Hertzberg.
Mrs. Nation talked of her father and RMC.

Her father was the repository of all virtues, she said, loyal to a fault, an orator, witty, attractive, and passionate in his duty. He loved his wife, doted on his daughters, and had great presence. He was also a bigot who disliked blacks and French Canadians except those in the Royal 22e Régiment. He was considerate to troops, once cutting off a padre at RMC after eight minutes because he kept the cadets standing in the sun too long. He was small, slight, and fit but seemed taller. He was hard outside and putty inside. He could tear strips off people and turn icy if someone offended him. His eyes teared up when the Battery Sergeant Major of RMC's class of 1942 asked him to lead the final church parade. He'd wanted to be a cadet, couldn't, and loved his postings there, though he thought it improper for an ex-cadet to be Commandant. He said if he'd gone to RMC, General C.F. Constantine would have been his Battery Sergeant Major.

There was a family story that he wouldn't make political appointments to suit Finance Minister J.L. Ralston and was thus sacked as Quartermaster General. "For God's sake, Hertz, bend a little," begged T.V. Anderson, the Chief of the General Staff. The RMC post was a demotion.

On the PF
Dagmar loved the PF. As her father was at the top of it, it provided a great chance to meet important people. But H.F.H. wouldn't let his wife use army cars, although the wives of District Officers Commanding could; and he

wouldn't push his kids forward (for example, when the Governor-General came to RMC, they were last in line to meet him). He taught his officers, and Mrs. H.F.H. taught their wives. She saw that the family ate well on little money, and they entertained a lot. She was a good cook – Andy McNaughton once rang up and said, "I haven't had one of your beef and kidney pies for a long time."

"All right, darling," she replied, "come to dinner."

She made clothes for herself and the kids, and was a trained social worker.

H.F.H. was a close friend of Air Marshal Gus Edwards in the RCAF, to whom he taught social niceties. He loved Admiral L.W. Murray of the Royal Canadian Navy and General Constantine.[14] He liked Generals Ken Stuart, E.C. Ashton, and Harry Crerar. Crerar's wife, Verse, was so lovely "and wicked" – at Government House she would chew gum during knitting bees. They loved the McNaughtons: Andy's wife, Mabel, would say, "When I'm with Charlie [C.S.L.] I like him best; and then with Dane [H.F.H.'s nickname], I like him best." Andy relaxed with them, and sometimes when he was out wandering deep in thought, Dagmar would be sent to look for him.

Her mother spent a lot of time calming wives who were griping over post-ings. "You married him, you knew he'd travel," and so forth. Dagmar herself went to nine schools.

In their District Officer Commanding quarters, there was a batman who was allowed only to look after H.F.H.'s clothing, a driver, a steward, and a cook-general paid for by the family.

Disappointments in 1940 and 1944

H.F.H. wanted to be GOC of the 2nd Division and was crushed when he didn't get it – "It almost broke his heart," her mother said.

Her brother, killed in Italy in late 1944, was in terrible trouble with a mar-ried woman in the United Kingdom and was sued in the divorce. As a kid, he'd had a difficult time with H.F.H., who demanded such perfection from him. But he was a charmer and H.F.H. adored him. His death was personally shattering for H.F.H., but his belief that it was for the country helped ease his pain.

....

14 Rear Admiral Leonard Murray rose to be Commander-in-Chief, Canadian North-west Atlantic, in command of a crucial sector in the Battle of the Atlantic from 1943 to 1945.

MRS. EVELYN LETT (1896-1999)

INTERVIEW | VANCOUVER, BC, 2 MARCH 1992

In her mid-nineties when I interviewed her, Mrs. Lett was the widow of Brigadier Sherwood Lett, who was wounded at Dieppe and again in Normandy.

Mrs. Lett talked briefly about senior officers.

Lett, she said, had greatly disliked UK generalship in the Great War but was less censorious in the Second World War. Mountbatten was no favourite, though, a reference to the Dieppe raid's failure.[15] Lett thought the Dieppe plan had been bad and refused to blame Hamilton Roberts, the GOC of the 2nd Division, for the disaster.

Major-General Victor Odlum was a local Vancouver notable (giving large sums to the University of British Columbia and starting its Aboriginal collections), and his wife was very kind to Mrs. Lett. She seemed to think that Odlum deserved command of the 2nd Division because of the way he'd kept the Militia together in Vancouver between the wars.

In 1944, Lett wrote to tell her that he'd been offered the post of Chief Justice of the Supreme Court, which he believed was a conspiracy by NDHQ and the government to deprive him of command of the 2nd Division. He was being pushed aside, just as Odlum had been when he was offered the High Commission in Australia. He knew Odlum hadn't been up to command, but he, Lett, had a very good record behind him. In the end, after being wounded in Normandy as a brigade commander on 18 July 1944, he retired, letting the Supreme Court position go to someone else. If he'd got the 2nd, he would have stayed in the army. She added that Lett knew that his friend George Pearkes also wasn't up to divisional command.

GEORGE MONTAGUE (1928-2011)

TELEPHONE CONVERSATION, TORONTO, 26 MAY 1992

He was the nephew of Lieutenant-General John Percival "Price" Montague who served at Canadian Military Headquarters in London as Quarter-

....

15 Admiral Mountbatten, who was Chief of Combined Operations, bore primary responsibility for planning the Dieppe raid of 19 August 1942.

> *master General, Judge Advocate General, and finally, in the rank of*
> *lieutenant-general, as Chief of Staff.*
> *The interview began with talk of his uncle.*

After the Great War, Price Montague loved the army and stayed with the Militia. He wasn't a joiner and his only interests were the law, the military, his fraternity, and horses.

In 1931, Montague was offered a judgeship by Prime Minister R.B. Bennett. He considered his senior partners in Pitblado, Hoskins, the Winnipeg law firm where he worked, and realized they'd probably live to be ninety. So he went to the Manitoba Court of King's Bench.

He went overseas in 1939, and George recalled hearing that he was touched when J.W. Dafoe of the *Winnipeg Free Press* saw him off at Winnipeg's railway station and praised his devotion to duty. The Liberal *Free Press* had chased after Montague's father, a Tory politician in Ottawa and Manitoba, and the family had snubbed Dafoe ever after.[16] But that scene at the station affected Montague. Like his father, Montague was a Tory, but as a man of duty, he had no problems serving a Liberal government during the Second World War.

Montague was not long overseas when his wife fell ill with cancer and soon died. He could not get back from overseas before her death.

He was quite fit and was very proud that he could keep up with General Montgomery, a fetishist about fitness, in climbing five flights of stairs. He also saw a lot of Charles de Gaulle in London during the war.

George recalled that officers who'd served with his uncle at CMHQ during the war were devoted to him – when George moved to Toronto, Montague gave introductions to some of them. They would have done anything for Price.

Personal life

As a child, George had seen Montague as a severe, disciplined man. After the war, he was much more relaxed and affable. Like his father, he was a good speaker, a raconteur who carried a joke book with him.

....

16 General Montague's father, Walter H. Montague, had served in Parliament during the 1880s and 1890s, been a minister from 1894 to 1896, and served in the Manitoba legislature as Minister of Public Works from 1913 to 1915.

As a lawyer and judge, he handled few great cases. George recalled hearing that Montague gave a large judgment to a man whose sex life was ruined when an airplane propeller cut off part of his penis. Later – and this was the kind of story Montague loved – the man appeared before him as co-respondent in a divorce case.

He was a great horseman and loved polo, even in the 1930s when money was tight. Montague's polo team, the Buffaloes, used to travel to the United States to play against US Army teams. The team brought him into contact with the Sifton family in Winnipeg. He continued riding after the war too.

Montague was an "old school" type, one who believed in standing up for what was right and fighting to protect it if necessary.

P.K. (PATRICIA KATHERINE) PAGE (1916-2010)
TELEPHONE CONVERSATION | VICTORIA, BC, 30 JULY 1992

The daughter of Major-General Lionel F. Page, she was a distinguished poet and painter. Her husband, Arthur Irwin, was editor of Maclean's *and served as High Commissioner to Australia in the 1950s.*
She spoke first of her father's background.

General Page was born in Yorkshire, the son of a well-off brewer from the landed gentry. His mother was well-off Irish. But the father died young, and somehow the money disappeared. Page went to Berkhamsted School, which George Pearkes had also attended, tried for and missed Sandhurst, and came to Canada at age seventeen on some school-assisted scheme to farm near Red Deer, Alberta. He acquired land and homesteaded, and he established a reputation as a daredevil with bucking broncos and bulls. She said he also rescued an Indian woman from drowning in a raging stream. Page had a business partnership of sorts, and just before the war he sold his farm for $25,000, but somehow there was never any money. He also brought his mother to live in Canada with him. The family was High Church, but he was a free-thinker and gave his kids no religion. He retained a slight British accent all his life.

General Page met his British wife in Red Deer when she was visiting her bank manager brother, but the marriage was delayed on the grounds that Page had no money. Nonetheless, they married in Britain during the Great War, and P.K. was born there in 1916.

He established a terrific reputation overseas – well decorated, brave, and loved by his men. On his return to Canada, he was carried through the streets of Red Deer. But he had a wife and child to support and no job – his business partner had decamped – so he drove a cab and sold insurance until joining the PF in the Lord Strathcona's Horse.

The PF

She remembered his groom leading the horse to the door so he could ride to work. Their quarters in Winnipeg were pretty bad. If a cigar were lit on the first floor, you could smell it on the third, and there was no money. But they liked it all. They camped under canvas every summer at Camp Sarcee, just off the base in Calgary, and Page finally built a shack there. Mrs. Page was a gypsy, P.K. said. Some other officers' wives camped too.

They entertained if they had the money, which was infrequent, from winnings on the races. They had a maid always, usually a Polish immigrant, and Page's batman. They got a car only when he became CO of the Lord Strathcona's Horse, and they were given a staff car when he became a brigadier. Her mother complained about being obliged to practise "ladylike" behaviour by the army. It was all a bit too prissy, with cards and calls, and too bourgeois.

General Page's views on the empire and the monarchy were conventional, but he was unorthodox on everything else: religion was out; he wanted a left-hander on his staff as he believed they thought differently; he was innovative, read a lot, and wrote short stories and doggerel. She didn't know of his professional writing, if any.

His friends were Maurice Pope, who was very dashing, and George Pearkes, a "dear idiot" whom Mrs. Page helped to buy a trousseau when he finally married. Page didn't like Harry Crerar; nor did P.K. She also disliked Ken Stuart.

General Officer Commanding in the Second World War

Page was very disappointed when he lost the job of GOC of the 4th Canadian Armoured Division, which he'd raised; but, he said, at least he'd now be able to see his family. He had heart problems and had suffered a serious heart attack in Calgary during the 1930s. He died in Halifax in 1944, and though he was a major-general, his widow received only a lieutenant-colonel's pension on the grounds that his illness had arisen when he was at that rank.

She was so furious that she swore she'd live to ninety, just to get a long run at the pension, and she did. Page's estate was only $8,000, consisting entirely of insurance.

P.K. said her husband, Arthur Irwin, went to Australia as High Commissioner in the 1950s, after Generals Victor Odlum and Léo Laflèche had held the post. She thought Odlum a dreadful man. Irwin had been an important figure at *Maclean's* when the Bren gun affair arose before the war, and Laflèche, who had been Deputy Minister of National Defence, had taken much of the blame. At the High Commissioner's residence in Australia, Laflèche had had the bell pulls labelled His Excellency, Her Excellency, and Little Excellency.

MRS. HELEN PRICE PERODEAU (1922-2014)
TELEPHONE INTERVIEW | SIDNEY, BC, 23 MARCH 1992

*Her father was Major-General C.B. Price, who was the commander of the 3rd Canadian Division. Mrs. Perodeau's spouse, **Giles Perodeau**, was a wartime Aide de Camp to General Crerar.*
She talked about General Price.

Admitting her biases, she described her father as a true gentleman, honourable, upright, and patriotic. He was terribly proud of his Great War service in the ranks and as an officer, proud of his decorations (Distinguished Conduct Medal and Distinguished Service Order) and of the Royal Montreal Regiment, and close to his wartime friends in the regiment. He loved the army, and she thought he would have stayed in the Permanent Force after the war if he could have done so, but her mother wasn't keen.

Her mother's family was well off; her father's was not. Price was managing director of her family's Elmhurst Dairy, and Mother held the purse strings. This might have caused some difficulty between them. Certainly, they lived a good middle-class life in the interwar years.

She thought her mother was pretty unhappy when Price went overseas in 1939 and even more so when he remained there with the Red Cross after he was removed from his division. But he so wanted to be involved in the war that he had to stay. He was terribly crushed when he lost his division – she said he had no killer instinct – but it was not in him ever to cause trouble.

Price blamed the PF for his removal, and indeed, as a good militiaman, didn't like PFers much. He wasn't too keen on Andy McNaughton either.

His son, her brother, was killed on air force training with bombers in the United Kingdom in 1942. She thought he and Price were not all that close, and she said that his death would not have affected Price's ability to carry out his duty.

He was a Conservative before the war but not very involved. He ran in 1945 in Montreal against Liberal Douglas Abbott and lost narrowly. It wasn't that he was especially angry with the government for sacking him – it was just that he had tunnel vision and hated Liberals. And Americans!

MRS. MARY PLOW (1906-99)

INTERVIEW | BROCKVILLE, ON, 19 DECEMBER 1991

She was the widow of Major-General E.C. Plow, who was Commander, Corps Royal Artillery, of the II Canadian Corps and Brigadier, Royal Artillery, of the First Canadian Army. He was an RMC classmate of Guy Simonds.

A vigorous eighty-five-year-old when interviewed at her home, Mrs. Plow began by talking of life in the PF.

She married Plow in 1937, when he was stationed at Winnipeg. He was in the RMC class of 1925, which produced four generals. They lived in the Fort Osborne Barracks on Tuxedo Avenue for a year, and she obviously loved it. She had connections in the town, and they got involved with the civilians. They had little money ($250 a month) and no private means to speak of, as the Plow family had gone bust in the 1920s. They were usually short of money but led a good life. The mess was lively, there was little formal calling, with the presentation of name cards, the young officers were studying all the time, and it was good. All were dedicated to the army, all were private-school upper-middle-class types (including the wives), and even "drink as the curse of the PF" was more than a little exaggerated (though the messes had liquor during Prohibition periods). Officers couldn't marry until they had been in the army for eleven years or had attained the rank of captain, which was good policy because it fostered mess life. They socialized a lot with parties, progressive dinners (where guests moved from house to house for each course), and sports.

In 1938, they went to Kingston to RMC; Guy Simonds, **S.F. Clark**, and Harry Crerar were also there. They lived in Hogan's Alley, the officers' quarters, and life was beautiful. Her husband failed his Staff College entrance exams on his first try in 1938 but made it the following year and then had to be persuaded to accept a place at the college. Then Crerar, the Commandant, refused to let him go. The war made it all irrelevant anyhow.

On the Simonds family

She and Guy Simonds's wife, Kay, got to know each other well, and Plow was godfather to the Simonds boy, Charles. Kay complained that Guy spent all his money on boots and books, leaving none for her. Later, when he was overseas, she moaned that he sent her no money but said that she'd saved $5,000 to $8,000 during the war. There was no doubt that Guy was selfish and ambitious, but Mrs. Plow had no sympathy for whiners. She added that when Guy went overseas in 1939, Kay took the bus to Ottawa to say goodbye. She looked terribly drab. She hadn't even fixed herself up to give him a good send-off.

One of Mrs. Plow's best friends was Doe Sinclair, widow of an RCAF pilot and later Guy Simonds's second wife. She introduced her to Simonds in Britain and then again, after the war, in Halifax. Doe had nothing to do with the breakup of the Simonds marriage and in fact didn't particularly like Guy at first. Still, after they were married, she civilized and humanized him. He got a divorce at Reno, Nevada, and they married in the United States so that Kay could get Simonds's pension – this was at Doe's insistence.

Everyone knew how difficult Simonds was. General Plow said it was "fortunate he never served under Guy," and it was just as well. He and Guy stayed friends. Simonds could be brutal. For example, when he fired Brigadier R.O.G. Morton, a brother artillery officer, in Italy, he didn't even look up from his desk.[17] It was widely said that Guy refused to have any officer under his command who was older than he or who had once been senior to him. When F.F. Worthington, at least a decade older than Simonds, heard that Guy was coming, he began packing, or so the story went. Some of Guy's behaviour, she said, was due to shyness.

....

17   Morton was Commander, Royal Artillery, of the 5th Canadian Armoured Division, and Simonds fired him in December 1943.

Overseas

The war was a good time for Mrs. Plow, as she had no children and was free to go overseas. So she did, sailing with perhaps a hundred wives of Canadian soldiers and disembarking in January 1940. She found space in Fleet, near London, in what was "the warmest house" in town – 39 degrees Fahrenheit. She remained overseas until after Dunkirk, when Harry Crerar decided that wives should return to Canada. Plow wanted her to leave: he couldn't worry about the war and her at the same time. Once in Canada, Mrs. Plow devoted herself to figuring out how to get back to England, which she did in March 1942 by taking a job with the Motorized Transport Corps, a volunteer ladies group. The British ladies in the corps were puzzled that so many Canadian wives wanted to be near their husbands when they all wanted to get away from theirs to snag a Yank. Then she got on with No. 1 Canadian General Hospital. The daughter of General R.M. Luton, the Director of Medical Services, was expecting a child and lived with her for a time.

Marriages survived the separations of war because moral standards were higher then, women weren't liberated, and they were much less independent. She knew that some senior officers had mistresses and didn't worry much about them. It was natural in the circumstances.

MR. JUSTICE JOSEPH POTTS (1925-2006)

INTERVIEW | TORONTO, 1 FEBRUARY 1992

The son of Major-General Arthur E. Potts, he served in the army from 1943 to 1946.
Potts began talking of his father's time during the Great War and in the Militia.

Born in Blyth, Scotland, General Potts was educated at Edinburgh University. He won a scholarship to Cornell University and then joined up in Montreal, where he'd gone for visits. He became engaged to his future wife while he was serving in the McGill University companies. His six brothers in the United Kingdom also joined the British Army, and three were killed during the war. Potts served with the Princess Patricia's Canadian Light Infantry (PPCLI) and won a commission in the field. In 1918, Walter Murray, President of the University of Saskatchewan, visited France to recruit faculty and signed up Potts, who became an agriculture professor. After his arrival on campus, he established the Canadian Officers Training Corps at the university and was its CO for the next twenty years. He also rose to colonel in the Militia and commanded a Militia brigade as the senior officer in Saskatchewan. The Militia was his hobby and his obsession, and Joe recalled his long-suffering mother being dumped at a cottage with six kids while Father went off to Dundurn Camp for a month of training every summer.

Potts also willingly sent his eldest son to RMC, and perhaps Joe's twin brother might also have attended, had the war not intervened. Potts liked the college and was on its Board of Visitors. He received an honorary RMC degree in 1979. Nor was he full of PF-Militia antipathy.

Second World War service overseas

On the outbreak of war, Potts expected to be called up for service immediately, but no call came. Then Andy McNaughton and George Pearkes, both friends, visited Saskatoon in November 1939 and discovered that the CO of the Saskatoon Light Infantry (SLI), a machine-gun battalion, was no good. They hit on Potts as his replacement, so they tracked him down at a movie theatre and suggested that he take over the SLI. He'd have to be dropped a rank, and they told him that he was scheduled for a brigade in the 2nd Division, but when they offered him the SLI, he agreed at once. He got the word on a Thursday and went overseas on Monday, leaving his wife without any money. She asked a bank manager for a loan to carry her over until the army pay had started but was refused. She had to borrow money from the brother-in-law of Potts's Adjutant, a local investment man.

Potts told his wife that he was going to make the SLI "a finer regiment than the Princess Patricia's Canadian Light Infantry," but when he asked the PPCLI for a corporal to become his Regimental Sergeant Major, he was told that none could be spared. That annoyed him with the PF, Joe recalled. The SLI was one of three machine-gun battalions that went overseas (the Toronto Scottish and the Royal Montreal Regiment were the other two), but after the 1st Division was reorganized to include just one machine-gun battalion, there was a competition between the three to see which one would win that position. When Joe came to Holland in March 1945 as a reinforcement officer to the SLI, a sergeant told him that the regiment had initially hated his father.

It was billeted with the Toronto Scottish at Aldershot, in southern England. The Toronto regiment would be eating its breakfast while the SLI was training. Hours later, when the Toronto Scottish was eating dinner, the SLI would still be training. The raw Saskatchewan farmers in the SLI didn't think much of this until their regiment had a shoot-off with the Toronto Scottish, and the SLI won handily. Then Potts was a god, as everyone realized what he'd done. The SLI, not the others, was put in the 1st Division.

Potts was the first lieutenant-colonel to be promoted to brigadier during the Second World War, though Joe said he may have been promoted because he was slated for a brigade anyhow. He soon led the Spitsbergen expedition and later remarked, "If there'd been any shots fired, I'd have got a Distinguished Service Order, not the Commander of the Order of the British Empire."[18]

General Potts was an admirer of George Pearkes, but when he took over the 2nd Brigade from Pearkes, he found that one of its COs was a dud. Courteously, he informed George, now GOC of the 1st Division, that he was going to sack the CO. "Of course, damn good idea," Pearkes said. But why, Potts wondered, hadn't Pearkes done it beforehand?

Defending the West Coast

Because of the threat to the West Coast, or so Joe said, Potts was sent back to Canada as a major-general to take over the new 6th Division, and Hardy Ganong took the 8th, both serving under Pearkes, who commanded on the West Coast.[19] Potts liked Ganong and thought highly of him – and his division.

Joe, who was on a university/army course at the University of British Columbia, saw his father quite a bit into 1943. After a visit by Field Marshal Sir John Dill from Washington, Joe, Potts, his mother, and Ganong went out to dinner – after first rolling dice to see who'd pay for the meal. Mrs. Potts lost and handed Joe a twenty-dollar bill, with which he paid. He remembered the waiter looking in disbelief while a private, seated with two generals,

....

18   In August 1941, the 2nd Brigade, commanded by Brigadier Potts, landed in Spitsbergen, a Norwegian archipelago, to destroy its facilities and coal stocks and to remove civilians. The operation was completed successfully. See Stacey, *Six Years of War*, 301-7.

19   See the different account in Granatstein, *The Generals*, 30-31.

paid the tab. Later, after D-Day, when General Potts was at Military District No. 2 in Toronto, Joe tried to get taken off an Officer Cadet Training Unit draft to Brockville so he could go overseas. His CO said, "If you think I'm going to do this with your father, a general, less than sixty miles away –." Joe had to get his father to sign a note saying it was OK.

The conscripts

Joe went overseas in early 1945 with the first conscript drafts. He liked the home defence conscripts and thought they were good soldiers. So did his father, who sympathized with them in their refusal to volunteer so that the government wouldn't have to impose conscription for overseas service. At one parade that General Potts attended, a Victoria Cross–winning CO asked the men why they hadn't volunteered, and a private stepped forward and said, "Why should we make up the government's mind?" Essentially, Potts came to the conclusion that voluntarism was unfair and that conscription was the way to go. He believed his 6th Division had been as good as any other division in the army, the large home defence conscripts component notwithstanding. Thus, when McNaughton became Defence Minister in November 1944, he felt betrayed by Andy's call for new efforts to convert home defence conscripts to general service. Ottawa had already squeezed out the maximum possible number on that front. Especially, he was furious at McNaughton's comments after meeting the District Officers Commanding in November 1944 that the infantry reinforcement crisis could be resolved, and he fired off letters and telegrams to Ottawa.[20] The friendship with McNaughton did not resume.

Joe said that the only time his father used influence for the family was when he and his two brothers wanted to get into the Pacific Force. The orders assigning them all (a major, a lieutenant, and a private) were duly issued.

On his own experience, Joe said that the reinforcement shortage was not apparent in March 1945 in the SLI or the Loyal Edmontons, to which he was attached. What did show, however, was wobbly training – gun crews that couldn't clean their machine guns and drivers who couldn't operate a Bren carrier. He also added that, although as the son of a general officer he ought

....

20   See ibid., Chaps. 3 and 8; and Granatstein and Hitsman, *Broken Promises*, Chap. 6.

to have been more attuned to this than most, it made little difference who the division or brigade commander was.

MRS. BETTY SPRY (1915-2005)

INTERVIEWS | OTTAWA, 21 JANUARY AND 18 MARCH 1992

Mrs. Spry was the wife of Major-General Daniel Spry, who served in England, Italy, and, as commander of the 3rd Division, in Northwest Europe.

Mrs. Spry began the interview by describing her husband's career.

Spry served in the PF with the Royal Canadian Regiment and was in England with the regiment. He attended Staff College and was Personal Assistant to Andy McNaughton. Then he was in Italy as a battalion and brigade commander, and in Northwest Europe as GOC of the 3rd Division and as commander of the Canadian Reinforcement Unit in England.

The PF and the war

Mrs. Spry met her husband when she was fifteen, while they were both students at Halifax Academy. They'd stayed in touch throughout the next decade, during which she worked on the social page of the *Halifax Chronicle*. Spry had attended Dalhousie University and, wanting to be a journalist, was editor of the university paper. She said that he'd criticized the president and been forced to leave Dalhousie.

As a result, he'd gone into the army – jobs were scarce during the Depression. He and Betty got married in 1939, Spry with a black eye from a mess party. His father, a PF officer who had retired as a major-general in the mid-1930s, was not pleased, thinking that marriage would hurt Spry's career. He sent only a curt telegram: "Best wishes, D.C.B. Spry." At twenty-six, Spry was too young to get the army's marriage allowance. When the war came, Betty accompanied him on the train to Valcartier, and after he went overseas in December 1939, she followed on the first available boat.

The Staff College course

She thought his time at Staff College in the United Kingdom was very difficult. He came first in his class, but he'd never worked so hard in his life.

She'd met General Montgomery somewhere, and he'd told her to accompany her husband to the course. There'd been suicides, he said, the pressure being so high. At the end of the course, Spry didn't get a posting in his mailbox like everyone else. Then a car came for him, took him to London, and he didn't come back. He was on Mountbatten's staff for a time.

On the McNaughtons

Spry was a great admirer of General McNaughton, though Andy was a hard case: "He didn't give anything of himself away." Mrs. McNaughton was a great lady. She once asked Betty how she liked the army, and Betty blurted out that it was fine – except for the senior officers' wives. Ever after, Mrs. McNaughton would jokingly say that Spry got on despite his wife. Betty added that, though Mrs. McNaughton was a strong Catholic and the kids were so raised, Andy was an atheist. The McNaughtons were very good to her in Britain. She had her first child in England, and at the baby's christening, McNaughton had to inform her that her husband was en route to Italy.

She also remembered that when her husband was stationed in the United Kingdom (probably as Personal Assistant to McNaughton), the body of a blonde woman was found under their bed in their flat. She'd belonged to the Polish underground (the Poles had their headquarters around the corner), and someone had waited until both Sprys were out to plant the corpse. Scotland Yard investigated, but it remained a mystery. Betty said that Spry embellished this tale quite shamelessly in subsequent retellings.

The war and the postwar riots

Spry never talked much of the war, except funny events. But she remembered he'd wake up with nightmares.

In the summer of 1945, impatient at the delays in shipping them home, Canadian soldiers rioted in the town of Aldershot, England. Spry was in command of the Canadian Reinforcement Unit at Aldershot. Curiously, his father as a lieutenant-colonel in 1919 had had to deal with the Great War riots by Canadian soldiers. Her husband insisted on driving his jeep into the rioting mob. She feared for his life and was more frightened than at any time during the war. It was the "longest night of the war," she said.

The Sprys came back to Canada in 1946 on the *Queen Mary*. His posting was as Vice Chief of the General Staff in Ottawa, but they were met at the pier by Jackson Dodds, the General Manager of the Bank of Montreal, who was powerful in the Boy Scouts of Canada, and he "just badgered" Spry into agreeing to take on the job of Canadian head of the Scouts.

Spry's brother, Graham Spry, was a major player in the agitation for a public broadcasting system in Canada during the 1930s and was later British Cabinet Minister Sir Stafford Cripps's wartime aide in the United Kingdom. Graham and her husband weren't close; nor was her husband really all that close to his father.

She spoke briefly about General H.F.H. Hertzberg. She knew him when he was District Officer Commanding in Halifax, liked him, and thought he was charming with the ladies but could be very stiff with men. His two daughters were hellions who swore like troopers.

MALCOLM (1917-99) AND ATHOLL SUTHERLAND-BROWN (1923-2006)
INTERVIEW | VICTORIA, BC, 27 FEBRUARY 1992

*Malcolm and Atholl were the sons of Brigadier-General James "Buster"
Sutherland-Brown, who was Director of Military Operations and Planning
at National Defence HQ during the 1920s.*[21] *He retired from the PF in the
mid-1930s. A third son was killed while serving in the RCAF. Malcolm was
a lieutenant-colonel in the Royal Canadian Engineers overseas and Atholl
was in the RCAF.*

*The two Sutherland-Browns began by speaking of their father's relations
with General Andrew McNaughton.*

The relationship with Andy McNaughton was difficult, though not at first. Andy was on the Imperial Defence College course, and Buster Sutherland-Brown was next in line to take the course, with a bit of an overlap. Their wives were staunch friends then.

But Andy and Buster fell out during the Depression, when unemployed men were housed in government work camps, treated like prisoners of war, and paid twenty cents a day. As District Officer Commanding in British Columbia, Sutherland-Brown had to cope with the bulk of this problem.

....

21   "Sutherland-Brown" originally lacked the hyphen, but Buster added it, and his sons
consistently referred to themselves as the Sutherland-Browns.

Hoping to improve conditions in the camps, he made ten recommendations to McNaughton, but nothing was done. In desperation, he wired "either accept recommendations or resignation." Ottawa did both, eventually implementing some eight of his ten suggestions. Buster retired from the army in 1936, and the dispute made him physically ill, aggravating his rheumatic fever from the Great War. Nonetheless, when Malcolm went to RMC in 1934, Buster told him "any feud in one generation shouldn't be carried on to the next." When Major-General B.W. "Sam" Browne was made Adjutant General in 1940, he told Buster, "It's you who should have got this job."

There was a moment of poetic justice in September 1939, when Malcolm was a Royal Canadian Engineers (RCE) officer in Calgary under George Pearkes. Although NDHQ hadn't approved funds for the construction of some huts, Pearkes got the project under way regardless, and when McNaughton came out to build up the 1st Division, he said to Pearkes, "Great, who's done it?" Pearkes pointed to his chief engineer, who in turn pointed to Malcolm. It made no difference to McNaughton that he was the son of Sutherland-Brown, and Mabel McNaughton had him to tea in the United Kingdom.

Malcolm and Atholl thought McNaughton had no talent for dealing with people and that Mabel kept him on the straight-and-narrow. He was very political, however, and definitely kept Buster out of the war after 1939.

The PF

As District Officer Commanding, Sutherland-Brown lived in quarters at Work Point, Esquimalt, in a house that held four officer families and the officers' mess. Built in 1898, it had tennis courts, a pool, and a great view, and there were always horses to exercise for the PF soldiers. Malcolm and Atholl had a nanny, and the family entertained a lot and spent all of Buster's pay. When he resigned, there was no pension until he turned sixty-five – indeed, he had to keep paying into it – and things were tight.

Buster was very pro-Militia, unlike McNaughton, who didn't believe in it. When he resigned, there was a big move to have a mass resignation, but Buster squelched this. Price Montague was a friend, as he and Buster had been administrative officers of Great War divisions.

Buster drafted Defence Plan No. 1 in the 1920s, which called for an invasion of the United States in the event of a British-American war. Although he came from a United Empire Loyalist background and had a dark view of the United States, he had no special commitment to the plan – it was just a job he'd been given to do. Indeed, the brothers recollected their father giving a talk praising the United States. However, on trips to visit friends in America, he continued to collect data!

Buster ran provincially and federally for the Tories. Malcolm remembered General E.J.C. Schmidlin, the Quartermaster General, visiting and saying to Buster, "You can't say those things about the Prime Minister."

"But they're true," retorted Buster.

"You still can't say them."

Schmidlin would have been smoking a cigarette all the way to the end, without knocking off the ash. And after 1939, he determined that every Royal Canadian Engineer Field Company must have at least one PF officer. The wealth of military engineering talent had to be spread.

Malcolm Sutherland-Brown's RCE career

Malcolm was Acting Chief Engineer in the 2nd Division, and he knew that Buster had recruited Charles Foulkes, commanding the division, into the Royal Canadian Regiment. He wasn't a bad GOC, Malcolm said, and in late 1944-45 in the Netherlands against an enemy that was on its last legs, a corps commander couldn't be bad.

Guy Simonds was an inhumane man whose first wife had a family connection to Buster. He was Malcolm's company commander at RMC and was very strict – no cadet ever went to him with a problem, and cadets saw George Pearkes as more of a comer than Simonds. They had to be sent to call on him; no one would go by choice. In Normandy, he used a Staghound armoured car to visit units, and there'd be trouble if anyone blocked his way. Malcolm recalled being given a direct order to discipline a sergeant who'd been mine-clearing on the road verges and had interfered with Simonds's progress.

Malcolm confirmed the story that C.S.L. Hertzberg refused his smallpox vaccination and subsequently died of the disease in India. But he spoke highly of Hertzberg, Chief Engineer of the Canadian Corps, as a good officer, saying he did great things in India. Brigadier J.L. Melville, Hertzberg's successor as Chief Engineer of the First Canadian Army, had been Liberal Cabinet Minister Chubby Power's right-hand man.

General Howard Kennedy, the Quartermaster General, was a forestry consultant. He was very capable and took advice. He was more human than

C.S.L. Hertzberg, who was distant (and really an architect) but who leaned on his staff a great deal.

W.F.R. STEIN (1929-2014)

INTERVIEW | NANAIMO, BC, 1 MARCH 1992

He was the son of Major-General C.R.S. Stein, who briefly commanded the 5th Canadian Armoured Division (January to October 1943) and was relieved on health grounds. General Stein led civil defence planning in British Columbia after the war.
Stein spoke of his father.

General Stein's father was the first chartered accountant in Vancouver and fairly prominent, though he didn't have much money. Stein went to RMC and left after a year in 1915, with a Special War Certificate. Classmate friends included Nick McCarter, Brigadier General Staff to E.L.M. Burns at the I Canadian Corps in Italy. Stein was commissioned in the Royal Canadian Engineers and served in France only in 1918. He rarely talked about the war.

The son claimed that he didn't know why Stein stayed in the PF. Nor did he know anything about his own mother, Stein's first wife, not even if they divorced or she died. Stein was a private man, who rarely talked to his son. He remarried in 1938 to Frances Stuart Ross, of the Quebec City Rosses, whom he probably met at an RMC ball. There was some money in the Ross family, and the marriage was a success. The son was largely raised by his grandmother, though when Stein went to Staff College in Quetta in 1929-31, he went with him.

He knew nothing about his father's war career, except that he was medically discharged.[22] But General Stein wanted to see action too, and his photo books suggested some pride in the 5th Armoured Division. A newspaper clipping noted that he had been posted to a British armoured division in 1941 to learn how to handle tanks.

General Stein was not a reader, but he kept up with current events, and though he drank, his son never saw him drunk. He was relatively athletic,

....

22   See Granatstein, *The Generals*, 192.

playing golf and boating. After the war, he worked for the United Nations Relief and Rehabilitation Administration in Poland, and in 1951, he joined the civil defence organization as BC co-ordinator.

COLONEL MALCOLM TURNER (1920-2002)
INTERVIEW | CHESTER, NS, 10 OCTOBER 1990

Colonel Turner was the son of Major-General Guy R. Turner, Deputy Adjutant and Quartermaster General to General McNaughton. Turner began by speaking of his father's early career.

Farmers of Scottish descent, Turner's family arrived in New Brunswick in 1784 via the United States, though they were not Loyalists, and settled at Aroostock Junction. Turner's parents were far from prosperous, though three of their four sons did very well – one a mayor, one a Bank of Montreal vice president, and the other, Guy, a general. The fourth son stayed home during the Great War to look after the widowed mother and to keep the family potato farm in operation. He also worked on the railway and died in a train crash during the 1920s. Turner's father died of typhoid when he himself was young; indeed, he had the disease at the same time. Turner went to Normal School and took some extramural courses at the University of New Brunswick but had no degree. He served in the Militia and joined up in the first contingent in 1914. He served with great distinction in the Canadian Engineers, winning a Distinguished Conduct Medal and two Military Crosses. He was commissioned in the field and wounded a couple of times. He married his prewar sweetheart, who was from Saint John and slightly better off, of United Empire Loyalist descent, and quite pretty to judge by photos taken in Britain in 1916. Malcolm was born in 1920. Turner, he said, qualified as an engineer on the basis of his military experience.

The Permanent Force
After the Great War, Turner left the army to work for the Department of Soldiers Civil Re-establishment, but the PF wanted him, so he joined as a captain. He had no private income and helped support his mother financially. Money was tight when he was in the PF, so much so that at one point he had to borrow against his insurance policy to send his family by train to New Brunswick for the summer. The family lived in married quarters in Winnipeg

or in rented accommodation and never had a car but did have a maid. He wasn't a drinker; the social life was cards, bridge, and mahjong for the wives; in Ottawa, social life was more impressive and would include Government House receptions. He had lots of military friends – in the PF, everyone knew everyone else. He liked the life and so did his wife.

He was selected for Staff College at Quetta in 1925 and stood first in the class in the two-year course. His wife couldn't join him during his first year – either army money problems or a Quetta rule prevented her – but she came out for the second year, and Malcolm had photos of ponies and birthdays there.

Turner was a hard, strict man, but fair. He had been a sportsman, and he played ball with his son and took him to games. He didn't want Malcolm to go to RMC – he preferred that he become a doctor – but he didn't stand in his way.

His favourites in the army were Andy McNaughton, who walked on water, and Georges Vanier, who was brave – unlike most French Canadians, who, Turner believed, were beyond the pale. Mrs. Turner was very friendly with Mrs. McNaughton. Turner didn't bring his wife to Britain in 1939, unlike Harry Crerar, McNaughton, and R.M. Luton, who brought their wives. He thought wives should be at home and also believed he shouldn't do what privates couldn't. Malcolm thought Turner was hurt that he didn't get a fighting command. General Percy Hobart, who commanded the 79th British Division, was a classmate at Quetta and of roughly the same age. Still, it was a young man's war.

Malcolm's war

Malcolm was born in 1920 and went to RMC in 1937; he graduated early after the war started. His wife was the daughter of a Signals officer who commanded at Camp Borden during the 1930s. He met her in 1940 and married her in 1946, but he didn't think most PF kids married other PF kids. Malcolm served in the Royal Canadian Engineers overseas and ended as a major, commanding the 3rd Field Squadron in 1945. He stayed in the army after the war and retired as a colonel. Guy Simonds had been the artillery staff officer and a company commander at RMC. Even then, he was seen as a comer, an exceptional staff officer, fair but firm. **Geoffrey Walsh** in the RCE was also at RMC on staff, and Malcolm had high regard for him. He was a bully, but if you stood up to him, there were no difficulties. Malcolm liked Chris Vokes, who was his brigade commander in 1942. Vokes had been at the Turners' house before the war.

On RMC

The RMC connection, he thought, didn't mean much at the junior ranks or in the United Kingdom. Indeed, it might even have hurt him, as did the fact that his dad was a general. Many people with whom he served weren't even aware that he'd gone to RMC, and he tended to think that all it gave you was a few months' head start. The civilian engineers learned the trade fast. Moreover, RMC grads could be found wanting and returned to Canada too.

Senior officers

Victor Odlum was "at the end of the line." F.F. Worthington had probably been first class at one point but was "too long in the tooth" by the war. Malcolm used to go out with E.W. Sansom's daughter Charmian. Bud Stein, pronounced "Steen," was staff adjutant at RMC when Malcolm was there.

MAJOR FRED VOKES (1932-)

INTERVIEW | OTTAWA, 24 SEPTEMBER 1991

> *He is the son of Major-General Christopher Vokes.*
> *We began by talking of his father.*

Fred was born in 1932; his brother Michael was born postwar. Their father was overseas from the beginning of the war until 1946 and never came home during this period.

As a father, Vokes was difficult. He didn't talk, just gave opinions or stated facts. He would "try you on" and could be a bully. Fred never had a conversation with him. Indeed, he basically grew up without a father, and after the war he was in boarding school. He decided to join the army, but his grades weren't good enough for him to attend RMC, as Vokes had wanted. His father repeatedly interfered: he chose Fred's corps (infantry, not armour) and then pushed him into the Canadian Guards from the Princess Patricia's Canadian Light Infantry. Fred had wanted the tanks – he wanted to be like his uncle, killed in Italy, not his father.

Postwar, Chris Vokes's life was not good. He'd done everything he was going to by 1945. He'd peaked. His wife was Constance Waugh from Winnipeg, where they met. Her father was in insurance and prominent, but the economic crash hurt the family. She wanted stability, so he stayed in the army. She died in 1969.

Vokes knew he wouldn't be Chief of the General Staff, disliked "Benzedrine Charlie Foulkes," and regretted that he hadn't gotten out of the service. But he never talked of this.

Vokes was very Irish, born in Armagh, and soft as mush and emotional. He didn't take Canadian citizenship until long after the war, when he was hassled at the American border. He was loyal to the empire, the Crown, and Canada. He once said, "One day, and it will be a great pity, Canada will become the 49th state."

He was keen on RMC, proud of his time there. He went to reunions and had friends in his class. He said, "In times of war you can always buy an engineer, but you can't buy a soldier."

He was not well off after retirement in 1959. He lived on the principle that in the PF you struggled on the pittance you got, and he didn't do well until the indexing of pensions. He had arthritis badly and suffered.

Vokes's friends

Vokes and General **Geoffrey Walsh** were friends, but Mrs. Vokes disliked Walsh. When Vokes retired as General Officer Commanding Western Command, Walsh was to take over. Though there were business opportunities out west, they moved to Oakville, Ontario, where the contacts he'd made when he was GOC Central Command were long gone.

Vokes had dogs, and he liked to fish and shoot. He never moaned, not even about his brother who was killed in Italy. He didn't get maudlin about casualties either.

His friends were Guy Simonds, Howard Graham, M.H.S. Penhale, who was "pear-shaped," **H.A. Sparling**, and **Des Smith** – in other words, the Italy officers.

HARVIE WALFORD

INTERVIEW | MONTREAL, 4 MAY 1992

He is the son of Major-General A.E. Walford, one of the key wartime army administrators as Deputy Adjutant and Quartermaster General of the First Canadian Army and Adjutant General in Ottawa.

The interview opened with Harvie describing General Walford's early career.

Like his father, A.E. Walford was a chartered accountant. The family came from Bristol, England, were Baptists, and were comfortable, but hardly wealthy. Walford was a keen Boy Scout (and believed a nation had to be prepared), a believer in Crown and empire and duty. His father cried when he went overseas in the Great War and said he didn't want him to go, but that if he hadn't gone, he'd have disowned him. His whole high school class joined up in 1916, and he won the Military Medal with Cape's Battery (3rd Battery, Canadian Siege Artillery), a unit created by a Montreal businessman. He took a commission in 1918, returned in 1919, and married in 1922. His wife was a schoolteacher from a humble background and was socially ambitious for him.

On the war

In 1939, by which time Walford was a Militia lieutenant-colonel, Andy McNaughton called him and asked him to handle "administrative" matters in the 1st Division. McNaughton chose him because of his business background and because he knew him from the Great War and afterward. When Walford went overseas in December 1939, it was a sad day for his wife and son. And when he came back in 1944 (on Defence Minister Ralston's bomber) to become Adjutant General at NDHQ, Ralston said he needed him in Ottawa right away. Mrs. Walford said, "Oh, Minister, he's been away five years." So Ralston gave them three or four days.

On senior officers

Walford was a McNaughton admirer but thought Andy loathed being Minister of National Defence. He was used to giving orders and seeing them carried out, and things didn't work that way for politicians. Walford disagreed with McNaughton on conscription – the burden of sacrifice had to be spread fairly, Harvie recalled.

Walford was a McNaughton-style nationalist, one who didn't take any crap from British officers. He and Harry Crerar once co-operated to thwart a British officer: Walford disobeyed an order, and Crerar backed him, Harvie claimed.

Walford told Harvie that Guy Simonds was heartily disliked by the troops, but they knew he won his battles and would therefore do anything for him.

Walford was keen on promoting subordinates, even if they left for other jobs. He knew they'd be under him again, and because he hadn't blocked their departure, they would have no resentment. He was no office politician, and his wife thought he was denied lieutenant-general rank because he wasn't PF. As he apparently told Crerar, he wanted to revert in rank so that he could have a field command, something that horrified Mrs. Walford and that Crerar dismissed.

Harvie didn't know how Walford voted. He knew he'd asked Mackenzie King in 1944 for guarantees that as Adjutant General he wouldn't be asked to do things for political reasons. The Prime Minister agreed to this condition and honoured his promise too, Harvie remembered.

Postwar
Walford was full of fun, didn't smoke, and was a social drinker. After the war, he was Honorary ADC to the Governor-General, Field Marshal Viscount Alexander, and he was high up in Henry Morgan's, the Montreal department store. He went to A.G.M. Cape, and later to Canadian Vickers. A prudent investor, he lived well in Westmount. When he died, his coffin was draped with a Canadian flag that he'd bought for the purpose, and his officer's cap and a Boy Scout hat were placed on top of it.

PETER WORTHINGTON (1927-2013)
INTERVIEW | TORONTO, 28 MARCH 1991

A well-known journalist, columnist, and Korean War veteran,
Worthington was the son of Major-General F.F. Worthington.
He started by talking of the Permanent Force and the Second
World War.

In his PF days, Worthy was no neutral figure. He had won a Military Medal and bar as well as a Military Cross and bar in the Great War, and that worked well with all ranks, though when he was in the United Kingdom attending courses, his Military Medals demonstrated that he'd been a ranker.[23] Peter thought he might have had some difficulty with RMC types too.

He had no British accent, though he called girls "gels." Peter thought he might have been born in the United States. There were lots of Worthingtons

----

23 The Military Medal was awarded only to Other Ranks, the Military Cross to junior officers.

in Cooperstown, New York, and Worthington's father might have been a black-sheep offspring.[24]

Worthy was an early advocate of armour, and he corresponded with British military thinkers J.F.C. Fuller, B.H. Liddell Hart, and Archibald Wavell, both before and after the Second World War. A reader, he marked up books. He was an innovator, a good mechanic, and an expert at figuring out things, and was interested in learning how to instruct better. Perhaps this explained his friendship with and admiration for Andy McNaughton, who also had a scientific bent. Worthy had run relief camps for McNaughton in the 1930s. He was a McNaughton man, and Peter thought that when McNaughton was relieved as GOC-in-C in 1943, this opened the way to Worthy's being replaced at the 4th Armoured Division. He saw a Simonds (pro-British) versus McNaughton (pro-Canadian) split there and put his father on the pro-Canadian side. (Worthy supported the new Canadian flag in 1965, and a single uniform and unification of the armed forces too.) Peter did say that in the 1950s, when Simonds seemed lonely, the Worthingtons had much to do with him, and Simonds apologized for his role in getting rid of Worthy.

During the interwar years, the PF was "heaven on earth." The story was that if they happened to be short of food, a cavalry horse would break a leg. The Worthington family had maids at least up to 1938. Peter acted as batman, shining buttons for five cents. The regiment seemed to be part of the family, and everyone exhibited a kind of reverse snobbery to civilians, who lived differently and separately. Worthy had military and RCMP friends. He was not a subtle man, and if he didn't like something, you knew it.

He was always a bit of a troublemaker. The PF war games in the 1920s always ended with a cavalry charge that was designed to defeat the infantry. Worthy had his Princess Patricia's soldiers wave blankets and towels that spooked the horses. Unfair!

In the Great War, Worthy had been called "Nappy," short for Napoleon. Peter thought it was a tribute to his vision and his innovative approach. That made the claim that he had been sacked for not knowing how to command a division even more hurtful. **George Kitching**, who took over the 4th Canadian Armoured Division from Worthy in early 1944, had nothing to do with

....

24   Cf. Jarymowycz, "General Guy Simonds," in Horn and Harris, *Warrior Chiefs*, 135n34.

the sacking and wrote Worthy to apologize for taking his division away. Worthy was very fit for his age, so he certainly wouldn't have been fired for physical or mental incapacity. He was sacked by the anti-McNaughton gang, Peter claimed. In the Second World War, the RMC products and Staff College types resented the Great War vets, and this, he said, may have played a role as well. His father hadn't attended Staff College.

On senior officers

Worthington liked Harry Crerar better than Crerar's wife, Verse, who never forgave him for once coming to tea with a dirty collar. Crerar was not Worthy's cup of tea.

He didn't get on with Ken Stuart – he wouldn't badmouth him, but had no warmth toward him or E.W. Sansom.

He liked E.L.M. Burns a lot; Burns commanded one of his armoured brigades at Debert, Nova Scotia. Worthy was very upset when Burns was sacked in Italy and felt he'd been misused.

After the war, Rod Keller was very bitter and had no spark of fun left. He hated Americans for what they had done to him in the accidental August 1944 bombing in Normandy. Worthington liked Keller and hunted with him. He and Peter went to the Keller place near Kelowna, British Columbia, to hunt. After a night of drinking, Peter accidentally fired a Luger pistol shot through Mrs. Keller's fur coat and narrowly missed both Kellers. No one noticed the close call.

Worthy laughed at Chris Vokes and thought he was very crude. Worthy would curse, but he was never obscene or vulgar.

He thought of George Pearkes as a Colonel Blimp and had no respect for his mind.

Worthy's views

Worthy was a good friend of Toronto broker and socialite Harold Crang, who played a role in organizing the public campaign for tanks in 1939. Worthy loathed politicians, and unlike most PF people, he liked the Militia. As he feared another war was coming in the 1930s, he knew the Militia was necessary.

His views on empire and Crown were conventional. He had no formal religion but was devout and read the Bible. He wasn't an authoritarian at home. He was permissive with his kids, Peter said, but he did mete out summary punishments on the spot. He was demanding as an officer, though he liked innovation and radicals. When he set up his 4th Armoured Division, for example, various troublemakers were dumped on him, but they were often people who disliked orthodoxy, and, Peter recalled, they worked out well under Worthy.

MRS. CLARA "LARRY" WORTHINGTON (1902-92)

INTERVIEW | OTTAWA, 23 MAY 1991

Married to General F.F. Worthington, she wrote his biography.[25]
Mrs. Worthington began by speaking of Worthy's politics.

He hated Mackenzie King and voted Tory when King was in power; but under Prime Ministers St. Laurent and Pearson, he probably voted Liberal.

On the PF

The PF was fun for her, she remembered. Though there was never enough money, it was a happy time. Their furniture wasn't good, and they shopped for second-hand items. Only "bloated plutocrats" in the PF had any money. The pay was very low, and deductions were made for her food (forty cents a day) and for a batman (fifteen dollars a month). The Worthingtons dispensed with the batman (who also got a five-dollar tip each month) and used a maid, who was cheaper – and her wages didn't come off the army pay. At Winnipeg, where they stayed for years, there was a nursery school at Fort Osborne Barracks. There was a lot of entertaining in Winnipeg but little in Toronto when they were posted there with other junior officers. Nothing was formal unless the colonel came to dinner. They played "Murder" on Saturday nights, rode to exercise the unit's horses, played tennis, and skied. There was little drinking, except among senior officers.

The married quarters at Fort Osborne weren't bad. There was a large apartment building with about twelve suites, and the space you were given depended on the size of your family. They even had their own tennis court.

....

25   Larry Worthington, *"Worthy": A Biography of Major-General F.F. Worthington, CB, MC, MM* (Toronto: Macmillan, 1961).

Worthy ran a relief camp in the 1930s, and when a deadline pressed, he could get the men to work overtime through force of personality. He was tough but reasonable, she said, and he listened.

On senior officers

Charles Foulkes tried to be a stuffed shirt. Guy Simonds was very superior even as a cadet, and his nose always looked as if he'd smelled something unpleasant. He was a British gentleman in the colonies, never one of the crowd of young officers at Winnipeg. Worthy and Foulkes got on well as junior officers because "no one else would talk to them."

Andy McNaughton was "a darling" and so was "Mrs. Mac."

E.W. Sansom's wife was a terror who thought she was the queen and that the officers' wives were her subjects.

Major-General Ronnie Alexander was a wonderful person and a good friend of Worthy's, a great gentleman.

WILLIAM YOUNG

INTERVIEW | ANCASTER, ON, 17 DECEMBER 1991

His father was Major-General J.V. Young, the Master General of the Ordnance from 1942 to 1945. William Young also served in the artillery and as an ADC to Harry Crerar in 1942.

He spoke first about General Young's military career.

General Young attended RMC, graduating in 1911. He went overseas in 1914 with the artillery, was severely wounded, and was released in 1916. His parents died in a U-boat sinking in 1915, and he took over the family business. He was a keen supporter of the RMC Club (and sent three sons there, one of whom was killed on D-Day in the 3rd Division), but he had no Militia connections. He went to Ottawa early in the war as a civilian to work in the Master General of the Ordnance (MGO) office, and in September 1941, now a colonel, he became Deputy MGO. Promoted to brigadier in early 1942, he became MGO as a major-general in July 1942 and held that post for the rest of the war.

Young enjoyed his wartime experiences, William said, but he wasn't a very military general. Unlike most of the wartime crew, he had no Militia experience. When he came to the United Kingdom, he would keep his hands in his pockets when he saw his sons, not returning salutes. It tickled him, however, that he, who had been a Great War lieutenant, was now a general. He had been made a general primarily because Victor Sifton, his predecessor as MGO, had perversely stayed a civilian. Sifton wouldn't get forced into the army mould, but Young, an RMC ex-cadet, had no problem there.

His friends from RMC included Colin Gibson, Ken Stuart, and Ian Hendrie. The link with Stuart strengthened when William was at RMC in the late 1930s and Stuart was General Staff Officer, Grade 1. When Young came down for RMC Club business or June balls, he always stayed with the Stuarts, and the wives were friends too. William thought this helped get Young the post of MGO, and Young had no difficulty working with Stuart as Chief of the General Staff.

Young was a small-c conservative politically, but he voted for Gibson, a Liberal, and might well have contributed to his campaign. He liked Colonel Ralston, but there was no hint that he was an admirer of Mackenzie King and certainly not of his manpower policies.

William occasionally wrote home with complaints, hoping his father could do something to address them. The troops' razor blade shortage, he said, seemed to ease after one such letter. His mother also sent a parcel to Harry Crerar with maple syrup, which Crerar gave to the mess. William told the General to get it back, that it almost certainly contained whisky. It did.

William's war

William graduated from RMC in October 1939. He thought the RMC link didn't hurt him in the war, but there was jealousy in the Militia toward ex-cadets, a feeling they were cliquish and standoffish. In his artillery unit, he was the only ex-cadet, as his proficiency at drill revealed. Although the Militia officers were ahead in gunnery, it didn't take long for everyone to even up. There was also tension between PFers and Militia officers, but this too eased as time went on. A lot of the older Militia officers had been weeded out by the time fighting began.

Early in the war, he served in Britain in Stan Todd's battery – or "Stan God," as he was known. Todd was a great commander who trained his men well.

Andy McNaughton made no impact and was scarcely seen. William saw him occasionally on exercises, but that was all.

In the period before Dieppe, William became ADC to Harry Crerar (**Henri Tellier** was the other ADC). Crerar and William's father had served in the same battery during the Great War, and the connection had been kept up. Moreover, Crerar was RMC Commandant when William was there.

William liked Crerar. As the junior officer in the A Mess at Canadian Corps HQ at Wakehurst, England, he ran the mess and screwed up the books so badly that he had to be rescued by General R.M. Luton, the Deputy Director of Medical Services. Crerar was pretty popular, and Churchill Mann used to play jokes on him, though he was the only one who dared to do that. A.E. Walford was also there, friendly enough but less warm than Crerar! William's job as ADC involved getting Harry to places on time, reading the maps in the UK, where the wartime blackout was in place and all the road signs had been taken down in case the enemy invaded. Harry could be sharp in questioning and kept him on his toes.

Crerar was quite shocked at the human cost of the Dieppe raid. He was especially worried by Hamilton casualties in the Royal Hamilton Light Infantry, went to see some of them in hospital, and wrote to the parents of those he knew. There was a lot of second-guessing after Dieppe and shock over errors in planning. And in the A Mess, the feeling existed that the enemy had known the raid was coming.

Later, when William was in Italy with the 2nd Medium Regiment, Crerar was I Canadian Corps commander. He never asked William to visit. Crerar was not warmly received by the troops, quite unlike Montgomery, who got a good reception. But then, the troops received no Canadian general with enthusiasm, save perhaps Chris Vokes. Charles Foulkes, in particular, tended to get the blame for a Hastings and Prince Edward Regiment attack that was hit by friendly fire and had heavy casualties.

William said his regiment in Italy had a lot of Québécois in it. They got on very well and were as anti-Zombie as the Anglos. French Canadian infantry regiments were highly thought of, he added.

Appendices

APPENDIX 1 | List of Canadian Generals of the Second World War

This listing includes only those fifty-one officers of major-general rank or higher who are mentioned in the interviews. The ranks given are the highest held during the war, and only the most important wartime posts are noted in parentheses. Other officers mentioned in the interviews may be located in the index.

Alexander, Major-General R.O. (GOC-in-C, Pacific Command)
Anderson, Major-General T.V. (CGS)
Ashton, Lieutenant-General E.C. (Inspector-General, Central Canada)

Burns, Lieutenant-General E.L.M. (GOC, 5th Canadian Armoured Division; GOC, I Canadian Corps)

Chisholm, Major-General B. (Director General of Medical Services)
Constantine, Major-General C.F. (District Officer Commanding, Military District No. 2)
Crerar, General H.D.G. (CGS; GOC, I Canadian Corps; GOC-in-C, First Canadian Army)

Elkins, Major-General W.H.P. (GOC-in-C, Atlantic Command)

Foster, Major-General H. (GOC, 4th Canadian Armoured Division; GOC, 1st Canadian Division)
Foulkes, Lieutenant-General C. (GOC, 1st Canadian Division; GOC, I Canadian Corps; CGS)

Ganong, Major-General H.N. (GOC, 8th Canadian Division)

Hertzberg, Major-General C.S.L. (Chief Engineer, First Canadian Army)
Hertzberg, Major-General H.F.H. (Commandant, RMC)

Hoffmeister, Major-General B.M. (GOC, 5th Canadian Armoured Division)

Keefler, Major-General R.H. (GOC, 3rd Canadian Division)
Keller, Major-General R.F.L. (GOC, 3rd Canadian Division)
Kitching, Major-General G. (GOC, 4th Canadian Armoured Division)

Laflèche, Major-General L. (Military Attaché in France)
Letson, Major-General H.F.G. (Adjutant General)
Luton, Major-General R.M. (Director of Medical Services, CMHQ)

MacQueen, Major-General J.V. (Master General of the Ordnance)
Matthews, Major-General A.B. (GOC, 2nd Canadian Division)
Matthews, Major-General H.H. (Adjutant General)
McNaughton, General A.G.L. (GOC, 1st Canadian Division; GOC, Canadian Corps; GOC-in-C, First Canadian Army; Minister of National Defence)
Montague, Lieutenant-General P.J. (Chief of Staff, CMHQ)
Murchie, Lieutenant-General J.C. (CGS)

Odlum, Major-General V.W. (GOC, 2nd Canadian Division)

Page, Major-General L.F. (GOC, 4th Canadian Armoured Division)
Panet, Major-General E. de B. (District Officer Commanding, Military District No. 4)
Pearkes, Major-General G. (GOC, 1st Canadian Division; GOC-in-C, Pacific Command)
Pope, Lieutenant-General M.A. (Military Assistant to the Prime Minister)
Potts, Major-General A.E. (GOC, 6th Canadian Division)
Price, Major-General C.B. (GOC, 3rd Canadian Division)

Renaud, Major-General E.J. (District Officer Commanding, Military District No. 4)
Roberts, Major-General J.H. (GOC, 2nd Canadian Division)

Salmon, Major-General H.L.N. (GOC, 1st Canadian Division)
Sansom, Lieutenant-General E.W. (GOC, II Canadian Corps)
Schmidlin, Major-General E.J.C. (Quartermaster General)
Simonds, Lieutenant-General G.G. (GOC, 1st Canadian Division; GOC, II Canadian Corps; Acting GOC-in-C, First Canadian Army)

Spry, Major-General D.C. (GOC, 3rd Canadian Division)
Stein, Major-General C.R.S. (GOC, 5th Canadian Armoured Division)
Stuart, Lieutenant-General K. (CGS; Acting GOC-in-C, First Canadian
    Army; Chief of Staff, CMHQ)

Tremblay, Major-General T.L. (Inspector-General, Eastern Canada)
Turner, Major-General G.R. (Deputy Adjutant and Quartermaster
    General, First Canadian Army)

Vanier, Major-General G.P. (District Officer Commanding, Military
    District No. 5)
Vokes, Major-General C. (GOC, 1st Canadian Division; GOC, 4th
    Canadian Armoured Division; GOC, Canadian Army Occupation Force)

Walford, Major-General A.E. (Deputy Adjutant and Quartermaster
    General, First Canadian Army; Adjutant General)
Weeks, Major-General E.G. (Major-General in charge of Administration,
    CMHQ)
Worthington, Major-General F.F. (GOC, 4th Canadian Armoured
    Division)

Young, Major-General H.A. (Quartermaster General)
Young, Major-General J.V. (Master General of the Ordnance)

APPENDIX 2 | Table of Army Ranks and Responsibilities

Officers   2nd Lieutenant
                   Lieutenant
                   Captain
                   Major
                   Lieutenant-Colonel
                   Colonel
                   Brigadier
                   Major-General
                   Lieutenant-General
                   General
                   Field Marshal

Other Ranks	Private/Gunner/Sapper/Trooper
	Lance Corporal
	Corporal
	Sergeant
	Quartermaster Sergeant
	Company/Battery/Squadron Sergeant Major
	Regimental Sergeant Major

A 2nd Lieutenant or Lieutenant ordinarily commanded an infantry platoon or armoured troop of some 30 men.

A Captain was usually a company/squadron commander or battalion/regiment adjutant.

A Major usually commanded a company/squadron of four platoons/troops or 120 or so men or was a battalion/regiment second-in-command.

A Lieutenant-Colonel commanded a battalion/regiment of some 700 to 900 men.

A Colonel was usually a senior staff officer.

Brigadiers commanded brigades of three battalions/regiments (roughly 3,000 to 4,000 men).

Major-Generals usually commanded divisions of three brigades plus supporting arms and services (approximately 17,500 to 21,000 men) or held senior posts in Ottawa or London.

Lieutenant-Generals commanded a corps of two or more divisions.

Generals commanded an army of two or more corps.

Field Marshals commanded two or more armies in an Army Group.

A Corporal or Lance Corporal usually led a section of up to ten men.

A Sergeant was usually second-in-command of a platoon/troop.

A Sergeant Major (Warrant Officer Class II) was responsible for discipline in a company or squadron.

A Regimental Sergeant Major (Warrant Officer Class I) was responsible for discipline in a battalion or regiment.

Selected Readings

CANADA'S SECOND WORLD WAR generals did not produce much by way of autobiography. Only Lieutenant-General E.L.M. Burns of the corps commanders published a memoir, *General Mud: Memoirs of Two World Wars* (Toronto: Clarke Irwin, 1970), which is focused on the Italian campaign. Burns also wrote *Manpower in the Canadian Army* (Toronto: Clarke Irwin, 1956). Guy Simonds drafted a memoir covering his life to 1939, but this manuscript, held by his son, has not been published in print. Christopher Vokes's *Vokes: My Story* (Ottawa: Gallery Books, 1985) is a tape-recorded, badly edited memoir that is not very helpful in assessing Vokes's competence. General Maurice Pope, whose war was spent primarily in Ottawa and Washington, wrote *Soldiers and Politicians: The Memoirs of Lt.-Gen. Maurice A. Pope, C.B., M.C.* (Toronto: University of Toronto Press, 1962), which is careful, precise, and occasionally very frank. George Kitching's *Mud and Green Fields: The Memoirs of General George Kitching* (Langley, BC: Battleline Books, 1986) leaves out too much, but Howard Graham's *Citizen and Soldier: The Memoirs of Lieutenant-General Howard Graham* (Toronto: McClelland and Stewart, 1983), again focused on Italy, is better. Only one wartime francophone brigadier wrote his story: *Mémoires du Général Jean V. Allard* (Boucherville, QC: Mortagne, 1985). The sole remaining autobiography by a senior officer, Brigadier J.A. Roberts's *The Canadian Summer* (Toronto: University of Toronto Press, 1981), is excellent in telling the story of an ice cream maker's rise from Militia lieutenant to a first-rate brigade commander.

There is much more luck in finding biographies. General McNaughton is the subject of John Swettenham's three-volume *McNaughton* (Toronto: Ryerson, 1968-69) and of John Rickard's *The Politics of Command: Lieutenant-General A.G.L. McNaughton and the Canadian Army, 1939-1943* (Toronto: University of Toronto Press, 2010). Paul Dickson's study of Harry Crerar, *A Thoroughly Canadian General* (Toronto: University of Toronto Press, 2007), is very competent and inclusive, which cannot be said of Peter V. Crerar's

My Father, the General (N.p.: privately printed, 2001). There is a very good chapter on Crerar in John A. English's *Patton's Peers: The Forgotten Allied Field Army Commanders of the Western Front, 1944-45* (Mechanicsburg, PA: Stackpole, 2009).

Dominick Graham's *The Price of Command: A Biography of General Guy Simonds* (Toronto: Stoddart, 1993) is good on Simonds's campaigns but suffers from a lack of broad archival research. It can usefully be supplemented by the documents, memoranda, and addresses collected in Terry Copp, *Guy Simonds and the Art of Command* (Kingston: Canadian Defence Academy, 2007). There is unfortunately no biography of General Charles Foulkes, though Douglas Delaney ably examines Foulkes, Burns, and Simonds in his *Corps Commanders: Five British and Canadian Generals at War, 1939-45* (Vancouver: UBC Press, 2011). There are essays on McNaughton, Crerar, Burns, and Simonds in B. Horn and S. Harris, eds., *Warrior Chiefs: Perspectives on Senior Canadian Military Leaders* (Toronto: Dundurn, 2001). The best biography of a general officer is Douglas Delaney's *The Soldiers' General: Bert Hoffmeister at War* (Vancouver: UBC Press, 2005). Reginald H. Roy wrote *For Most Conspicuous Bravery: A Biography of Major-General George R. Pearkes, V.C., through Two World Wars* (Vancouver: UBC Press, 1977), a thorough but largely uncritical life of George Pearkes.

There are many memoirs by officers and soldiers. No such listing can omit George Blackburn's three volumes: *Where the Hell Are the Guns?; The Guns of Normandy;* and *The Guns of Victory* (Toronto: McClelland and Stewart, 1995-97), which are a superb account of an artillery Forward Observation Officer's war, nor Donald Pearce's *Journal of a War* (Toronto: Macmillan, 1965), one junior officer's fine account. I also found good material in Charly Forbes, *Fantassin* (Quebec City: Septentrion, 1994); Donald Tansley, *Growing Up and Going to War, 1925-1945* (Waterloo: Laurier Centre for Military Strategic and Disarmament Studies, 2005); Charles Martin, *Battle Diary* (Toronto: Dundurn, 1994); and Gerald Levenston, *My Darling Mom* (ebook, Vancouver: n.p., 2012), a little-known but very useful collection of letters home by a staff officer at the II Canadian Corps. There is also much excellent material including letters, memoirs, and battle studies in the pages of the journal *Canadian Military History,* most especially the run of excellent letters by Captain Hal MacDonald of the North Shore Regiment that stretches over several issues from 2002 to 2006 and covers all the war years.

I have made use here of several of the books I wrote on Canada and the Second World War in shaping how I viewed the successes and failures of the Canadian Army's senior officers. Most notably, I relied on *Broken Promises: A History of Conscription in Canada* (Toronto: Oxford University Press, 1977; Oakville, ON: Rock's Mills Press, 2015), co-authored with J.M. Hitsman; *Canada's War: The Politics of the Mackenzie King Government, 1939-45* (Toronto: Oxford University Press, 1990; Oakville, ON: Rock's Mills Press, 2015); *Canada's Army: Waging War and Keeping the Peace* (Toronto: University of Toronto Press, 2002); *The Best Little Army in the World: The Canadians in Northwest Europe, 1944-1945* (Toronto: HarperCollins, 2015); and, with Dean Oliver, *The Oxford Companion to Canadian Military History* (Toronto: Oxford University Press, 2010). *The Oxford Companion* has substantial entries on military biography and autobiography that should be read in conjunction with *The Weight of Command*. I also took advantage of the material that Norman Hillmer and I collected for two books of documents: *First Drafts: Eyewitness Accounts from Canada's Past* (Toronto: Thomas Allen, 2002); and *Battle Lines: Eyewitness Accounts from Canada's Military History* (Toronto: Thomas Allen, 2004). Peter Neary and I edited another collection, *The Good Fight: Canadians and World War II* (Toronto: Copp Clark, 1995).

The basic texts on the army at war remain the official histories by Charles Stacey: *Six Years of War* (Ottawa: Queen's Printer, 1955); *The Victory Campaign* (Ottawa: Queen's Printer, 1960); and *Arms, Men and Governments* (Ottawa: Queen's Printer, 1970). *The Canadians in Italy, 1943-1945* (Ottawa: Queen's Printer, 1957), by Stacey's colleague G.W.L. Nicholson, is a useful discussion. These are fine pieces of work, with excellent maps and notes, among the best official histories by any of the combatant nations. So too are the official Canadian navy and air force histories.

There are scores of regimental histories, far too many to list. David Bercuson's history of the PPCLI, *The Patricias* (Fredericton: Goose Lane, 2013), is valuable, and his *Battalion of Heroes* (Calgary: Calgary Highlanders, 1994) is very frank on the successes and failures of the Calgary Highlanders; so too is Gordon Brown and Terry Copp, *Look to Your Front* (Waterloo: Laurier Centre for Military Strategic and Disarmament Studies, 2001), on the Regina Rifles.

If I cannot cite all such histories, neither can I detail all the excellent campaign studies. Terry Copp's books, based on detailed research into war diaries and close study of the ground, include *The Brigade: The Fifth Canadian Infantry Brigade in World War II* (Mechanicsburg, PA: Stackpole, 2007); *Fields of Fire: The Canadians in Normandy* (Toronto: University of Toronto Press, 2003); *Cinderella Army: The Canadians in Northwest Europe, 1944-1945*

(Toronto: University of Toronto Press, 2003); and, with Bill McAndrew, *Battle Exhaustion: Soldiers and Psychiatrists in the Canadian Army, 1939-1945* (Montreal and Kingston: McGill-Queen's University Press, 1990). Copp has changed the way in which the Canadian soldier's war in Northwest Europe is viewed (and his *Fields of Fire* has an extensive bibliography that is especially good on regimental histories). Marc Milner's *Stopping the Panzers: The Untold Story of D-Day* (Lawrence: University Press of Kansas, 2014) is also very challenging, most valuable, and based on sound documentation and study of the terrain. It is by far the most revisionist account of the Canadian role in the D-Day landings. Also very helpful are the essays in Geoffrey Hayes, Mike Bechthold, and Matt Symes, eds., *Canada and the Second World War: Essays in Honour of Terry Copp* (Waterloo: Wilfrid Laurier University Press, 2012).

Just as important as these studies is the very critical work by Lieutenant-Colonel John A. English, *The Canadian Army and the Normandy Campaign: A Study of Failure in High Command* (Westport, CT: Praeger, 1991). English also wrote *Surrender Invites Death: Fighting the Waffen SS in Normandy* (Mechanicsburg, PA: Stackpole, 2011). Another fine book, the very model of a battle study (not least for its superb graphics), is Brian Reid's *No Holding Back: Operation Totalize, Normandy, August 1944* (Toronto: Robin Brass Studio, 2005). There are four excellent volumes by Denis Whitaker and Shelagh Whitaker on Dieppe (1992), Normandy (2000), the Scheldt (1984), and the Rhineland (1989). Whitaker, as a captain at Dieppe and later as CO of the Royal Hamilton Light Infantry in 1944-45, offers his unique perspective.

There are many more books on Dieppe, including David O'Keefe's uni-dimensional *One Day in August* (Toronto: Knopf, 2013); and Robin Neillands, *The Dieppe Raid* (Bloomington: Indiana University Press, 2005). On Hong Kong, two little-known volumes add much: H.B. McInnis, *Letters to Harvelyn* (Toronto: HarperCollins, 2002); and L.B. Corrigan, *A Hong Kong Diary Revisited* (Baltimore, ON: Frei Press, 2008). On the control of information, the best study is Timothy Balzer, *The Information Front* (Vancouver: UBC Press, 2011), which is much superior to Mark Bourrie's *The Fog of War* (Vancouver: Douglas and McIntyre, 2011). David Halton's excellent biography of his father, CBC war correspondent Matthew Halton, *Dispatches from the Front* (Toronto: McClelland and Stewart, 2014), is most helpful. On the wartime homefront, Jeffrey Keshen's *Saints, Sinners, and Soldiers* (Vancouver: UBC Press, 2004) is unrivalled.

Larry Rose's ably done *Mobilize! Why Canada Was Unprepared for the Second World War* (Toronto: Dundurn, 2013) examines the pathetic state of the military in 1939 and its consequences; so too does Stephen Harris's *Canadian Brass: The Making of a Professional Army, 1860-1939* (Toronto: University of Toronto Press, 1988). Michael Stevenson discusses National Selective Service in *Canada's Greatest Wartime Muddle* (Montreal and Kingston: McGill-Queen's University Press, 2001). Daniel Byers's *Zombie Army: Canada, the Canadian Army, and Conscription in the Second World War* (Vancouver: UBC Press, 2016) adds much to what we know of the National Resources Mobilization Act men, and Dean Oliver, "When the Battle's Won: Military Demobilization in Canada, 1939-46" (PhD diss., York University, 1996), explains the process of demobilization. Volume 1 of Tim Cook's *The Necessary War* (Toronto: Allen Lane, 2014) covers the war from 1939 to 1943; Volume 2, *Fight to the Finish*, which goes to the end of the war, appeared in late 2015. John A. Macdonald's very good RMC 1992 master's thesis, "In Search of Veritable: Training the Canadian Army Staff Officer, 1899 to 1945," is most informative. And no listing would be complete without the extraordinary multi-volume Canadian Battle Series by Mark Zuehlke, which includes good books on the campaigns in Sicily and Italy and in Northwest Europe.

The literature on the Second World War is vast. Especially useful are J.W. Pickersgill's first two volumes of *The Mackenzie King Record* (Toronto: University of Toronto Press, 1960, 1968); C.P. Stacey, *Canada and the Age of Conflict,* vol. 2 (Toronto: University of Toronto Press, 1981); David Bercuson, *Our Finest Hour* (Toronto: HarperCollins, 2015); and John W. Holmes, *The Shaping of Peace,* vol. 1 (Toronto: University of Toronto Press, 1979). British and American scholarship includes David Reynolds, *In Command of History: Churchill Fighting and Writing the Second World War* (New York: Random House, 2005), which is superb, as is his *Rich Relations: The American Occupation of Britain, 1942-1945* (New York: Random House, 1995), which also talks about the Canadians in Britain. The first two volumes of Nigel Hamilton's *Monty* (London: Hamish Hamilton, 1981, 1986) remain important, as do Max Hastings, *Overlord* (repr., London: Pan, 2015); Russell Weigley, *Eisenhower and His Lieutenants* (Bloomington: Indiana University Press, 1981); John Buckley, *Monty's Men: The British Army and the Liberation of Europe, 1944-5* (New Haven: Yale University Press, 2013); Ben Kite, *Stout Hearts: The British and Canadians in Normandy, 1944* (Solihull, UK: Helion, 2014); Russell Hart, *Clash of Arms: How the Allies Won in Normandy* (Norman: University of Oklahoma Press, 2001); Richard Overy's excellent *The Bombing War* (London:

Allen Lane, 2013); Brian Bond, *Britain's Two World Wars against Germany: Myth, Memory and the Distortion of Hindsight* (Cambridge: Cambridge University Press, 2014); John Ellis, *Brute Force* (New York: Viking, 1990); Stephen Hart, *Montgomery and "Colossal Cracks": 21st Army Group in Northwest Europe, 1944-45* (Mechanicsburg, PA: Stackpole, 2007); Max Hastings, *Armageddon: The Battle for Germany, 1944-1945* (New York: Vintage, 2005); Andrew Roberts's two volumes: *The Storm of War* (Toronto: HarperCollins, 2009) and *Masters and Commanders* (London: Penguin, 2009); and A. Danchev and D. Todman, eds., *Alanbrooke War Diaries, 1939-1945* (London: Weidenfeld and Nicolson, 2001). There are many more fine books, with more being published every year. The seventy-fifth anniversary years of the Second World War will unquestionably produce a print bonanza.

Index

Note: Where known, military ranks listed are the highest achieved.

STUDIES IN CANADIAN MILITARY HISTORY

Timothy Balzer, *The Information Front: The Canadian Army and News Management during the Second World War*

Andrew B. Godefroy, *Defence and Discovery: Canada's Military Space Program, 1945-74*

Douglas E. Delaney, *Corps Commanders: Five British and Canadian Generals at War, 1939-45*

Timothy Wilford, *Canada's Road to the Pacific War: Intelligence, Strategy, and the Far East Crisis*

Randall Wakelam, *Cold War Fighters: Canadian Aircraft Procurement, 1945-54*

Andrew Burtch, *Give Me Shelter: The Failure of Canada's Cold War Civil Defence*

Wendy Cuthbertson, *Labour Goes to War: The CIO and the Construction of a New Social Order, 1939-45*

P. Whitney Lackenbauer, *The Canadian Rangers: A Living History*

Teresa Iacobelli, *Death or Deliverance: Canadian Courts Martial in the Great War*

Graham Broad, *A Small Price to Pay: Consumer Culture on the Canadian Home Front, 1939-45*

Peter Kasurak, *A National Force: The Evolution of Canada's Army, 1950-2000*

Isabel Campbell, *Unlikely Diplomats: The Canadian Brigade in Germany, 1951-64*

Richard M. Reid, *African Canadians in Union Blue: Volunteering for the Cause in the Civil War*

Andrew B. Godefroy, *In Peace Prepared: Innovation and Adaptation in Canada's Cold War Army*

Nic Clarke, *Unwanted Warriors: The Rejected Volunteers of the Canadian Expeditionary Force*

David Zimmerman, *Maritime Command Pacific: The Royal Canadian Navy's West Coast Fleet in the Early Cold War*

Cynthia Toman, *Sister Soldiers of the Great War: The Nurses of the Canadian Army Medical Corps*

Daniel Byers, *Zombie Army: The Canadian Army and Conscription in the Second World War*

Brandon R. Dimmel, *Engaging the Line: How the Great War Shaped the Canada-US Border*

Douglas E. Delaney and Serge Marc Durflinger, eds., *Capturing Hill 70: Canada's Forgotten Battle of the First World War*

Colin McCullough, *Canada's Peacekeeping Past*

STUDIES IN CANADIAN MILITARY HISTORY
Published by UBC Press in association with the Canadian War Museum.

Printed and bound in Canada by Friesens

Set in Helvetica Condensed, Baskerville, and Minion
by Artegraphica Design Co. Ltd.

Text design: Irma Rodriguez

Copy editor: Deborah Kerr
Proofreader: Frank Chow